The Tutorverse
MAKING THE UNIVERSE BRIGHTER, ONE STUDENT AT A TIME

HSPT Mathematics and Quantitative Reasoning: 1,300+ Practice Questions

HSPT Mathematics and Quantitative Reasoning: 1,300+ Practice Questions

March 2024

Published in the United States of America by:

The Tutorverse, LLC

222 Broadway, 19th Floor

New York, NY 10038

Web: www.thetutorverse.com

Email: hello@thetutorverse.com

Copyright © 2024 The Tutorverse, LLC. All rights reserved. Except as permitted under the Copyright Act of 1976, no part of this publication may be reproduced or distributed in any forms or by any means, or stored in a database or retrieval system, without the prior written permission of the publisher.

Third party materials used to supplement this book may be subject to copyright protection vested in their respective publishers and are likewise not reproducible under any circumstances.

For information about buying this title in bulk or to place a special order, please contact us at hello@thetutorverse.com.

ISBN-13: 978-1-7321677-7-3

ISBN-10: 1-7321677-7-X

HSPT® is a registered trademark of the Scholastic Testing Service, Inc., which was not involved in the production of, and does not endorse, sponsor, or certify this product.

Neither the author or publisher claim any responsibility for the accuracy and appropriateness of the content in this book, nor do they claim any responsibility over the outcome of students who use these materials.

The views and opinions expressed in this book do not necessarily reflect the official policy, position, or point of view of the author or publisher. Such views and opinions do not constitute an endorsement to perform, attempt to perform, or otherwise emulate any procedures, experiments, etc. described in any of the passages, excerpts, adaptations, cited materials, or similar information. Such information is included only to facilitate the development of questions, answer choices, and answer explanations for purposes of preparing for the HSPT.

Available in Print & eBook Formats
visit thetutorverse.com/books

View or Download Answer Explanations
at thetutorverse.com/books

Table of Contents

Table of Contents 4
Welcome 7
How to Use This Book 8
Diagnostic Practice Test 11
Quantitative Skills 30
    Number Series (Sequence) 31
        Arithmetic 32
        Geometric 34
        Other 37
    Geometric Comparison 41
        Comparison of Angles 42
        Comparison of Polygons 45
    Non-Geometric Comparison 48
        Algebraic Comparison 49
        Counting 50
        Fractions, Decimals, Percents 53
        Graphs 55
        Measurements 59
        Order of Operations 62
        Slope 64
    Number Manipulation (Reasoning) 68
        Fractions, Percents, Decimals 69
        Whole Numbers 71
Mathematics 73
    Concepts 74
        Algebraic 75
        Geometry 76
        Measurements 82
        Numbers & Operations 83
    Problem-Solving 86
        Algebraic Concepts 87
        Data & Probability 91
        Measurements 101
        Numbers & Operations 103

Practice Test 1	112
Practice Test 2	150
Answer Keys	189
Diagnostic Test	189
Quantitative Skills	189
Mathematics	189
Exercises	189
Quantitative Skills	189
Mathematics Concepts	190
Mathematics Problem Solving	191
Practice Test 1	192
Verbal Skills	192
Quantitative Skills	192
Reading	192
Mathematics	192
Language Skills	192
Practice Test 2	193
Verbal Skills	193
Quantitative Skills	193
Reading	193
Mathematics	193
Language Skills	193

HSPT Mathematics and Quantitative Reasoning: 1,300+ Practice Questions

Welcome

Dear Students, Parents, and Educators,

We believe that the key to scoring well on the High School Placement Test (HSPT) is practice—lots of practice. While test-taking tips and tricks can be helpful, we believe a solid foundation of core learning and subject-matter proficiency is the bedrock on which high-performance relies.

That's why this workbook contains over 1,300 practice math questions. We've painstakingly identified core concepts and crafted questions of varying difficulty to help prepare students for the exam. Our questions help to build confidence, test mastery, and introduce new concepts, skills, and knowledge.

The HSPT is a speed test. Testing students on nearly 300 questions in about 2 hours and 30 minutes, the HSPT asks students to complete about two problems per minute—a heavy lift for many 8th graders, for many of whom this is their first experience with this kind of test. Because students can only take the HSPT once, it's of vital importance that they go into the testing site as prepared for what they're going to see as possible. That preparation comes in many forms: developing content knowledge, test understanding, and the self-confidence that comes from thorough study.

The test may be intimidating, but with practice students can confidently master its tricks. Taking the time to go through the material, some of which is beyond what students cover in average grade-level courses, is essential. This is what our workbook offers.

Test preparation is a long, arduous journey, with plenty of challenges ahead for parents and students alike. Though the process might be at times discouraging, we are here to support you every step of the way.

This workbook helps students to identify skills and concepts requiring further development. It also provides ample practice for many of the subject areas on the HSPT. Whether you use this workbook for independent study or with a professional tutor or teacher, we believe that the practice you will receive will benefit you both on the HSPT and far beyond.

Best wishes, good luck, and welcome to The Tutorverse!

Regards,

The Team at The Tutorverse

www.thetutorverse.com

How to Use This Book

Overview

The purpose of this workbook is to provide students, parents, and educators with practice math materials for the HSPT. Though this workbook includes information regarding the test's structure and content, our primary goal is to provide students with copious practice materials that reinforce their learning and introduce them to new words, concepts, and skills as necessary.

Organization

This workbook is organized into four main sections. Each section is designed to accomplish different objectives. These sections and objectives are as follows:

- Diagnostic Test
  This section is designed to help students identify topics requiring the most practice. Though not the full length of a real HSPT test (as the diagnostic only features math questions), students can use this diagnostic to familiarize themselves with the speed at which the test moves and to build their stamina and endurance for the full-length practice tests at the end of the book. This first test should be used as a gauge to estimate the amount of additional practice needed on each topic, and not as an estimate of how the student will perform on the actual test.

- Quantitative Skills
  This is the first of two practice sections. The topics tested in this section are number series, comparisons, and number manipulation (reasoning). These topics are further divided into sub-sections, including geometric and non-geometric comparisons, which can help students more accurately focus their study.

- Mathematics
  This section is the second of the two practice sections in this workbook and includes questions in concepts and problem-solving. There are many algebra, geometry, and data analysis topics in this section, organized as indicated in the table of contents.

- Practice Tests 1 and 2
  These practice tests help to familiarize students with the format, organization, and time allotment of the HSPT. Both in length and material, these practice tests mirror the actual exam, including ELA material in addition to the math. These tests should be taken once students have completed the diagnostic tests and spent sufficient time studying topics in the practice sections that they found challenging.

At the beginning of each of the above listed sections are detailed instructions. Students should carefully review these instructions, as they contain important information about the actual exam and how best to practice.

Strategy

Every student has different strengths and abilities. We don't think there is any one strategy that will help every student ace the exam. Instead, we believe there are core principles to keep in mind when preparing for the HSPT. These principles are interrelated and cyclical in nature.

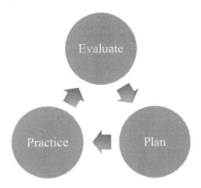

- Evaluate
  A critical step in developing a solid study plan is to have a clear idea of how to spend your time. What subjects are more difficult for you? Which types of questions do you frequently answer incorrectly? Why? These and many other questions should be answered before developing any study plan. The diagnostic test is just one way to help you evaluate your abilities.

- Plan
  Once you've taken stock of your strengths and abilities, focus on actions. How much time do you have before the test? How many areas do you need to work on during that time, and which areas do you need to work on? How many questions (and of which type) do you need to do each day, or each week? The answers to these and other questions will help you determine your study and practice plan.

- Practice
  Once you settle on a plan, try to stick with it as much as you can. To study successfully requires discipline, commitment, and focus. Try turning off your phone, TV, tablet, or other distractions. Not only will you learn more effectively when you're focused, but you may find that you finish your work more quickly, as well.

- Reevaluate
  Because learning and studying is an ongoing process, it is important to take stock of your improvements along the way. This will help you see how you are progressing and allow you to make adjustments to your plan. The practice test at the end of this workbook is designed to help you gauge your progress.

Calculators

Students are not permitted to use calculators on the HSPT. To ensure your study is as effective as possible, try to complete the problems in this book without the use of a calculator. If you have a diagnosed learning disability which requires the use of a calculator, contact your testing site to organize special accommodations.

Help

Preparing for a standardized test such as the HSPT can be difficult and trying. In addition to challenging material, preparing for a standardized test can often feel like an extra responsibility on top of students' already busy lives. For these reasons, it's important to recognize when students need extra help.

Because not all schools cover the same material at the same level, some students may find material in this workbook to be difficult or entirely new. This is normal and to-be-expected, as certain material included in this workbook may not yet have been taught to some students.

We encourage you to reach out to trusted educators to help you prepare for the HSPT. Strong tutors, teachers, mentors, and consultants can help you with many aspects of your preparation—from evaluating your needs, to creating an effective plan, to helping you make the most of your practice, reaching out for help when you need it is always a smart move.

Looking for a tutor?

Look no further—we're The Tutorverse for a reason! We offer one-one-one tutoring in-home or online. Our tutoring is the ultimate test-prep and supplemental educational service.

TO LEARN MORE, SCAN THE QR CODE OR VISIT:

thetutorverse.com/hspt

QUESTIONS? SEND US AN EMAIL:

hello@thetutorverse.com

Looking for ELA practice?

This is not the only book in the Tutorverse library dedicated to helping students boost their scores on the HSPT! Check out our book "HSPT Reading Comprehension, Verbal, and Language: 1,700+ Practice Questions!" Developed by a team of educators with combined decades of test-prep experience, this book offers students studying for the HSPT

- over **1,700** professionally written and edited **practice questions!**
- **2 full-length practice tests** featuring questions for both English and math!
- **detailed answer explanations** available online for **every question**!

TO LEARN MORE, VISIT US ONLINE AT

thetutorverse.com/books

The Tutorverse
www.thetutorverse.com

Diagnostic Practice Test

Overview

The first step in an effective study plan is to know your strengths and areas for improvement.

This diagnostic test assesses your mastery of certain skills and concepts that you may see on the actual exam. The main difference between the diagnostic and practice tests and the actual test is that the diagnostic tests are scored differently from how the actual exam is scored. On the actual exam, your score will be determined by how well you did compared to other students in your grade. On the diagnostic and practice tests, however, we will score every question in order to gauge your mastery over skills and concepts. In addition to this, the diagnostic test only concerns material **covered in this book**, meaning only material in the quantitative skills and mathematics sections.

This diagnostic test should *not* be used as a gauge of how you will score on the test.

Format

The format of the diagnostic test is similar to that of the actual test. The number of questions included in each section mirror those of the actual test, *even though the actual test includes questions that will not be scored*. This is done by design, in order to help familiarize you with the actual length of each section.

The diagnostic includes the following sections:

Diagnostic Test Section	Questions	Time Limit
Quantitative Skills	52	30 minutes
Mathematics	64	45 minutes
Total	**116**	**1h 15 minutes**

Breaks: Generally, 2 brief breaks are given between sections of the test; however, the timing and duration of the breaks are determined by the individual school that is administering the exam. For the purpose of this diagnostic test, either take no break or take a brief break in-between Quantitative Skills and Mathematics.

Calculators

Students are not permitted to use calculators on the HSPT. **To ensure the results of the diagnostic test are as accurate as possible, do not use a calculator on this exam**. If you have a diagnosed learning disability which requires the use of a calculator, contact your testing site to organize special accommodations and continue to practice with a calculator as you need.

Answering

Use the answer sheet provided on the next page to record your answers. You may wish to tear this page out of the workbook.

www.thetutorverse.com

Diagnostic Test Answer Sheet

[Carefully tear or cut out this page.]

Section 1: Quantitative Skills

1. Ⓐ Ⓑ Ⓒ Ⓓ
2. Ⓐ Ⓑ Ⓒ Ⓓ
3. Ⓐ Ⓑ Ⓒ Ⓓ
4. Ⓐ Ⓑ Ⓒ Ⓓ
5. Ⓐ Ⓑ Ⓒ Ⓓ
6. Ⓐ Ⓑ Ⓒ Ⓓ
7. Ⓐ Ⓑ Ⓒ Ⓓ
8. Ⓐ Ⓑ Ⓒ Ⓓ
9. Ⓐ Ⓑ Ⓒ Ⓓ
10. Ⓐ Ⓑ Ⓒ Ⓓ
11. Ⓐ Ⓑ Ⓒ Ⓓ
12. Ⓐ Ⓑ Ⓒ Ⓓ
13. Ⓐ Ⓑ Ⓒ Ⓓ
14. Ⓐ Ⓑ Ⓒ Ⓓ
15. Ⓐ Ⓑ Ⓒ Ⓓ
16. Ⓐ Ⓑ Ⓒ Ⓓ
17. Ⓐ Ⓑ Ⓒ Ⓓ
18. Ⓐ Ⓑ Ⓒ Ⓓ
19. Ⓐ Ⓑ Ⓒ Ⓓ
20. Ⓐ Ⓑ Ⓒ Ⓓ
21. Ⓐ Ⓑ Ⓒ Ⓓ
22. Ⓐ Ⓑ Ⓒ Ⓓ
23. Ⓐ Ⓑ Ⓒ Ⓓ
24. Ⓐ Ⓑ Ⓒ Ⓓ
25. Ⓐ Ⓑ Ⓒ Ⓓ
26. Ⓐ Ⓑ Ⓒ Ⓓ
27. Ⓐ Ⓑ Ⓒ Ⓓ
28. Ⓐ Ⓑ Ⓒ Ⓓ
29. Ⓐ Ⓑ Ⓒ Ⓓ
30. Ⓐ Ⓑ Ⓒ Ⓓ
31. Ⓐ Ⓑ Ⓒ Ⓓ
32. Ⓐ Ⓑ Ⓒ Ⓓ
33. Ⓐ Ⓑ Ⓒ Ⓓ
34. Ⓐ Ⓑ Ⓒ Ⓓ
35. Ⓐ Ⓑ Ⓒ Ⓓ
36. Ⓐ Ⓑ Ⓒ Ⓓ
37. Ⓐ Ⓑ Ⓒ Ⓓ
38. Ⓐ Ⓑ Ⓒ Ⓓ
39. Ⓐ Ⓑ Ⓒ Ⓓ
40. Ⓐ Ⓑ Ⓒ Ⓓ
41. Ⓐ Ⓑ Ⓒ Ⓓ
42. Ⓐ Ⓑ Ⓒ Ⓓ
43. Ⓐ Ⓑ Ⓒ Ⓓ
44. Ⓐ Ⓑ Ⓒ Ⓓ
45. Ⓐ Ⓑ Ⓒ Ⓓ
46. Ⓐ Ⓑ Ⓒ Ⓓ
47. Ⓐ Ⓑ Ⓒ Ⓓ
48. Ⓐ Ⓑ Ⓒ Ⓓ
49. Ⓐ Ⓑ Ⓒ Ⓓ
50. Ⓐ Ⓑ Ⓒ Ⓓ
51. Ⓐ Ⓑ Ⓒ Ⓓ
52. Ⓐ Ⓑ Ⓒ Ⓓ

Section 2: Mathematics

53. Ⓐ Ⓑ Ⓒ Ⓓ
54. Ⓐ Ⓑ Ⓒ Ⓓ
55. Ⓐ Ⓑ Ⓒ Ⓓ
56. Ⓐ Ⓑ Ⓒ Ⓓ
57. Ⓐ Ⓑ Ⓒ Ⓓ
58. Ⓐ Ⓑ Ⓒ Ⓓ
59. Ⓐ Ⓑ Ⓒ Ⓓ
60. Ⓐ Ⓑ Ⓒ Ⓓ
61. Ⓐ Ⓑ Ⓒ Ⓓ
62. Ⓐ Ⓑ Ⓒ Ⓓ
63. Ⓐ Ⓑ Ⓒ Ⓓ
64. Ⓐ Ⓑ Ⓒ Ⓓ
65. Ⓐ Ⓑ Ⓒ Ⓓ
66. Ⓐ Ⓑ Ⓒ Ⓓ
67. Ⓐ Ⓑ Ⓒ Ⓓ
68. Ⓐ Ⓑ Ⓒ Ⓓ
69. Ⓐ Ⓑ Ⓒ Ⓓ
70. Ⓐ Ⓑ Ⓒ Ⓓ
71. Ⓐ Ⓑ Ⓒ Ⓓ
72. Ⓐ Ⓑ Ⓒ Ⓓ
73. Ⓐ Ⓑ Ⓒ Ⓓ
74. Ⓐ Ⓑ Ⓒ Ⓓ
75. Ⓐ Ⓑ Ⓒ Ⓓ
76. Ⓐ Ⓑ Ⓒ Ⓓ
77. Ⓐ Ⓑ Ⓒ Ⓓ
78. Ⓐ Ⓑ Ⓒ Ⓓ
79. Ⓐ Ⓑ Ⓒ Ⓓ
80. Ⓐ Ⓑ Ⓒ Ⓓ
81. Ⓐ Ⓑ Ⓒ Ⓓ
82. Ⓐ Ⓑ Ⓒ Ⓓ
83. Ⓐ Ⓑ Ⓒ Ⓓ
84. Ⓐ Ⓑ Ⓒ Ⓓ
85. Ⓐ Ⓑ Ⓒ Ⓓ
86. Ⓐ Ⓑ Ⓒ Ⓓ
87. Ⓐ Ⓑ Ⓒ Ⓓ
88. Ⓐ Ⓑ Ⓒ Ⓓ
89. Ⓐ Ⓑ Ⓒ Ⓓ
90. Ⓐ Ⓑ Ⓒ Ⓓ
91. Ⓐ Ⓑ Ⓒ Ⓓ
92. Ⓐ Ⓑ Ⓒ Ⓓ
93. Ⓐ Ⓑ Ⓒ Ⓓ
94. Ⓐ Ⓑ Ⓒ Ⓓ
95. Ⓐ Ⓑ Ⓒ Ⓓ
96. Ⓐ Ⓑ Ⓒ Ⓓ
97. Ⓐ Ⓑ Ⓒ Ⓓ
98. Ⓐ Ⓑ Ⓒ Ⓓ
99. Ⓐ Ⓑ Ⓒ Ⓓ
100. Ⓐ Ⓑ Ⓒ Ⓓ
101. Ⓐ Ⓑ Ⓒ Ⓓ
102. Ⓐ Ⓑ Ⓒ Ⓓ
103. Ⓐ Ⓑ Ⓒ Ⓓ
104. Ⓐ Ⓑ Ⓒ Ⓓ
105. Ⓐ Ⓑ Ⓒ Ⓓ
106. Ⓐ Ⓑ Ⓒ Ⓓ
107. Ⓐ Ⓑ Ⓒ Ⓓ
108. Ⓐ Ⓑ Ⓒ Ⓓ
109. Ⓐ Ⓑ Ⓒ Ⓓ
110. Ⓐ Ⓑ Ⓒ Ⓓ
111. Ⓐ Ⓑ Ⓒ Ⓓ
112. Ⓐ Ⓑ Ⓒ Ⓓ
113. Ⓐ Ⓑ Ⓒ Ⓓ
114. Ⓐ Ⓑ Ⓒ Ⓓ
115. Ⓐ Ⓑ Ⓒ Ⓓ
116. Ⓐ Ⓑ Ⓒ Ⓓ

The Tutorverse
www.thetutorverse.com

Quantitative Skills

Questions 1-52, 30 Minutes

1. In the sequence 2, 4, 8, 16..., which number should come next?
   (A) 20
   (B) 24
   (C) 32
   (D) 36

2. Examine I, II, and III and find the *best* answer:

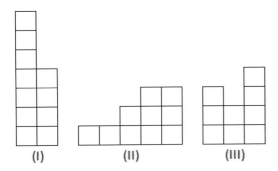

   (A) III is greater than II which is equal to I
   (B) II is greater than I, which is greater than III
   (C) I is greater than II, and II is greater than III
   (D) I and III are equal, and both are greater than II

3. What number added to 14 gives you 8 less than the difference of 60 and 25?
   (A) 13
   (B) 43
   (C) 63
   (D) 79

4. Examine I, II, and III and find the *best* answer:

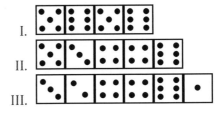

   (A) I = II < III
   (B) I + III < II
   (C) III < I = II
   (D) III = I > II

5. In the sequence 30, 10, $\frac{10}{3}, \frac{10}{9}$..., which number should come next?
   (A) $\frac{5}{3}$
   (B) $\frac{5}{6}$
   (C) $\frac{10}{12}$
   (D) $\frac{10}{27}$

6. What number when subtracted from 38 is 5 less than $\frac{1}{3}$ of 27?
   (A) 24
   (B) 27
   (C) 31
   (D) 34

7. Examine the following and find the best answer:

   I. $-4 - 11$
   II. $-(4 - 11)$
   III. $4 - 11$

   (A) I is greater than II, which is greater than III
   (B) I is smaller than II, which is smaller than III
   (C) I is smaller than III, which is smaller than II
   (D) I is greater than III, which is greater than II

8. In the sequence 3, 8, 6, 11, 9…, what three numbers should come next?
   (A) 7, 5, 3
   (B) 14, 19, 24
   (C) 14, 12, 17
   (D) 14, 12, 10

9. Examine the line graph and find the *best* answer.

   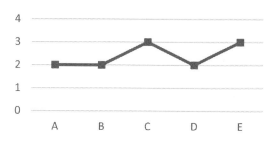

   (A) A plus B is equal to E
   (B) A, B, and E are equal
   (C) A plus B is equal to C plus D
   (D) A, B, and D are equal

10. Examine the following and find the best answer:

    I. 16^0
    II. 2^4
    III. 16^1

    (A) I is greater than II and III, which are equal
    (B) I is smaller than II and III, which are equal
    (C) I is smaller than II, which is smaller than III
    (D) I is greater than II, which is greater than III

11. In the sequence 0.14, 0.98, 6.86…, what should come next?
    (A) 7.84
    (B) 13.72
    (C) 34.04
    (D) 48.02

12. Examine the following and find the best answer:

    I. $2(5 + 7)$
    II. $-(4 - 28)$
    III. $12 + 12$

    (A) I is greater than II, which is greater than III
    (B) I, II, and III are equal
    (C) II is smaller than III and I, which are equal
    (D) I is greater than III, which is greater than II

13. Examine I, II, and III and find the best answer.

   I. the slope of the line shown
   II. the slope of $y = -\frac{1}{2}x - 8$
   III. the slope of $2x + y = -1$

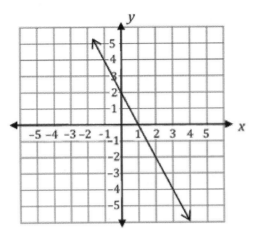

   (A) I is equal to II
   (B) I is greater than III
   (C) II is greater than III
   (D) III is less than I

14. What number added to 15 gives you the difference of 34 and the product of 6 and 3?
   (A) 1
   (B) 16
   (C) 31
   (D) 37

15. Examine the angles A, B, and C in the right triangle and find the best answer.

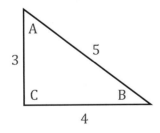

   (A) $\angle A > \angle B > \angle C$
   (B) $\angle A + \angle B = \angle C$
   (C) $\angle A = \angle B = \angle C$
   (D) $\angle A - \angle B = \angle C$

16. What number added to 23 gives you 10 less than the sum of 22 and 13?
   (A) 2
   (B) 4
   (C) 12
   (D) 22

17. Below are a rectangle and right triangle. Find the best answer.

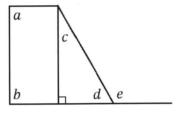

   (A) $c + d < a$
   (B) $c + d = b$
   (C) $c = d$
   (D) $d = e$

18. What number is 200% of the difference of 15 and 5?
   (A) 5
   (B) 10
   (C) 15
   (D) 20

19. In the sequence $1, \frac{1}{4}, \frac{1}{16}, \frac{1}{64}...$, which number should come next?
   (A) $\frac{1}{256}$
   (B) $\frac{1}{128}$
   (C) $\frac{1}{112}$
   (D) $\frac{1}{80}$

20. Examine I, II, and III and find the *best* answer if $x = 10$.

    I. $\frac{x}{2}$
    II. $\frac{x}{5} + 2$
    III. $x - 4 - 2$

    (A) I and III are greater than II
    (B) II and III are equal
    (C) III is greater than II
    (D) III is greater than I

21. Examine the following and find the best answer.

    I. The area of:

    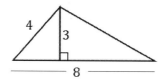

    II. The area of:

    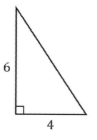

    III. The area of:

    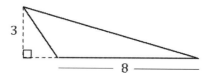

    (A) I and II are equal, and both are less than III
    (B) I and III are equal, and both are greater than II
    (C) I, II, and III are all equal
    (D) II is less than I, and I is less than III

22. In the sequence 17, 25, 33, 41..., what number should come next?
    (A) 39
    (B) 43
    (C) 47
    (D) 49

23. What number divided by 5 is 25% of 60?
    (A) 3
    (B) 65
    (C) 75
    (D) 100

24. Examine I, II, and III and find the *best* answer.

    I.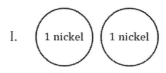

    II.

    III.

    (A) The sum of II and III is equal to I
    (B) I is greater than III
    (C) I and II are equal, and both are less than III
    (D) III is less than II

25. Examine I, II, and III and find the *best* answer if $x = 5$.

    I. $8 - x + 2$
    II. $\frac{x^2}{5}$
    III. $2x - 4$

    (A) I and III are equal
    (B) I and II are equal, and II is less than III
    (C) I and II are equal, and I is greater than III
    (D) I and II are equal, and III is less than II

26. Examine I, II, and III and find the best answer.

   I. the slope of $y = 2x - 8$
   II. the slope of $2x + y = 8$
   III. the slope of the line shown

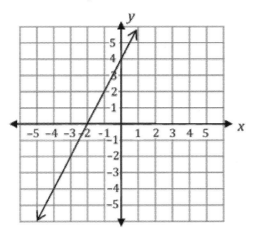

   (A) I is greater than II
   (B) I is less than III
   (C) II is greater than III
   (D) III is less than I

27. Examine I, II, and III and find the *best* answer if $x = 2$.

   I. $3x^3$
   II. $x - 6 + 1$
   III. $\frac{6}{x}$

   (A) II and III are equal
   (B) III is greater than I
   (C) III is greater than I and II
   (D) I is greater than III, and III is greater than II.

28. Examine I, II, and III and find the *best* answer if $x = 6$.

   I. $2x - 3$
   II. $3x$
   III. $7 - x + 4$

   (A) I is greater than II
   (B) II is greater than I
   (C) I is less than III
   (D) II and III are equal

29. Examine I, II, and III and find the *best* answer:

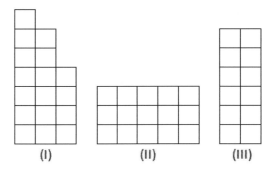

   (A) I > II > III
   (B) I = II > III
   (C) III > I = II
   (D) II > I > III

30. In the sequence 77, 80, 83, 86..., what number should come next?
   (A) 88
   (B) 89
   (C) 90
   (D) 91

31. In the sequence 93, 98, 103, 108..., what number should come next?
   (A) 113
   (B) 115
   (C) 118
   (D) 128

32. Examine I, II, and III and find the *best* answer:

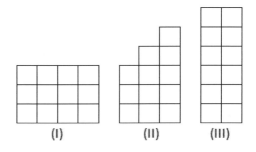

   (A) I = II < III
   (B) I = II = III
   (C) II = III < I
   (D) III > I = II

33. Examine I, II, and III, and find the *best* answer.

   I. $\frac{2}{3}$
   II. $\frac{3}{4}$
   III. $\frac{3}{5}$

   (A) I > II > III
   (B) I = II = III
   (C) II > I > III
   (D) III > II > I

34. Examine I, II, and III, and find the *best* answer.

   I. $\frac{2}{3}$
   II. $\frac{5}{6}$
   III. $\frac{8}{12}$

   (A) I > III > II
   (B) I = III < II
   (C) I = III > II
   (D) I = II = III

35. Examine the following and find the best answer:

   I. measure of ∠a
   II. the sum of measures ∠a and ∠b
   III. measure of ∠c

   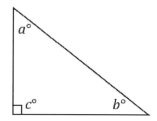

   (A) III is greater than II, and II is greater than I
   (B) I is less than II, and II and III are equal
   (C) I is less than II, and II is less than III
   (D) I is less than II, and II is greater than III

36. In the sequence 72, 24, 30, 10..., what number comes next?
   (A) −10
   (B) $\frac{10}{3}$
   (C) 0
   (D) 16

37. Examine I, II, and III, and find the *best* answer.

   I.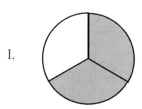

   II.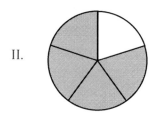

   III.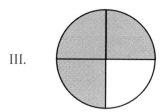

   (A) II is shaded more than I, and I is shaded more than III
   (B) I and II are equally shaded, and III is the most shaded
   (C) II is the most shaded, and III is more shaded than I
   (D) II and III are equally shaded, and I is the least shaded

38. Examine I, II, and III and find the *best* answer:

   (A) I = II > III
   (B) I = II < III
   (C) I + II < III
   (D) I = II = III

39. Examine I, II, and III, and find the *best* answer.

   I. $\frac{4}{6}$
   II. $\frac{5}{9}$
   III. $\frac{15}{18}$

   (A) I = II = III
   (B) II < III < I
   (C) III < I < II
   (D) III > I > II

40. The following bar graph tracks two different variables over five weeks. Find the *best* answer.

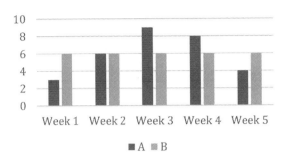

   (A) The sum of A over five weeks was greater than the sum of B over five weeks
   (B) The sum of A over five weeks was less than the sum of B over five weeks
   (C) The sum of A over five weeks was equal to the sum of B over five weeks
   (D) A was greater than B in week 5

41. In the sequence 6, 1, 3, −2, −6, −11..., what number should come next?
   (A) −33
   (B) −16
   (C) 6
   (D) 11

42. What number added to 40 gives you 12 more than the product of 6 and 7?
   (A) 10
   (B) 14
   (C) 15
   (D) 20

43. In the sequence 4, 7, 14, 17, 34..., what number should come next?
   (A) 37
   (B) 44
   (C) 47
   (D) 68

44. Examine the following and find the best answer.

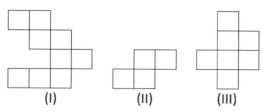

(A) I - II > III
(B) II + III > I
(C) II + II = I
(D) III > I

45. The following graph shows the five states with the most electoral votes. Find the *best* answer. (*Note: bars for states appear in order from left to right as in key*)

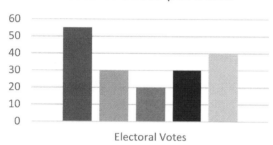

(A) New York has more electoral votes than Florida
(B) Texas has fewer electoral votes than Florida
(C) The sum of California and Texas is less than the sum of New York and Florida
(D) Texas has more electoral votes than Florida

46. Examine I, II, and III and find the best answer.

   I. the slope of $y = x - 8$
   II. the slope of the line shown
   III. the slope of $x + 3y = 8$

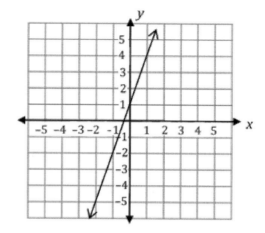

(A) I is equal to II
(B) I is equal to III
(C) I is greater than III
(D) II is less than III

47. What number is 25% of the sum of 12 and 20?
(A) 7.5
(B) 8
(C) 9.5
(D) 10

48. Examine I, II, and III and find the *best* answer:

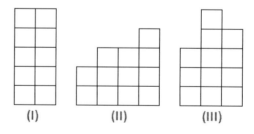

(A) III < I < II
(B) I < II = III
(C) III > I > II
(D) II > III > I

49. What number subtracted from 3^3 is $\frac{1}{2}$ of 24?
    (A) 15
    (B) 19
    (C) 25
    (D) 39

50. In the sequence 26, 32, 38, 44..., what number should come next?
    (A) 46
    (B) 48
    (C) 50
    (D) 52

51. What number added to 34 gives you 5 more than 6 times 9?
    (A) 1
    (B) 10
    (C) 15
    (D) 25

52. Given that m is parallel to n, examine angles A, B, C, D, E, F, G, and H and find the best answer.

    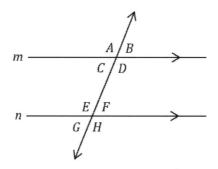

    (A) $\angle A = \angle C$
    (B) $\angle B = \angle H$
    (C) $\angle D = \angle E$
    (D) $\angle E = \angle G$

Mathematics

Questions 53-116, 45 Minutes

53. Solve: $-34x < 68$.
    (A) $x < -2$
    (B) $x > -2$
    (C) $x < 2$
    (D) $x < 2$

54. What is the radius of a circle with a diameter of 13 ft?
    (A) 5 ft
    (B) 5.5 ft
    (C) 6 ft
    (D) 6.5 ft

55. A parallelogram is made up of two right triangles with an area of 5 square cm each, and a square with a perimeter of 20 cm. What is the area of the parallelogram?

    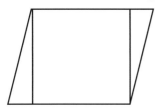

    (A) 20 square cm
    (B) 25 square cm
    (C) 30 square cm
    (D) 35 square cm

56. If the area of a circle is 36π sq. ft, what is the diameter of the circle in <u>inches</u>?
    (A) 6 in.
    (B) 12 in.
    (C) 72 in.
    (D) 144 in.

57. What is the LCM of 3, 5, and 6?
    (A) 15
    (B) 18
    (C) 30
    (D) 60

58. Which number is in the hundreds place after simplifying $(3 \times 10^3) + (2 \times 10^2) + (5 \times 10^1)$?
    (A) 1
    (B) 2
    (C) 3
    (D) 5

59. Two triangles each with an area of 72 square centimeters fit into a square, as shown. What is the perimeter of the square?

    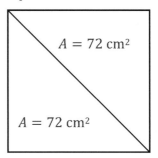

    (A) 48 centimeters
    (B) 52 centimeters
    (C) 72 centimeters
    (D) 144 centimeters

60. What is equivalent to $8^3 \times 8^3$?
    (A) 8^6
    (B) 8^9
    (C) 16^3
    (D) 64^9

61. A rectangular prism has a length of 4 cm, a width of 3 cm, and a height of 10 cm. What is its volume?
    (A) 17 cm^3
    (B) 82 cm^3
    (C) 120 cm^3
    (D) 164 cm^3

62. What is equivalent to $\frac{2^8}{2^4}$?
    (A) 1^2
    (B) 1^4
    (C) 2^2
    (D) 2^4

63. Five hundredths can be written as
    (A) 0.005
    (B) 0.05
    (C) 500
    (D) 5,000

64. A regular hexagon with side length of 12 is has the same perimeter as a equilateral triangle. What is the length of each side of the triangle?
    (A) 12
    (B) 18
    (C) 24
    (D) 72

65. Find the LCM of 4, 8, and 10.
    (A) 2
    (B) 20
    (C) 40
    (D) 80

66. Which of the following fractions does NOT equal $\frac{1}{4}$?
    (A) $\frac{5}{20}$
    (B) $\frac{7}{28}$
    (C) $\frac{9}{32}$
    (D) $\frac{10}{40}$

67. Which number is in the hundreds place after simplifying $(4 \times 10^2) + (7 \times 10^3) + (1 \times 10^1)$?
    (A) 1
    (B) 2
    (C) 4
    (D) 7

68. All of the following fractions are equal EXCEPT:
    (A) $\frac{4}{5}$
    (B) $\frac{6}{10}$
    (C) $\frac{9}{15}$
    (D) $\frac{12}{20}$

69. What is the GCF of 5, 10, and 15?
    (A) 1
    (B) 5
    (C) 15
    (D) 30

70. What is the surface area of this object?

    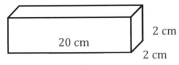

    (A) 24 cm²
    (B) 80 cm²
    (C) 84 cm²
    (D) 168 cm²

71. What is the GCF of 4, 9, and 6?
    (A) 1
    (B) 12
    (C) 18
    (D) 72

72. In a regular pentagon, what is the measure of the sum of two adjacent angles?
    (A) 90°
    (B) 180°
    (C) 360°
    (D) 540°

73. Which of the following would be the most appropriate unit to record the distance between the Moon and Earth?
    (A) acres
    (B) inches
    (C) kilometers
    (D) square feet

74. Which unit would be most appropriate to record the temperature on a sunny day?
    (A) Fahrenheit
    (B) millimeters
    (C) percentage
    (D) yards

75. What type of triangle is shown?

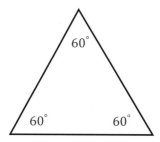

    (A) right
    (B) obtuse
    (C) scalene
    (D) equilateral

76. Which statement best describes the inequality: $5x \leq x - 7$?
    (A) Five times a number is less than seven less than that number.
    (B) Five times a number is less than or equal to seven less than that number.
    (C) Five times a number is less than or equal to seven times that number.
    (D) Five times a number is less than seven less than that number.

77. What is the slope of a line perpendicular to the line $y = -\frac{5}{7}x - 3$?
    (A) -3
    (B) $-\frac{5}{7}$
    (C) $\frac{5}{7}$
    (D) $\frac{7}{5}$

78. What is the slope of a line perpendicular to the line $y = -4x + 2$?
    (A) $-\frac{1}{4}$
    (B) $\frac{1}{4}$
    (C) 2
    (D) 4

79. Express the fraction $\frac{8}{25}$ as a percent.
    (A) 8%
    (B) 30%
    (C) 32%
    (D) 80%

80. Which of the following numbers is divisible by 6?
    (A) 1,010
    (B) 1,011
    (C) 1,101
    (D) 1,110

Problem Solving

81. Jason is three years younger than Chris. Tamara is eight years older than Chris. The sum of Jason, Chris, and Tamara's ages is equal to five times Jason's age. How old is Tamara?
    (A) 7
    (B) 10
    (C) 15
    (D) 18

82. Solve: $(-7) \times (-3) \times 5 =$
    (A) -100
    (B) -80
    (C) 100
    (D) 105

83. How many cups fit in a pint?
    (A) 2 cups
    (B) 4 cups
    (C) 6 cups
    (D) 8 cups

84. Solve: $\frac{3}{8} + \frac{2}{5} =$
    (A) $\frac{5}{13}$
    (B) $\frac{2}{3}$
    (C) $\frac{3}{4}$
    (D) $\frac{31}{40}$

85. Frederick has taken three tests and has an average of 88. What score does he need on his fourth test to make sure he has an average of 90?
    (A) 92
    (B) 93
    (C) 94
    (D) 96

86. A box of chocolates has four different kinds of chocolates. There are 6 dark chocolates, 3 milk chocolates, 5 white chocolates, and 1 chocolate cherry. What is the probability of choosing a milk chocolate at random?
    (A) $\frac{1}{15}$
    (B) $\frac{1}{5}$
    (C) $\frac{1}{3}$
    (D) $\frac{2}{5}$

87. Solve for x: $-4x = \frac{1}{8} \times 12$
    (A) -6
    (B) $-\frac{3}{8}$
    (C) $\frac{3}{8}$
    (D) 6

88. If $3^x = 27$, then $x =$?
    (A) 2
    (B) 3
    (C) 4
    (D) 9

89. Which information is best displayed on a pie chart?
    (A) grocery prices over time
    (B) student absences over a semester
    (C) survey results asking about favorite sports
    (D) average grades on a test

90. Jenetta is baking a cake that requires a tablespoon of baking soda. If one cup is equivalent to 16 tablespoons, approximately what percent of a cup of baking soda is the amount required by the recipe? (Round your answer to the nearest tenth)
    (A) 2.3%
    (B) 4.8%
    (C) 6.3%
    (D) 8.4%

91. Which of the following would equal 3.9 when rounded to the tenths place?
    (A) $1.48 + 1.36$
    (B) $2.23 + 1.85$
    (C) $1.68 + 2.26$
    (D) $3.07 + 1.13$

92. An architect is drawing a floor plan for a building with overall dimensions of 72 feet by 45 feet. If the scale of the floor plan is to be 1 inch is equal to 6 feet, how long will the shortest side be on the drawing?
    (A) 6 inches
    (B) 7.5 inches
    (C) 9 inches
    (D) 12 inches

93. What is $6.15 + 0.006 + 0.01 + 0.61$ rounded to the nearest hundredth?
    (A) 6.77
    (B) 6.776
    (C) 6.78
    (D) 6.8

94. If $3\sqrt{8} = x\sqrt{2}$, find x.
    (A) 6
    (B) 8
    (C) 9
    (D) 10

95. Which of the following figures describes the shape of a school textbook?
    (A) cylinder
    (B) isosceles triangle
    (C) rectangular prism
    (D) triangular prism

96. The band sold cupcakes and cookies at the bake sale. They sold 4 cupcakes for $3.50 each and 8 cookies for $1.25 each. How much total money did they make from these sales?
    (A) $10.00
    (B) $14.00
    (C) $24.00
    (D) $30.50

97. The drive from school to Darron's house takes fifteen minutes at 24 miles per hour. How far away is school from his house?
    (A) $\frac{15}{24}$ miles
    (B) 6 miles
    (C) 12 miles
    (D) 20 miles

98. The following Venn diagram represents the choice students made as to what subjects they are taking in school. What does the region where the "B" is placed represent?

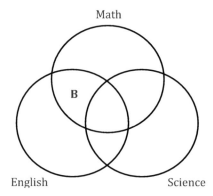

    (A) students who are taking only math
    (B) students who are taking English and math but are not taking science
    (C) students who are taking English and science but are not taking math
    (D) students who are taking math and science but are not taking English

99. What is the value of 160% of 90?
    (A) 5.4
    (B) 54
    (C) 144
    (D) 14,400

100. 4 lb. 6 oz. equals:
    (A) 22 oz.
    (B) 46 oz.
    (C) 60 oz.
    (D) 70 oz.

101. There are three kinds of cards in an animal deck: 5 whales, 3 sharks, and 2 dolphins. If Wesley randomly selects two cards and keeps them both, what is the probability that he chooses two whales?
    (A) $\frac{1}{10}$
    (B) $\frac{2}{9}$
    (C) $\frac{1}{4}$
    (D) $\frac{5}{18}$

102. Due to deforestation, researchers expect the deer population to decline by 10% every year. If the current deer population is 10,000 deer, what is the size of the deer population after 2 years?
    (A) 8,000
    (B) 8,100
    (C) 9,000
    (D) 9,800

103. If $(\frac{2}{3})^x = \frac{8}{27}$, then $x =$?
    (A) -3
    (B) $\frac{1}{3}$
    (C) 3
    (D) 4

104. Solve: $10,080 - (-8,120) =$
    (A) $-1,960$
    (B) 1,960
    (C) 18,100
    (D) 18,200

105. Dyani plays basketball and has scored 18, 10, 21, and 17 points in her last four games. How many points does she need to score in her next game to average 20 points over those five games?
    (A) 20
    (B) 22
    (C) 26
    (D) 34

106. In a choir, the ratio of tenor voices to alto voices is 6 to 5. If there are 30 alto voices in a choir, how many tenors are there?
    (A) 25
    (B) 30
    (C) 32
    (D) 36

107. What is the name of this polygon?

    (A) heptagon
    (B) hexagon
    (C) octagon
    (D) pentagon

108. A class of 30 seniors is surveyed about whether they own a bike or a car. Three seniors say they own neither, 24 seniors own a bike, and 4 seniors own both. How many seniors own just a car?
    (A) 2
    (B) 3
    (C) 6
    (D) 20

109. If the square root of 27 is added to the square root of 75, what is the final value?
    (A) $5\sqrt{3}$
    (B) $8\sqrt{3}$
    (C) 8
    (D) 13

110. Joe is saving up money to buy a new cell phone that costs $850. He earns $75 a day working at the country club, plus an additional $2 for each plate he washes in the restaurant. If he works Monday through Friday for two weeks, how many plates must he wash to make enough money to afford the cell phone?
    (A) 50
    (B) 70
    (C) 235
    (D) 388

111. Huda is taking a cross-country road trip. If she wants to travel 400 miles today in 8 hours or driving, how fast does she have to go?
    (A) 50 miles per hour
    (B) 55 miles per hour
    (C) 60 miles per hour
    (D) 65 miles per hour

112. Solve for y: $\frac{5}{3} + (-\frac{7}{6}) = \frac{1}{4} - \frac{1}{3}y$
    (A) $-\frac{3}{4}$
    (B) $-\frac{1}{2}$
    (C) $\frac{1}{2}$
    (D) $1\frac{1}{2}$

113. 20% of 50% of 300 is what value?
    (A) 210
    (B) 70
    (C) 50
    (D) 30

114. Solve: $\frac{0.6+0.6+0.6+0.6+0.6}{5} =$
    (A) 0.12
    (B) 0.3
    (C) 0.48
    (D) 0.6

115. The following graph shows the number of times each student in Mr. Lee's class was absent this year. Which two students had the fewest absences?

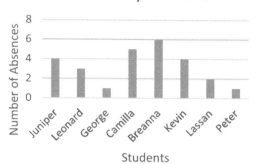

(A) George & Lassan
(B) Camilla & Breanna
(C) George & Peter
(D) Juniper & Leonard

116. Jasmine's piggy bank has a combination of nickels, dimes, and quarters for a total of 12 coins. The number of dimes is three times the number of nickels, and the number of quarters is twice the number of nickels. How many dimes does Jasmine have?
    (A) 2
    (B) 4
    (C) 6
    (D) 8

Scoring the Diagnostic Practice Test

Using your answer sheet and referring to the answer key at the back of the book, calculate the percentage of questions you answered correctly in each section by taking the number of questions you answered correctly in that section and dividing it by the number of questions in that section. Multiply this number by 100 to determine your percentage score. The higher the percentage, the stronger your performance in that section. The lower the percentage, the more time you should spend practicing that section.

Note that the actual test will not evaluate your score based on percentage correct or incorrect. Instead, it will evaluate your performance relative to all other students in your grade who took the test.

Record your results here:

Section	Questions Correct	Total Questions	Percent Questions Correct
Quantitative Skills	____	52	____%
Mathematics Achievement	____	64	____%

Carefully consider the results from your diagnostic test when coming up with your study plan. Remember that, depending on the curriculum at your school, there may be material on this test that you have not yet been taught. If this is the case, and you would like to improve your score beyond what is expected of your grade, consider outside help from an adult—such as a tutor or teacher—who can help you learn more about the topics that are new to you.

Answer Key

The keys are organized by section, and each question has an answer associated with it. Remember: there are detailed answer explanations available online at www.thetutorverse.com/books. Be sure to obtain permission before going online.

Quantitative Skills

On the Actual Test

In the Quantitative Skills section of the HSPT, you will encounter four types of questions:

- Number Series (Sequence)
- Geometric Comparison
- Non-Geometric Comparison
- Number Manipulation (Reasoning)

There will be 52 questions on the Quantitative Skills section, which you will have 30 minutes to complete.

Calculators

Students are <u>not</u> permitted to use calculators on the HSPT. To help your study, we recommend <u>not</u> using a calculator as you work through the problems in this book. Your brain is like a muscle, and by doing mental math, you exercise and prepare it for the conditions of the actual test, where you're not allowed to use a calculator without a diagnosed learning disability and special accommodation from your testing site.

In This Practice Book

This book gives you the chance to practice many questions from these four areas covered in the Quantitative Skills section. By practicing each question type individually, you will develop the correct reasoning strategies. Repeated practice and exposure to each of these question types is the key to success!

Remember: there are detailed and searchable answer explanations available online at www.thetutorverse.com/books. Be sure to obtain permission before going online.

Number Series (Sequence)

Overview

This section tests your ability to find relationships between a series of numbers (and sometimes letters or a combination of both) and then find the element that fits with that series based on the pattern.

In order to find the pattern, you have to use logical reasoning and then apply that to the series.

Think through the different ways that the numbers or letters could be related. Some possible relationships to consider are:

- Arithmetic sequences with addition and subtraction
- Geometric sequences with multiplication and division
- Mixed operations (such as alternating between addition and multiplication, etc.)
- Pattern within a pattern (such as +2, +3, +4, etc.).

How to Use This Section

As determined by your study plan, including the results of your diagnostic tests, we encourage you to focus on the topics that are most challenging to you. This section will give you exposure to the different types of questions that are presented in number series, and give you the practice to finding the path to the correct answer. Are the single operation questions a breeze? Practice more of the mixed operations to polish your skills. If you find that you are challenged by this area and need additional help, remember to reach out to a trusted educator. Don't get discouraged! Take the materials to a teacher or tutor if you need additional enrichment in any given topic.

Tutorverse Tips!

Remember that on the HSPT, there is no penalty for guessing. If you don't know an answer to a question, take your best guess.

Looking for a tutor?

Look no further—we're The Tutorverse for a reason! We offer one-one-one tutoring in-home or online. Our tutoring is the ultimate test-prep and supplemental educational service.

TO LEARN MORE, SCAN THE QR CODE OR VISIT:
thetutorverse.com/hspt

QUESTIONS? SEND US AN EMAIL:
hello@thetutorverse.com

Number Series (Sequence) Exercises

Arithmetic

1. In the sequence 109, 121, 133, 145..., what number should come next?
   (A) 151
   (B) 153
   (C) 155
   (D) 157

2. In the sequence 38, 58, 78, 98..., what number should come next?
   (A) 108
   (B) 113
   (C) 118
   (D) 128

3. In the sequence 44, 37, 30, 23..., what number should come next?
   (A) 16
   (B) 17
   (C) 18
   (D) 19

4. In the sequence 127, 118, 109, 100..., what number should come next?
   (A) 80
   (B) 89
   (C) 90
   (D) 91

5. In the sequence 35, 31, 27, 23..., what number should come next?
   (A) 17
   (B) 19
   (C) 21
   (D) 22

6. In the sequence −29, −26, −23, −20..., what number should come next?
   (A) −18
   (B) −17
   (C) −16
   (D) −15

7. In the sequence −34, −28, −22, −16..., what number should come next?
   (A) −22
   (B) −12
   (C) −10
   (D) −8

8. In the sequence −17, −13, −9, −5..., what number should come next?
   (A) −4
   (B) −3
   (C) −2
   (D) −1

9. In the sequence −52, −44, −36, −28..., what number should come next?
   (A) −20
   (B) −18
   (C) −16
   (D) −8

10. In the sequence −110, −95, −80, ___, −50, what number should fill in the blank?
    (A) −70
    (B) −65
    (C) −60
    (D) −55

11. In the sequence −2, −5, −8, −11..., what number should come next?
    (A) −16
    (B) −15
    (C) −14
    (D) −13

12. In the sequence −22, −29, −36, ___, −50, what number should fill in the blank?
    (A) −43
    (B) −42
    (C) −41
    (D) −40

13. In the sequence 97, 89, 81, ___, 65, what number should fill in the blank?
    (A) 69
    (B) 71
    (C) 72
    (D) 73

14. In the sequence 90, 102, ___, 126, 138, what number should fill in the blank?
    (A) 108
    (B) 110
    (C) 114
    (D) 118

15. In the sequence 21, 25, 31, 36, 41..., one number is *wrong*. That number should be:
    (A) 26
    (B) 32
    (C) 35
    (D) 46

16. Complete the series: 2, 4, 6, ___, 10, 12
    (A) 7
    (B) 8
    (C) 9
    (D) 6

17. In the sequence −4, 2, 8..., what number should come next?
    (A) 10
    (B) 11
    (C) 12
    (D) 14

18. In the sequence 19, 17, 15..., what number should come next?
    (A) 11
    (B) 12
    (C) 13
    (D) 14

19. In the sequence 41, 45, 49, 53..., what number should come next?
    (A) 54
    (B) 55
    (C) 56
    (D) 57

20. In the sequence 16, −2, −20..., what number should come next?
    (A) −37
    (B) −38
    (C) −39
    (D) −40

21. In the sequence 50, 81, 112..., what number should come next?
    (A) 141
    (B) 142
    (C) 143
    (D) 144

22. In the sequence 121, 112, 103..., what number should come next?
    (A) 93
    (B) 94
    (C) 95
    (D) 96

23. In the sequence 17, 30, 43..., what number should come next?
    (A) 56
    (B) 57
    (C) 58
    (D) 59

24. In the sequence 11, 28, 45..., what number should come next?
    (A) 60
    (B) 62
    (C) 65
    (D) 66

25. In the sequence 71, 62, 53..., what number should come next?
    (A) 41
    (B) 42
    (C) 44
    (D) 45

Quantitative Skills

26. In the sequence −18, −3, 12..., what number should come next?
    (A) 25
    (B) 26
    (C) 27
    (D) 28

27. In the sequence −27, −24, −21..., what number should come next?
    (A) −18
    (B) −19
    (C) −20
    (D) −21

28. In the sequence 101, 45, −11..., what number should come next?
    (A) −65
    (B) −66
    (C) −67
    (D) −68

29. In the sequence 11, 25, 39..., what number should come next?
    (A) 50
    (B) 51
    (C) 52
    (D) 53

30. In the sequence 1, −2, −5..., what number should come next?
    (A) −7
    (B) −8
    (C) −9
    (D) −10

Geometric

31. Fill in the blank in this series: 5, 30, ___, 1080...
    (A) 108
    (B) 180
    (C) 900
    (D) 1800

32. Fill in the blank in this series: 100, 20, ___, 0.8...
    (A) 1
    (B) 2
    (C) 4
    (D) 8

33. In the series 8, 56, ___, 2744..., what number should fill in the blank?
    (A) 392
    (B) 448
    (C) 881
    (D) 1080

34. In the sequence 10, 1, 0.1 ..., what number should come next?
    (A) 0.101
    (B) 0.01
    (C) 0.001
    (D) 0.0001

35. In the sequence 0.45, 9, ___, 3600..., what number should fill in the blank?
    (A) 180
    (B) 360
    (C) 720
    (D) 1800

36. In the sequence $\frac{1}{3}, -\frac{1}{6}, \frac{1}{12}$ ..., what number should come next?
    (A) $-\frac{1}{18}$
    (B) $-\frac{1}{24}$
    (C) $\frac{1}{24}$
    (D) $\frac{1}{18}$

37. Fill in the blank in this series:
    0.022, ___, 2.2, 22...
    (A) 0.2
    (B) 0.22
    (C) 1.2
    (D) 2.0

38. Fill in the blank in this series:
    1, 11, ___, 1331, ...
    (A) 110
    (B) 121
    (C) 131
    (D) 133

39. In this series: 1440, 120, ___, $\frac{10}{12}$..., what number should fill in the blank?
    (A) 8
    (B) 10
    (C) 12
    (D) 16

40. Fill in the blank in this series:
    13, ___, 117, 351, ...
    (A) 39
    (B) 52
    (C) 65
    (D) 78

41. Fill in the blank in this series:
    312, ___, 78, 39, ...
    (A) 13
    (B) 104
    (C) 156
    (D) 158

42. In the sequence 4, 12, 36 ..., what number should come next?
    (A) 48
    (B) 54
    (C) 72
    (D) 108

43. In the sequence 9, 9, 9..., what number should come next?
    (A) 0.9
    (B) 9
    (C) 10
    (D) 99

44. In the sequence 256, 64, 16 ..., what number should come next?
    (A) 2
    (B) 4
    (C) 6
    (D) 8

45. In the sequence 7, 1, $\frac{1}{7}$..., what number should come next?
    (A) $\frac{1}{49}$
    (B) $\frac{1}{28}$
    (C) $\frac{1}{14}$
    (D) $\frac{2}{7}$

46. In the sequence 1, 5, 25..., what number should follow?
    (A) 50
    (B) 75
    (C) 100
    (D) 125

47. Fill in the blank in this series:
    14, 7, ___, 1.75, ...
    (A) 3.5
    (B) 4.5
    (C) 4
    (D) 2.5

48. In this series: 1, −3, 9, ___, 81..., what number should fill in the blank?
    (A) −27
    (B) −18
    (C) 18
    (D) 27

49. Fill in the blank in this series:
    −2, ___, −50, 250, ...
    (A) −10
    (B) −5
    (C) 5
    (D) 10

50. In the sequence 70, 140, 280..., what number should come next?
    (A) 360
    (B) 420
    (C) 360
    (D) 560

51. In the sequence 12, 6, 3..., what number should come next?
    (A) $\frac{1}{2}$
    (B) $\frac{2}{3}$
    (C) 1
    (D) $\frac{3}{2}$

52. In the sequence 5,819, −5,819, 5,819, −5,819..., what number should come next?
    (A) −5,981
    (B) −5,819
    (C) 5,819
    (D) 5,981

53. In the sequence 405, 135, 45..., what number should come next?
    (A) 5
    (B) 10
    (C) 15
    (D) 30

54. In the sequence 1,728, 288, 48..., what number should come next?
    (A) 3
    (B) 4
    (C) 6
    (D) 8

55. In this series: −1, 8, −64..., what number should come next?
    (A) −512
    (B) −8
    (C) 8
    (D) 512

56. Fill in the blank in this series: 10, 50, ___, 1250...
    (A) 100
    (B) 200
    (C) 250
    (D) 550

57. In this series: 56, ___, 224, 448..., what number should fill in the blank?
    (A) 92
    (B) 102
    (C) 112
    (D) 118

58. In this series: 40, 800, 16,000..., what number should come next?
    (A) 32,000
    (B) 48,000
    (C) 320,000
    (D) 640,000

59. Fill in the blank in this series: 1, 6, ___, 216...
    (A) 16
    (B) 26
    (C) 36
    (D) 106

60. In the sequence 729, 81, 9..., what number should come next?
    (A) $\frac{1}{9}$
    (B) 1
    (C) 2
    (D) 4.5

Other

61. In the sequence 2, 10, 40, 120..., what number comes next?
    (A) 140
    (B) 200
    (C) 240
    (D) 360

62. In the sequence 0, 1, 3, 6, 10..., what comes next?
    (A) 13
    (B) 15
    (C) 16
    (D) 20

63. What element should come next in this series: 20, 17, 13, 8, ___?
    (A) 2
    (B) 3
    (C) 4
    (D) 5

64. In the sequence 240, 48, ___, 4, 2, what number should fill in the blank?
    (A) 8
    (B) 12
    (C) 16
    (D) 32

65. In the sequence 1, 2, 6, 24..., what number comes next?
    (A) 42
    (B) 48
    (C) 96
    (D) 120

66. In the sequence 10, 3, −3, −8..., what number comes next?
    (A) −14
    (B) −12
    (C) 8
    (D) 12

67. In the sequence 1, 10, 18, 25..., what number comes next?
    (A) 31
    (B) 32
    (C) 33
    (D) 34

68. In the sequence 48, 48, 24, ___, 2, what number fills in the blank?
    (A) 1
    (B) 4
    (C) 8
    (D) 24

69. In the sequence 3, 6, 10, 15..., what three numbers come next?
    (A) 20, 25, 30
    (B) 20, 26, 33
    (C) 21, 27, 33
    (D) 21, 28, 36

70. In the sequence 40, 31, 23, 16..., what number comes next?
    (A) 7
    (B) 8
    (C) 9
    (D) 10

71. In the sequence 0, 0, 3, 9, 6, 36..., what number should come next?
    (A) 7
    (B) 9
    (C) 36
    (D) 91

72. In the sequence 5, 25, 6, 36, 7..., what number comes next?
    (A) 8
    (B) 27
    (C) 37
    (D) 49

73. In the sequence 81, 9, 64, 8..., what three numbers should come next?
    (A) 7, 6, 5
    (B) 7, 49, 6
    (C) 49, 7, 36
    (D) 49, 36, 7

74. In the sequence H, K, N..., what comes next?
    (A) M
    (B) O
    (C) P
    (D) Q

75. In the sequence BA, DC, FE..., what should come next?
    (A) GH
    (B) HG
    (C) HI
    (D) IH

76. Which letter should come next in this series: Y, W, U, ___?
    (A) V
    (B) T
    (C) S
    (D) R

77. What number should fill in the blank in this series: I, V, IX, ___?
    (A) X
    (B) XI
    (C) XII
    (D) XIII

78. What number should fill in the blank in this series: A-I, ___, C-III, D-IV?
    (A) A-II
    (B) B-II
    (C) B-III
    (D) E-V

79. In the sequence 30K, 34L, 28M..., what term should come next?
    (A) 32M
    (B) 32N
    (C) 34M
    (D) 34N

80. In the sequence VII, 6, V..., what term comes next?
    (A) 4
    (B) 5
    (C) IV
    (D) VIII

81. In the sequence A6, E8, I16, M18..., what two terms should come next?
    (A) P20, T40
    (B) Q20, U40
    (C) P36, T38
    (D) Q36, U38

82. In the sequence B+23, C+24, E+26, H+29..., what comes next?
    (A) I+30
    (B) J+31
    (C) K+32
    (D) L+33

83. In the sequence 17×V, 16×U, 15×T..., what should come next?
    (A) 13×R
    (B) 13×S
    (C) 14×S
    (D) 14×T

84. What term should come fill in the blank in this series: I, 4, II, 8, ___, 12, IV?
    (A) 3
    (B) 6
    (C) III
    (D) XI

85. What number should fill in the blank in this series: QR, RS, ST, ___?
    (A) TU
    (B) TV
    (C) UV
    (D) UW

86. What number should fill in the blank in this series: 125, ___, 5, 1?
    (A) 5
    (B) 10
    (C) 15
    (D) 25

87. What number should fill in the blank in this series: 5, ___, 17, 34, 41?
    (A) 7
    (B) 10
    (C) 12
    (D) 15

88. What number should fill in the blank in this series: 0, 9, ___, 12, 4, 13?
    (A) 1
    (B) 2
    (C) 3
    (D) 6

89. In the sequence II, 4, III, 6, IV..., what three terms should come next?
    (A) 8, 5, X
    (B) XIII, 5, 10
    (C) 8, V, 10
    (D) XIII, V, X

90. In the sequence 500, 250, 50, 25..., what number comes next?
    (A) 5
    (B) 10
    (C) 15
    (D) 20

91. In the sequence 6, 12, 19, 25..., what should come next?
    (A) 29
    (B) 31
    (C) 32
    (D) 36

92. In the sequence 2, 4, 16, 32, 128, 256..., which number should come next?
    (A) 512
    (B) 612
    (C) 824
    (D) 1024

93. In the sequence 3, 13, 4, 14, 5..., which number should come next?
    (A) 6
    (B) 15
    (C) 16
    (D) 25

94. In the sequence $1, \frac{1}{3}, \frac{1}{6}, \frac{1}{18}, \frac{1}{36}$..., which number should come next?
    (A) 0
    (B) $\frac{1}{81}$
    (C) $\frac{1}{72}$
    (D) $\frac{1}{108}$

95. In the sequence $30, 10, 10, \frac{10}{3}, \frac{10}{3}, \frac{10}{9}$..., which number should come next?
    (A) $\frac{5}{3}$
    (B) $\frac{5}{6}$
    (C) $\frac{10}{9}$
    (D) $\frac{10}{27}$

96. In the sequence A140, D14, G70, J7..., what should come next?
    (A) M35
    (B) L45
    (C) N65
    (D) P110

97. In the sequence 3, 7, 15, 27..., which number should come next?
    (A) 31
    (B) 35
    (C) 43
    (D) 51

98. In the sequence 2, 18, 27, 243, 252..., which number should come next?
    (A) 261
    (B) 455
    (C) 557
    (D) 2268

99. Which number should fill the blank in the following sequence: 80, __, 38, 19, 17.
    (A) 40
    (B) 41
    (C) 50
    (D) 63

100. Which letter should fill the blank in the following sequence: A, F, __, P.
     (A) G
     (B) H
     (C) J
     (D) K

101. In the sequence 1111, 111, 11, 1..., which number should come next?
     (A) 0
     (B) $\frac{1}{11}$
     (C) $\frac{1}{10}$
     (D) −1

102. In the sequence NC45, QF40, TI35..., what should come next?
     (A) LX25
     (B) MX25
     (C) WL30
     (D) YL30

103. Which number should fill the blank in the following sequence: 1003, 1001, 1, −1, __, −1003, −2003?
     (A) −999
     (B) −1000
     (C) −1001
     (D) −1002

104. Which number should fill the blank in the following sequence: 2, −1, __, −10, −70, −73, −511?
     (A) −6
     (B) −7
     (C) −8
     (D) −9

Geometric Comparison

Overview

In this section, students are presented with geometric figures and are asked to choose the answer choice that correctly compares quantities related to these figures.

You will be asked to compare such elements as:

- Angles formed by lines
- Angles formed by shapes such as triangles, rectangles, and other polygons
- Lengths of radii, diameters, and chords in circles
- Area and circumference of circles
- Area and perimeter of polygons

How to Use This Section

As determined by your study plan, including the results of your diagnostic tests, we encourage you to focus on the topics that are most challenging to you. This section will give you exposure to the different types of questions that are presented in geometric comparison, and give you the practice to finding the path to the correct answer. If you find that you are challenged by this area and need additional help, remember to reach out to a trusted educator. Don't get discouraged! Take the materials to a teacher or tutor if you need additional enrichment in any given topic.

Tutorverse Tips!

With all comparison questions, it is a good idea to write down each value as you find it. This will make evaluation of the relationship between the choices easier. Find the value, write it down, and then compare!

Looking for a tutor?

Look no further—we're The Tutorverse for a reason! We offer one-one-one tutoring in-home or online. Our tutoring is the ultimate test-prep and supplemental educational service.

TO LEARN MORE, SCAN THE QR CODE OR VISIT:
thetutorverse.com/hspt

QUESTIONS? SEND US AN EMAIL:
hello@thetutorverse.com

Geometric Comparison Exercises
Comparison of Angles

1. Examine the angles below and find the *best* answer.

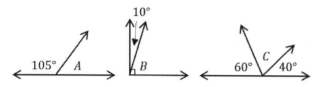

(A) ∠A > ∠B = ∠C
(B) ∠A > ∠C > ∠B
(C) ∠C > ∠B > ∠A
(D) ∠A < ∠B = ∠C

2. Examine the angles below and find the *best* answer.

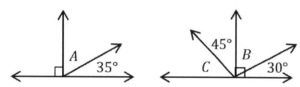

(A) ∠B > ∠A > ∠C
(B) ∠B = ∠C
(C) ∠A > ∠B > ∠C
(D) ∠A = ∠C

3. Examine the angles below and find the *best* answer.

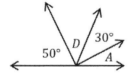 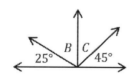

(A) ∠A = ∠D
(B) ∠B + ∠C = ∠A + ∠D
(C) ∠A + ∠D < ∠B + ∠C
(D) ∠B = ∠C

4. Examine the angles A, B, and C in the right triangle and find the *best* answer.

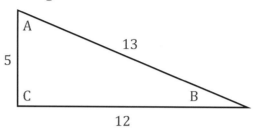

(A) ∠C = ∠A > ∠B
(B) ∠A = ∠C < ∠B
(C) ∠C = ∠B + ∠A
(D) ∠C < ∠A = ∠B

5. Examine the angles A, B, and C and find the *best* answer. (Note: Figure not drawn to scale)

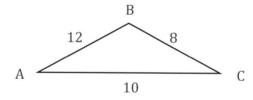

(A) ∠A = ∠C > ∠B
(B) ∠A > ∠C > ∠B
(C) ∠A < ∠B < ∠C
(D) ∠A < ∠B = ∠C

6. Examine the sides A, B, and C and find the *best* answer.

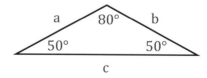

(A) c > b = a
(B) b = c < a
(C) b < a < c
(D) a = b > c

7. Examine the angles A, B, and C and find the *best* answer. (Note: Figure not drawn to scale)

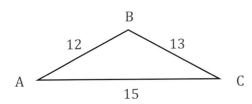

(A) ∠B > ∠A > ∠C
(B) ∠A < ∠B = ∠C
(C) ∠A = ∠B = ∠C
(D) ∠C = ∠A > ∠B

8. Below are a rectangle and right triangle. Find the *best* answer.

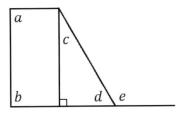

(A) $c + d = e$
(B) $b = d$
(C) $e > a$
(D) $a > b$

9. Below are two rectangles, with a diagonal dividing one of them. Find the *best* answer.

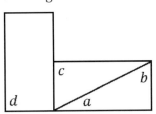

(A) $a + c < d$
(B) $a + b > d$
(C) $b = c$
(D) $a + b + c = 180$

10. Given that m is parallel to n, examine angles A, B, C, D, E, F, G, and H and find the best answer.

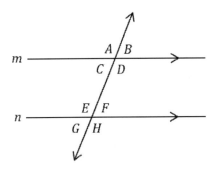

(A) ∠A = ∠G
(B) ∠B = ∠E
(C) ∠D = ∠G
(D) ∠A = ∠E

11. Examine the angles and find the *best* answer.

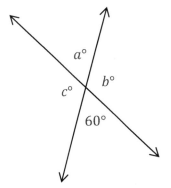

Note: Figure not drawn to scale.

(A) $a = c$
(B) $b = a + a$
(C) $a + c > b + 60$
(D) $b - a = c$

12. Examine the angles and find the *best* answer.

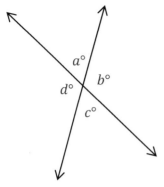

   (A) $a + c = b + d$
   (B) $a = b = c = d$
   (C) $a = c$
   (D) $b + c < a + d$

13. Examine the angles and find the *best* answer.

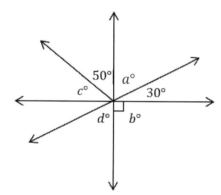

   (A) $d = b$
   (B) $c < a < b$
   (C) $a + c = b$
   (D) $b = c$

14. Examine the angles and find the best answer.

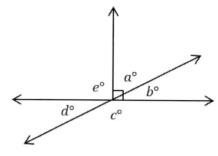

   (A) $b = c$
   (B) $d + e < a + b$
   (C) $a + b = e$
   (D) $b + c = a + e$

15. Examine the angles in rectangle ABCD and find the *best* answer.

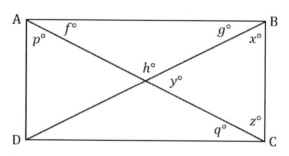

   (A) $g + h = g + x$
   (B) $f = z$
   (C) $f + g + h = x + y + z$
   (D) $g + x > q + z$

16. Examine the angles in rectangle ABCD and find the *best* answer.

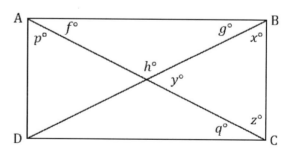

   (A) $f + p = q + z$
   (B) $f + h = x + y$
   (C) $y + z = g + x$
   (D) $h + y = g + x$

Comparison of Polygons

17. Examine the following and find the best answer.

    I. The length of SU, a chord of circle Q
    II. The length of PQ, where Q is the center of the circle
    III. The sum of the lengths of QT and QR, where Q is the center of the circle

    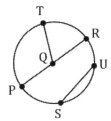

    (A) III is greater than I
    (B) I, II, and III are all equal
    (C) I is greater than III
    (D) II is greater than III

18. Examine the following and find the best answer.

    I. The area of a triangle with a base of 10 and a height of 6
    II. The area of a triangle with a base of 8 and a height of 8
    III. The area of a right triangle with legs of length 6 and 8

    (A) I is less than II, and II is less than III
    (B) III is greater than II, and I is greater than II
    (C) II is greater than I, and I is greater than III
    (D) I and III are equal, and both are less than II

19. Examine the following and find the best answer.

    I. The area of a rectangle with length 12 and width 4
    II. The area of a circle with radius of 5
    III. The area of a circle with diameter of 6

    (A) III is greater than II, and II is greater than I
    (B) II is greater than I, and I is greater than III
    (C) III is greater than I, and I is greater than II
    (D) III is greater than II, and I and II are equal

20. Examine the following and find the best answer.

    I. The area of a circle with radius 4
    II. The area of a circle with radius 5
    III. The area of a circle with diameter 8

    (A) I is less than II, and II and III are equal
    (B) I is less than II, and II is less than III
    (C) III is greater than II, and II is greater than I
    (D) II is greater than I, and I and III are equal

21. Examine the following and find the best answer.

    I. The area of a triangle with a base of 8 and a height of 12
    II. The area of a parallelogram with a base of 8 and a height of 12
    III. The area of a rectangle with length of 12 and width of 8

    (A) I = II = III
    (B) II = III > I
    (C) I = II < III
    (D) I < II < III

22. Examine the following and find the best answer.

    I. The area of a 45-45-90 triangle with base of 8
    II. The area of a square with side 8
    III. The area of a circle with diameter 8

    (A) II > III > I
    (B) I = II < III
    (C) I < II < III
    (D) I = III < II

23. Examine the following and find the best answer.

    I. The area of a parallelogram with base of 7 and height of 5
    II. The area of a 45-45-90 triangle with base of 6
    III. The area of a rectangle with length of 9 and height of 4

    (A) I and III are equal, and both are greater than II
    (B) II is less than III, and III is less than I
    (C) II is greater than I, and I is greater than III
    (D) III is greater than I, and I is greater than II

24. Examine the following and find the best answer.

    I. The circumference of a circle with radius 5
    II. The perimeter of an equilateral triangle with side 10
    III. The perimeter of a rectangle with width of 7 and length of 9

    (A) II is less than I, and I is less than III
    (B) II is greater than I, and I is greater than III
    (C) III is greater than I, and I is equal to II
    (D) I, II, and III are all equal

25. Examine the square and find the best answer.

    I. the sum of the length of sides AB and AC
    II. the length of diagonal BC
    III. the perimeter of square ABDC

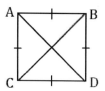

    (A) III > I = II
    (B) I < II < III
    (C) I > II > III
    (D) II < I < III

26. Examine the square and find the best answer.

    I. the length of diagonal BC
    II. the length of leg BD
    III. the length of leg CD

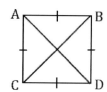

    (A) II + III < I
    (B) I > II = III
    (C) I = II = III
    (D) II + III = I

27. Examine the following rectangle and find the best answer.

    I. the measure of ∠PON
    II. the sum of the angles ∠MNP and ∠MPN
    III. the sum of the angles ∠ONP and ∠NPO

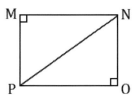

   (A) I > II = III
   (B) II + III = I
   (C) I, II, and III are all equal
   (D) I > II > III

28. Examine the following triangle and find the best answer.

    I. the measure of ∠A
    II. the measure of ∠B
    III. the measure of ∠C

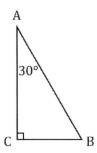

   (A) III is greater than I, and I and II are equal
   (B) III is greater than II, and II is greater than I
   (C) The sum of I and II is greater than III
   (D) The sum of I and II is less than III

29. Examine the following and find the best answer.

    I. the length of diameter AC
    II. the circumference of circle O
    III. the length of diameter BD

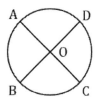

   (A) I and III are equal, and both are less than II
   (B) I is less than III, and III is less than II
   (C) The sum of I and III is equal to II
   (D) II is less than I, and I and III are equal

30. Examine the following and find the best answer.

    I. The sum of the angles of a pentagon
    II. The sum of the angles of a triangle
    III. The sum of the angles of a square

   (A) II < III < I
   (B) II > III > I
   (C) III > II > I
   (D) Not enough information is given to solve the problem

Non-Geometric Comparison

Overview

Non-geometric comparison questions test your ability to see relationships between numbers or equations. You will determine three quantities, and then choose an answer that correctly relates the three quantities.

The types of comparisons you will make include:

- Algebraic comparisons: solving or reducing expressions to compare values
- Counting: finding values given boxes, dice, pictures with a key
- Fractions, decimals, and percents
- Values from line graphs, bar graphs, and pie charts
- Measurements with different units
- Order of operations
- Slopes and intercepts of lines from equations and graphs

How to Use This Section

As determined by your study plan, including the results of your diagnostic tests, we encourage you to focus on the topics that are most challenging to you. This section will give you exposure to the different types of questions that are presented in non-geometric comparison, and give you the practice to finding the path to the correct answer. If you find that you are challenged by this area and need additional help, remember to reach out to a trusted educator. Don't get discouraged! Take the materials to a teacher or tutor if you need additional enrichment in any given topic.

Tutorverse Tips!

With all comparison questions, it is a good idea to write down each value as you find it. This will make evaluation of the relationship between the choices easier. Find the value, write it down, and then compare!

Looking for a tutor?

Look no further—we're The Tutorverse for a reason! We offer one-one-one tutoring in-home or online. Our tutoring is the ultimate test-prep and supplemental educational service.

TO LEARN MORE, SCAN THE QR CODE OR VISIT:
thetutorverse.com/hspt

QUESTIONS? SEND US AN EMAIL:
hello@thetutorverse.com

Non-Geometric Comparison Exercises
Algebraic Comparison

1. Examine I, II, and III and find the *best* answer if $x = 2$.

   I. $x + 6$
   II. $2x^2 + x$
   III. $x^2 + 4$

   (A) I = III < II
   (B) II = III
   (C) I = II < III
   (D) I < II < III

2. Examine I, II, and III and find the *best* answer if $x = 5$.

   I. $2x - 2$
   II. $2(x - 1)$
   III. $x + 2$

   (A) I > II > III
   (B) II < III
   (C) I = II > III
   (D) I = III > II

3. Examine I, II, and III and find the *best* answer if $x = 1$.

   I. $\frac{x+3}{2}$
   II. $4 - 2x$
   III. $x^3 + 1$

   (A) I = II < III
   (B) I = III > II
   (C) I = II = III
   (D) I < II = III

4. Examine I, II, and III and find the *best* answer if $x = 0$.

   I. $x^4 + 4$
   II. $2x^3 + x$
   III. $5 - x$

   (A) III > II > I
   (B) II > III
   (C) I > III
   (D) II < I < III

5. Examine I, II, and III and find the *best* answer when *x* and *y* are both positive.

   I. $x + 2y$
   II. $-(-x - 2y)$
   III. $2(x + y)$

   (A) I = II = III
   (B) I = II < III
   (C) I < II < III
   (D) I > II

6. Examine I, II, and III and find the *best* answer when *x* and *y* are both positive.

   I. $2x - 2y$
   II. $\frac{4x+2y}{2}$
   III. $3x - y - x$

   (A) II > III > I
   (B) III > II
   (C) I > II
   (D) II = III

7. Examine I, II, and III and find the *best* answer when *x* and *y* are both positive.

   I. $-x + 3y + x$
   II. $3(y - x)$
   III. $x + 3y$

   (A) III > II > I
   (B) I = II
   (C) II = III
   (D) II < I < III

8. Examine I, II, and III and find the *best* answer if $x = 4$.

   I. $2x + 3$
   II. x^2
   III. $3(x - 2)$

   (A) III < I < II
   (B) II > III > I
   (C) I > II
   (D) I = III

9. Examine I, II, and III and find the *best* answer if $x = 3$.

   I. $\frac{2x}{3}$
   II. $2x - 4$
   III. $5 - x$

   (A) II = III > I
   (B) II > III
   (C) I = II = III
   (D) I < II

10. Examine I, II, and III and find the *best* answer if $x = 10$.

    I. $4x$
    II. $\frac{x^2}{2}$
    III. $2(x + 5)$

    (A) I > II
    (B) I < III
    (C) II > I > III
    (D) II < I < III

11. Examine I, II, and III and find the *best* answer if $x = 1$.

    I. $3x^3$
    II. $4x$
    III. $2x^2 + 2$

    (A) I = II
    (B) II = III > I
    (C) I < II < III
    (D) II > III > I

Counting

12. Examine I, II, and III and find the *best* answer:

    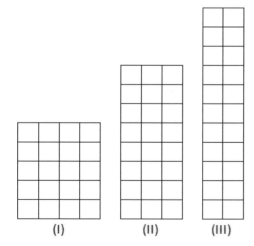

    (A) II < III < I
    (B) III < II < I
    (C) II > III > I
    (D) II < III = I

13. Examine I, II, and III and find the *best* answer:

    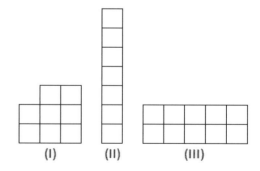

    (A) I = II < III
    (B) II < III < I
    (C) II > I > III
    (D) II < I < III

14. Examine I, II, and III and find the *best* answer:

    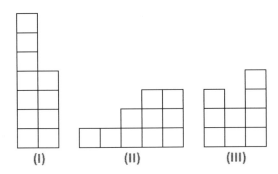

    (A) I equals II, but both are less than III
    (B) III is greater than II which is greater than I
    (C) I, II, and III are equal
    (D) I is greater than II which is greater than III

15. Examine I, II, and III and find the *best* answer:

    KEY

    Circle = 5

    Star = 1

    answer:

    (A) I < II < III
    (B) II > III > I
    (C) II = III > I
    (D) II = III < I

16. Examine I, II, and III and find the *best* answer:

    KEY

    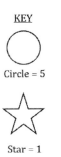

    Circle = 5

    Star = 1

    answer:

    (A) The sum of II and III is equal to I
    (B) II is less than I which is less than III
    (C) II is equal to III which is less than I
    (D) The sum of II and III is less than I

17. Examine I, II, and III and find the *best* answer:

    KEY

    Large House = 10 houses

    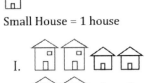

    Small House = 1 house

    (A) I = II > III
    (B) I < II < III
    (C) I + II > III
    (D) III > I > II

18. Examine I, II, and III and find the *best* answer:

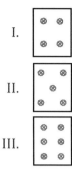

I.

II.

III.

(A) I + III < II
(B) I + II > III
(C) I + II = III
(D) III < II < I

19. Examine I, II, and III and find the *best* answer:

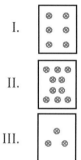

I.

II.

III.

(A) II is greater than III which is greater than I
(B) The sum of II and III is less than I
(C) I is greater than II which is greater than III
(D) The sum of I and III is less than II

20. Examine I, II, and III and find the *best* answer:

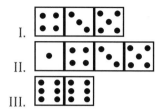

I.

II.

III.

(A) I = II > III
(B) I = II = III
(C) II > III > I
(D) II > III = I

21. Examine I, II, and III and find the *best* answer:

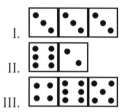

I.

II.

III.

(A) III > II > I
(B) III > II = I
(C) I > II > III
(D) III < I + II

Fractions, Decimals, Percents

22. Examine I, II, and III, and find the *best* answer.

    I. $\frac{1}{2}$
    II. $\frac{3}{5}$
    III. $\frac{6}{10}$

    (A) I = II > III
    (B) I < II < III
    (C) I < III < II
    (D) I < II = III

23. Examine I, II, and III, and find the *best* answer.

    I. 2.874
    II. $\sqrt{9}$
    III. $\frac{19}{6}$

    (A) I > II = III
    (B) I = II < III
    (C) III < II < I
    (D) III > II > I

24. Examine I, II, and III, and find the *best* answer.

    I. 108%
    II. $\sqrt{1}$
    III. $\frac{7}{5}$

    (A) II < III < I
    (B) II < I < III
    (C) III < II < I
    (D) I < II < III

25. Examine I, II, and III, and find the *best* answer.

    I. 25% of 32
    II. $\frac{1}{2}$ of 24
    III. $\frac{2}{3}$ of 18

    (A) III > II > I
    (B) I < II = III
    (C) I = II < III
    (D) III = I > II

26. Examine I, II, and III, and find the *best* answer.

    I. 8 ÷ 0.4
    II. 8 ÷ 4
    III. 0.8 ÷ 0.4

    (A) I = II = III
    (B) I = II > III
    (C) I > II = III
    (D) I > III > II

27. Examine I, II, and III, and find the *best* answer.

    I. 1.2 ÷ 4
    II. 1.2 × 4
    III. 1.2 × 0.4

    (A) I = II = III
    (B) I = II < III
    (C) I = III < II
    (D) I < III < II

28. Examine I, II, and III, and find the *best* answer.

    I. $\frac{8}{100} + \frac{7}{10} + 2$
    II. $\frac{9}{100} + \frac{3}{10} + 4$
    III. $\frac{6}{100} + \frac{9}{10} + 2$

    (A) I > II > III
    (B) II > I > III
    (C) II > III > I
    (D) II > I = III

29. Examine I, II, and III, and find the *best* answer.

I.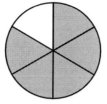

II.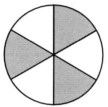

III.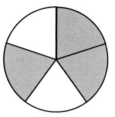

(A) I is more shaded than II, and II and III are equally shaded
(B) I is more shaded than III, and III is more shaded than II
(C) I is less shaded than II, and II is less shaded than III
(D) I is less shaded than II, and II and III are equally shaded

30. Examine I, II, and III, and find the *best* answer.

I. $\frac{7}{10} + \frac{3}{100} + 7$
II. $\frac{4}{100} + \frac{9}{10} + 7$
III. $\frac{6}{100} + \frac{2}{10} + 7$

(A) II > I > III
(B) I = III < II
(C) II < I < III
(D) I > II = III

31. Examine I, II, and III, and find the *best* answer.

I. $6 + \frac{4}{10} + \frac{8}{100}$
II. $\frac{5}{100} + \frac{6}{10} + 8$
III. $8 + \frac{6}{100} + \frac{2}{10}$

(A) II = III > I
(B) I > III > II
(C) II > I > III
(D) I < III < II

32. Examine I, II, and III, and find the *best* answer.

I. $11 + \frac{4}{100} + \frac{8}{1000}$
II. $\frac{1}{100} + \frac{3}{10} + 11$
III. $10 + \frac{9}{100} + \frac{7}{10}$

(A) I > II > III
(B) I = II > III
(C) III < II < I
(D) II > I > III

33. Examine I, II, and III, and find the *best* answer.

I. 0.1011
II. 0.011
III. 0.00101

(A) III < II < I
(B) I = III < II
(C) I < II < III
(D) II > I > III

Graphs

34. Examine the line graph and find the *best* answer.

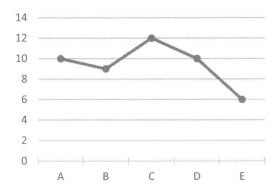

(A) A equals D
(B) B is greater than D
(C) D plus E equals A plus B
(D) A, B, and D are equal

35. Examine the line graph and find the *best* answer.

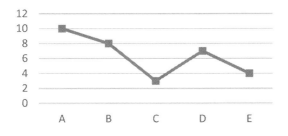

(A) C plus D equals A
(B) B and D are equal
(C) D plus E is less than A
(D) C and E are equal

36. Examine the line graph and find the *best* answer.

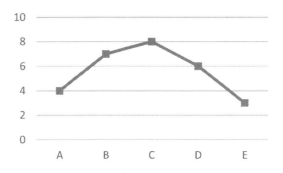

(A) E is less than D, and D is less than A
(B) Twice A equals C
(C) B plus D equals A plus C
(D) B equals D

37. The following graph shows how many hours of television Tracy and Darren watched on each day of the week. Find the *best* answer.

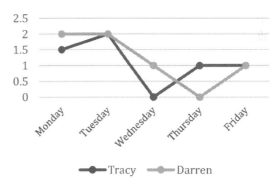

(A) Darren and Tracy watched the same amount on Thursday
(B) Darren watched more than Tracy on Friday
(C) The lowest amount of television Darren watched was on Tuesday.
(D) The highest amount of television Tracy watched was on Tuesday.

38. Mrs. Taylor and Mr. Dunable keep track of how many students in their class have a birthday each month, and the following graph records that information. Find the *best* answer.

Number of Birthdays Each Month

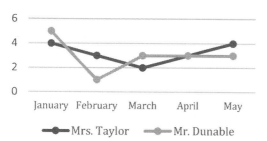

(A) More students have a birthday in March in Mrs. Taylor's class
(B) Fewer students have a birthday in May in Mrs. Taylor's class
(C) More students have a birthday in February in Mr. Dunable's class
(D) Fewer students have a birthday in May in Mr. Dunable's class

39. The following graph records how many students received a particular grade on a test in Mr. Bradford's and Mr. Trimble's math classes. Find the *best* answer.

Number of Students Receiving a Certain Letter Grade

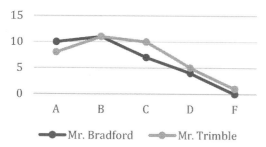

(A) In both classes, more students got a B on the test than any other grade
(B) More students got a C in Mr. Bradford's class than In Mr. Trimble's
(C) Fewer students got an A in Mr. Bradford's class than In Mr. Trimble's
(D) More students got a B in Mr. Trimble's class than In Mr. Bradford's

40. The following graph shows how many hours Mark and Jamal spent doing homework each day of the week. Find the *best* answer.

Hours Spent on Homework

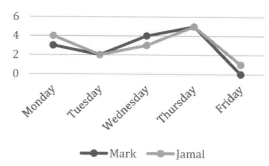

(A) On Monday, Mark spent more time doing homework than Jamal did.
(B) The sums of Jamal's hours and Mark's hours are the same.
(C) The sum of Jamal's hours was higher than the sum of Mark's hours
(D) The sum of Mark's hours was higher than the sum of Jamal's hours

41. The graph below shows how many pages Teresa read each week. Find the *best* answer.

Pages Read by Teresa

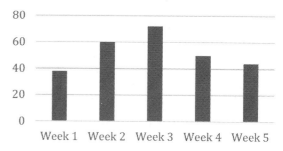

(A) Teresa read the greatest number of pages in week 1
(B) Teresa read more in week 5 than week 4
(C) Teresa read the greatest number of pages in week 3
(D) Teresa read the least number of pages in week 5

42. Examine the bar graph and find the *best* answer.

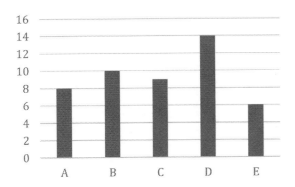

(A) The sum of A and E is equal to D
(B) The sum of B and C is less than D
(C) The sum of A and E is less than B
(D) The sum of A and B is equal to the sum of D and E

43. Examine the bar graph and find the *best* answer.

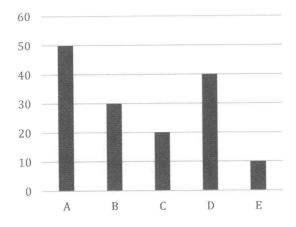

(A) C is smaller than both D and E
(B) B is greater than D
(C) The sum of A and B is twice the value of D
(D) The sum of B and E is greater than A

44. The following graph records how many points Jamila and Darcy scored in the first five games of the basketball season. Find the *best* answer.

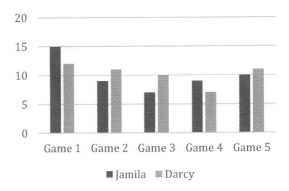

(A) Jamila and Darcy each had their lowest-scoring game in game 4
(B) Jamila outscored Darcy in game 5
(C) Jamila and Darcy each had their highest-scoring game in game 1
(D) Darcy outscored Jamila in game 4

45. The following graph records how many students in Mrs. Henderson's and Mrs. Vo's classes brought a canned good for the food drive. Find the *best* answer.

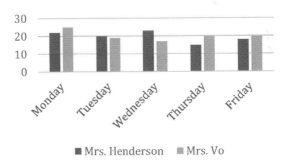

(A) Mrs. Vo's class had more students participate in three of the five days
(B) Mrs. Henderson's class had more students participate in three of the five days
(C) Mrs. Henderson's and Mrs. Vo's classes tied on one of the days
(D) Thursday was the lowest day of participation for Mrs. Vo's class

46. The following bar graph tracks two different variables over five weeks. Find the *best* answer.

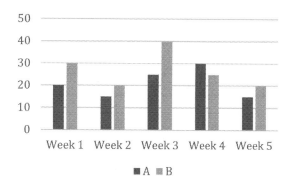

(A) The sum of A over all five weeks was greater than the sum of B all five weeks
(B) The sum of A over all five weeks was equal to the sum of B all five weeks
(C) B was greater than A in each of the five weeks
(D) B was greater than A in four of the five weeks

47. The following bar graph tracks two different variables over five weeks. Find the *best* answer.

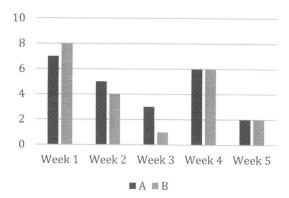

(A) The sum of A over five weeks was greater than the sum of B over five weeks
(B) The sum of A over five weeks was less than the sum of B over five weeks
(C) A and B were never equal in any of the five weeks
(D) A was greater than B in three of the five weeks

48. The following circle graph shows the value of four variables. Find the *best* answer.

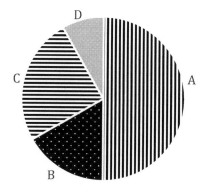

(A) A > B > C
(B) A > C > B
(C) A > D > B
(D) B > C > D

Measurements

49. Examine I, II, and III and find the *best* answer.

    I. 5 oz.
    II. 7 oz.
    III. 9 oz.

    (A) The sum of I and II is less than III
    (B) The difference of III and I is equal to II
    (C) The difference of III and II is equal to the difference of II and I
    (D) The sum of I, II, and III is greater than 24 oz.

50. Examine I, II, and III and find the *best* answer.

    I. 8 mm
    II. 2 cm
    III. 11 mm

    (A) I + III < II
    (B) I + II < III
    (C) III - I > II
    (D) I + II = III

51. Examine I, II, and III and find the *best* answer.

    I. 47 mm
    II. 38 mm
    III. 5 cm

    (A) I > II > III
    (B) II < III < I
    (C) III > I > II
    (D) I + II < III

52. Examine I, II, and III and find the *best* answer.

    I. 1 L
    II. 500 ml
    III. 750 ml

    (A) III is greater than I, and I is greater than II
    (B) I is greater than III, and III is greater than II
    (C) III is greater than II, and II is equal to I
    (D) I is greater than II, and II is greater than III

53. Examine I, II, and III and find the *best* answer.

    I. 90 mm
    II. 3 cm
    III. 6 cm

    (A) II is less than III, and III is less than I
    (B) The sum of II and III is greater than I
    (C) The sum of II and III is less than I
    (D) I is greater than II, and II is greater than III

54. Examine I, II, and III and find the *best* answer.

    I. The perimeter of a triangle with sides 5, 4, and 7
    II. The perimeter of a triangle with sides 3, 6, and 8
    III. The perimeter of equilateral triangle shown:

    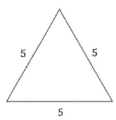

    (A) III < II < I
    (B) III < I < II
    (C) II > III > I
    (D) I = II

55. Examine I, II, and III and find the *best* answer.

   I. The perimeter of a triangle with sides 6, 4, and 9
   II. The perimeter of equilateral triangle shown:

   III. The perimeter of a triangle with sides 6, 5, and 9

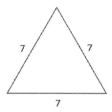

   (A) I < II < III
   (B) I < II = III
   (C) I = II = III
   (D) II > III > I

56. Examine I, II, and III and find the *best* answer.

   I. The perimeter of a triangle with sides 2, 2, and 2
   II. The perimeter of a right triangle with legs of 3 and 4
   III. The perimeter of isosceles triangle shown:

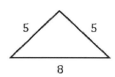

   (A) The sum of I and II is equal to III
   (B) The sum of I and II is greater than III
   (C) The sum of I and II is less than III
   (D) The sum of I and III is equal to II

57. Examine I, II, and III and find the *best* answer.

   I. The perimeter of a triangle with sides 3, 3, and 4
   II. The perimeter of the right triangle shown:

   III. The perimeter of a triangle with sides 4, 4, and 4

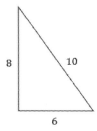

   (A) The difference of II and III is greater than I
   (B) III is greater than I, which is greater than II
   (C) The sum of I and III is greater than II
   (D) The sum of I and III is equal to II

58. Examine I, II, and III and find the *best* answer.

   I. The area of the rectangle shown below:
   II. The area of a 5 x 3 rectangle
   III. The area of a 3 x 2 rectangle

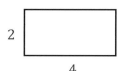

   (A) I < III < II
   (B) II - III < I
   (C) I + III < II
   (D) II > I = III

59. Examine I, II, and III and find the *best* answer.

   I. The area of a 6 x 5 rectangle
   II. The area of the rectangle shown below:
   III. The area of a 5 x 3 rectangle

   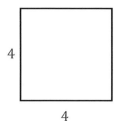

   (A) II + III < I
   (B) II = III < I
   (C) III > I - II
   (D) II < III < I

60. Examine I, II, and III and find the *best* answer.

   I. The area of the rectangle shown below:
   II. The area of a 3 x 3 rectangle
   III. The area of a 4 x 2 rectangle

   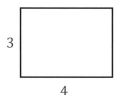

   (A) III is less than II, which is less than I
   (B) III is less than I, which is less than II
   (C) The sum of II and III is less than I
   (D) II and III are equal, and both are less than I

61. Examine I, II, and III and find the *best* answer.

   I. The area of a 6 x 4 rectangle
   II. The area of a 5 x 5 rectangle
   III. The area of the rectangle shown below:

   (A) III is less than I, which is less than II
   (B) I and III are equal, and both are less than II
   (C) I, II and III are all equal
   (D) I and III are equal, and both are greater than II

62. Examine I, II, and III and find the *best* answer.

   I. 120 seconds
   II. 100 seconds
   III. 2 minutes

   (A) I > II > III
   (B) I + II < III
   (C) III > II > I
   (D) I = III > II

63. Examine I, II, and III and find the *best* answer.

   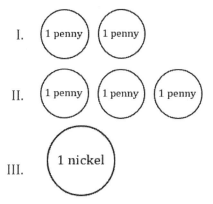

   (A) I is less than II, which is equal to III
   (B) III is less than I, which is less than II
   (C) The sum of I and II is equal to III
   (D) The difference of III and II is less than I

Order of Operations

64. Examine the below. Find the best answer:
    I. 2^{-2}
    II. $(-2)^2$
    III. $(-2)^{-2}$

    (A) I and III are equal
    (B) II and III are equal
    (C) I is smaller than III
    (D) III is greater than II

65. Examine the below. Find the best answer:
    I. $-(3^2)$
    II. $(-3)^2$
    III. $(-3)^{-2}$

    (A) I, II, III are equal
    (B) II and III are equal
    (C) I is smaller than III
    (D) I is greater than II

66. Examine the below. Find the best answer:
    I. $-(2^3 + 1)$
    II. $(-2)^3 + 1$
    III. $(-2 + 1)^3$

    (A) I, II, III are equal
    (B) II and III are equal
    (C) I is smaller than III
    (D) I is greater than II

67. Examine the below. Find the best answer:
    I. $9 \times (10 + 3)$
    II. $(10 \times 9) + 27$
    III. $(3 \times 40) + 9$

    (A) I and II are equal
    (B) II and III are equal
    (C) I is greater than III
    (D) I is greater than II

68. Examine the below. Find the best answer:
    I. 9×10^2
    II. $(10 \times 10) \times 9^2$
    III. 0.090×10^3

    (A) I and II are equal
    (B) II and III are equal
    (C) I is greater than II
    (D) I is greater than III

69. Examine the below. Find the best answer:
    I. 32^2
    II. 2^6
    III. 4^4

    (A) I < II < III
    (B) I > III > II
    (C) III > II > I
    (D) III > I > II

70. Examine the below. Find the best answer:
    I. 16^1
    II. 2^4
    III. 4^2

    (A) I < II < III
    (B) I > III = II
    (C) I = III < II
    (D) I = II = III

71. Examine the below. Find the best answer:
    I. 2×3^2
    II. $2^3 \times 2$
    III. 3×2^2

    (A) I < III < II
    (B) I = III = II
    (C) I = II > III
    (D) I > II > III

72. Examine the below. Find the best answer:

   I. 8.01×10^2
   II. 8^2
   III. 0.801×10^1

   (A) I and III are equal
   (B) II and III are equal
   (C) I is smaller than III
   (D) II is greater than III

73. Examine the below. Find the best answer:

   I. $6 \times (1 + 2)$
   II. $1 + (5 \times 1) + 2$
   III. $(1 + 5) \times (1 + 2)$

   (A) I and III are equal
   (B) II and III are equal
   (C) I is smaller than III
   (D) II is greater than III

74. Examine the below. Find the best answer:

   I. $-3 \times (5 + 2) - 6$
   II. $-(3 \times 5) + 2 - 6$
   III. $(-3 \times 5) - (2 - 6)$

   (A) I is greater than III
   (B) II and III are equal
   (C) I is smaller than III
   (D) II is greater than III

75. Examine the below. Find the best answer:

   I. $-(2 + 3) - 6(4 - 1)$
   II. $(-2 + 3) + 6(-4 - 1)$
   III. $-(2 - 3) - 6(4 + 1)$

   (A) I is smaller than III
   (B) II and III are equal
   (C) I is smaller than II
   (D) III is greater than II

76. Examine the below. Find the best answer:

   I. $-8 + 13$
   II. $-(8 + 13)$
   III. $13 - 8$

   (A) I is greater than II, which is greater than III
   (B) II is smaller than I and III, which are equal
   (C) II and III are equal and smaller than I
   (D) I is greater than III, which is greater than II

77. Examine the below. Find the best answer:

   I. $-2 \times (3 + 11)$
   II. $(-2 \times 3) + 11$
   III. $-(2 \times 3) + 11$

   (A) I is greater than II
   (B) II is smaller than III
   (C) I is smaller than III
   (D) I is greater than III

78. Examine the below. Find the best answer:

   I. $-(1 + 15) + 3$
   II. $(-1 + 15) + 3$
   III. $-1 - 15 - 3$

   (A) I is greater than II, which is greater than III
   (B) I is smaller than II, which is smaller than III
   (C) III is smaller than I, which is smaller than II
   (D) I is greater than III, which is greater than II

79. Examine the below. Find the best answer:

   I. 1.043×10^6
   II. $1,043,000$
   III. $1,043 \times 10^3$

   (A) I, II, and III are equal
   (B) I is greater than II, which is greater than III
   (C) I is smaller than II, which is smaller than III
   (D) II is greater than III, which is greater than I

Slope

80. Examine I, II, and III and find the best answer.

   I. the *y*-intercept of the line shown
   II. the *y*-intercept of $y = 0x - 3$
   III. the *y*-intercept of $-x + y = 3$

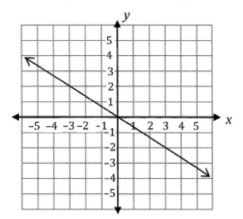

   (A) I = II > III
   (B) II = III > I
   (C) I < II = III
   (D) II < I < III

81. Examine I, II, and III and find the best answer.

   I. the *y*-intercept of $y = 2x - 2$
   II. the *y*-intercept of the line shown
   III. the *y*-intercept of $2x + 2y = -2$

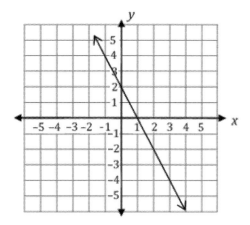

   (A) II > III > I
   (B) I > III > II
   (C) I = III < II
   (D) I = II = III

82. Examine I, II, and III and find the best answer.

   I. the *y*-intercept of $y = 2x - 8$
   II. the *y*-intercept of $2x + y = 8$
   III. the *y*-intercept of the line shown

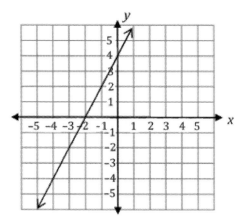

   (A) I is greater than II
   (B) I is less than III
   (C) II is equal to III
   (D) III is less than I

83. Examine I, II, and III and find the best answer.

   I. the *y*-intercept of the line shown
   II. the *y*-intercept of $y = -\frac{1}{2}x - 2$
   III. the *y*-intercept of $2x + y = -1$

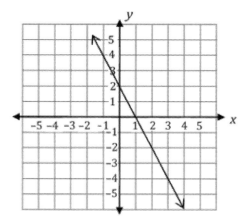

   (A) I is equal to II
   (B) I is greater than III
   (C) II is greater than III
   (D) III is equal to I

84. Examine I, II, and III and find the best answer.

   I. the y-intercept of $y = x + 3$
   II. the y-intercept of the line shown
   III. the y-intercept of $x + 3y = 3$

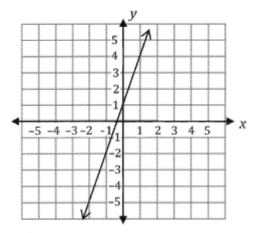

(A) I is equal to II
(B) II is equal to III
(C) I is greater than III
(D) III is greater than II

85. Examine I, II, and III and find the best answer.

   I. the slope of $x + y = -2$
   II. the y-intercept of $y = 2x - 5$
   III. the slope of the line shown

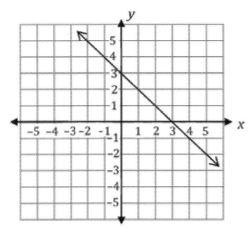

(A) I is equal to II
(B) I is equal to III
(C) II is equal to III
(D) II is greater than I

86. Examine I, II, and III and find the best answer.

   I. the y-intercept of the line shown
   II. the slope of $4x + 2y = 10$
   III. the y-intercept of $y = 2x - 10$

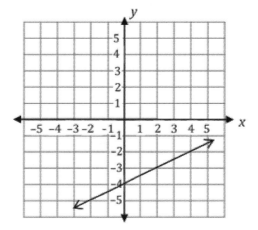

(A) I > II
(B) I = III
(C) I > III
(D) II < III

87. Examine I, II, and III and find the best answer.

   I. the slope of $y = 6x - 3$
   II. the y-intercept of $6x + 3y = 1$
   III. the slope of the line shown

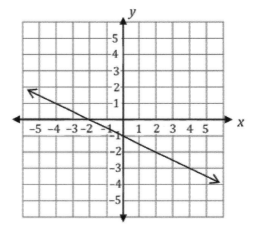

(A) I < II
(B) II < III
(C) I > III
(D) I = III

88. Examine I, II, and III and find the best answer.

   I. the *y*-intercept of $4x - y = 2$
   II. the slope of the line shown
   III. the *y*-intercept of $y = 4x - 8$

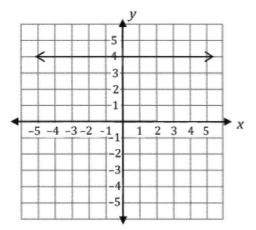

(A) I > II
(B) II > I
(C) III > II
(D) I = II

89. Examine I, II, and III and find the best answer.

   I. the *y*-intercept of the line shown
   II. the y-intercept of $y = 3x - 4$
   III. the slope of $3x + y = 4$

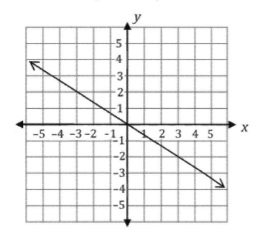

(A) I is less than II
(B) I is less than III
(C) II is greater than III
(D) III is greater than II

90. Examine I, II, and III and find the best answer.

   I. the *y*-intercept of the line shown
   II. the *y*-intercept of $y = 5x - 3$
   III. the slope of $x + 3y = 2$

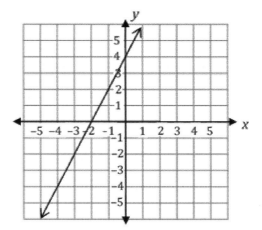

(A) I > II
(B) II > III
(C) I < III
(D) I = III

91. Examine I, II, and III and find the best answer.

   I. the slope of the line shown
   II. the *y*-intercept of $y = 2x - 3$
   III. the *y*-intercept of $4x + 3y = 2$

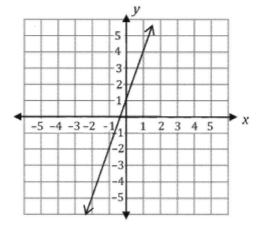

(A) II > III
(B) II > I
(C) II = III
(D) II < III

92. Examine I, II, and III and find the best answer.

   I. the y-intercept of the line shown
   II. the slope of $y = 2x - 3$
   III. the slope of $-3x + y = 2$

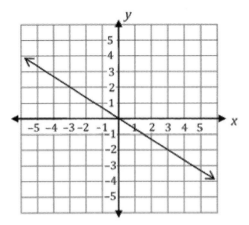

   (A) I > II > III
   (B) II > I > III
   (C) I < II = III
   (D) I < II < III

93. Examine I, II, and III and find the best answer.

   I. the slope of the line shown
   II. the slope of a line parallel to the line shown
   III. the slope of a line perpendicular to the line shown

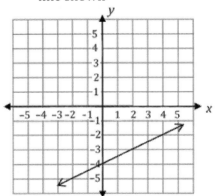

   (A) III = II = I
   (B) III = II > I
   (C) III < II = I
   (D) III > II = I

94. Examine I, II, and III and find the best answer.

   I. the slope of the line shown
   II. the slope of a line parallel to the line shown
   III. the slope of a line perpendicular to the line shown

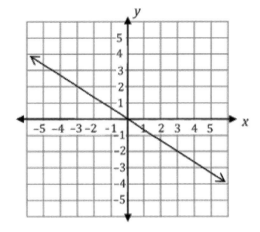

   (A) I > II > III
   (B) II > I > III
   (C) I < II = III
   (D) I = II < III

Number Manipulation (Reasoning)

For these questions, students need to translate a mathematical statement into an equation to solve.

You can expect to perform operations with:

- Fractions
- Percents
- Decimals
- Exponents
- Averages
- Whole numbers

How to Use This Section

As determined by your study plan, including the results of your diagnostic tests, we encourage you to focus on the topics that are most challenging to you. This section will give you exposure to the different types of questions that are presented in the number manipulation section, and give you the practice to finding the path to the correct answer. If you find that you are challenged by this area and need additional help, remember to reach out to a trusted educator. Don't get discouraged! Take the materials to a teacher or tutor if you need additional enrichment in any given topic.

Tutorverse Tips!

Many of these questions require students to perform more than one operation. A good approach can be to start with the last operation in the sentence and work backward. Plan an approach and then solve!

Looking for a tutor?

Look no further—we're The Tutorverse for a reason! We offer one-one-one tutoring in-home or online. Our tutoring is the ultimate test-prep and supplemental educational service.

TO LEARN MORE, SCAN THE QR CODE OR VISIT:
thetutorverse.com/hspt

QUESTIONS? SEND US AN EMAIL:
hello@thetutorverse.com

Number Manipulation (Reasoning) Exercises

Fractions, Percents, Decimals

1. What number is 200% of the difference of 40 and 34?
   (A) 6
   (B) 12
   (C) 14
   (D) 18

2. What number subtracted from 4^3 is $\frac{1}{3}$ of 27?
   (A) 3
   (B) 21
   (C) 55
   (D) 59

3. What number when subtracted from 22 is 4 less than $\frac{1}{4}$ of 32?
   (A) 4
   (B) 8
   (C) 18
   (D) 26

4. What number divided by 5 is 25% of 20?
   (A) 1
   (B) 5
   (C) 25
   (D) 100

5. What number multiplied by 2 is $\frac{1}{3}$ of 66?
   (A) 5.5
   (B) 11
   (C) 22
   (D) 44

6. What number subtracted from $\frac{1}{4}$ of 60 is 10% of 30?
   (A) 3
   (B) 12
   (C) 15
   (D) 18

7. What number is 7 less than the product of 3^3 and 2?
   (A) 11
   (B) 18
   (C) 47
   (D) 54

8. What number added to 4^2 is $\frac{1}{2}$ of 70?
   (A) 16
   (B) 19
   (C) 35
   (D) 51

9. What number divided by 4 is $\frac{2}{3}$ of 24?
   (A) 1
   (B) 8
   (C) 16
   (D) 64

10. What number is 5 more than the product of 25% of 20 and $\frac{1}{2}$ of 10?
    (A) 5
    (B) 20
    (C) 25
    (D) 30

11. What number is $\frac{2}{5}$ of the median of 50, 70, and 120?
    (A) 14
    (B) 28
    (C) 32
    (D) 70

12. What number is 10 less than the average of 5, 15, 25, and 35?
    (A) 10
    (B) 15
    (C) 20
    (D) 25

13. What is $\frac{1}{6}$ of the sum of $\sqrt{36}$ and 36?
    (A) 2
    (B) 6
    (C) 7
    (D) 12

14. What number is 10% of 20% of 400?
    (A) 0.8
    (B) 8
    (C) 10
    (D) 80

15. What number when subtracted from $\frac{2}{7}$ of 28 is $\frac{1}{3}$ of 18?
    (A) 2
    (B) 6
    (C) 8
    (D) 14

16. What number divided by 2^2 is 40% of 20?
    (A) 2
    (B) 8
    (C) 16
    (D) 32

17. What number is $\frac{1}{3}$ of the difference of 3^4 and 3?
    (A) 3
    (B) 9
    (C) 26
    (D) 27

18. What number when added to 12 makes twice as much as $\frac{2}{3}$ of 33?
    (A) 10
    (B) 12
    (C) 22
    (D) 32

19. What number is 10 less than the sum of 10% of 70 and $\frac{1}{4}$ of 60?
    (A) 5
    (B) 12
    (C) 22
    (D) 32

20. What number is $\frac{1}{5}$ of the product of 5, 6, and 10?
    (A) 30
    (B) 60
    (C) 90
    (D) 120

Whole Numbers

21. What number subtracted from the product of 8 and 11 makes 25 more than 38?
    (A) 6
    (B) 14
    (C) 19
    (D) 25

22. What number multiplied by 7 leaves 10 less than 38?
    (A) 4
    (B) 5
    (C) 6
    (D) 7

23. What number multiplied by 6 leaves the sum of 25, 31, and 16?
    (A) 4
    (B) 6
    (C) 8
    (D) 12

24. What number multiplied by 3 is equal to the difference of 50 and 11?
    (A) 12
    (B) 13
    (C) 20
    (D) 58

25. What number multiplied by 5 is equal to the range of the numbers 20, 5, 15, and 95?
    (A) 9
    (B) 12
    (C) 18
    (D) 27

26. What number multiplied by 2 is equal to the sum of 8 and the difference of 9 and 3?
    (A) 1
    (B) 7
    (C) 10
    (D) 12

27. What number is 12 less than the median of 28, 31, 98, 46, and 17?
    (A) 16
    (B) 19
    (C) 32
    (D) 208

28. What number subtracted from 24 is equal to the average of the numbers 12, 9, 8, and 3?
    (A) 8
    (B) 15
    (C) 16
    (D) 32

29. What number is equal to the difference of 57 and the product of 6 and 8?
    (A) 9
    (B) 11
    (C) 43
    (D) 55

30. What number is 10 more than the average of the numbers 6, 7, 3, 5, 7, 6, and 8?
    (A) 4
    (B) 16
    (C) 17
    (D) 52

31. What number times 8 is the sum of 24 and the product of 8 and 2?
    (A) 4
    (B) 5
    (C) 6
    (D) 7

32. Which of the following numbers leaves a remainder of 4 when divided by 5?
    (A) 102
    (B) 105
    (C) 107
    (D) 109

33. Which of the following numbers leaves a remainder of 1 when divided by 4?
    (A) 52
    (B) 53
    (C) 56
    (D) 58

34. What number subtracted from 68 leaves you with the range of the numbers 28, 50, 16, 55, and 43?
    (A) 17
    (B) 25
    (C) 29
    (D) 124

35. The median of the numbers 26, 8, 97, 75, and 54 is equal to the sum of what number and 13?
    (A) 37
    (B) 39
    (C) 41
    (D) 62

36. The median of the numbers 108, 87, 6, 13, and 92 is equal to the difference of what number and 20?
    (A) 47
    (B) 67
    (C) 87
    (D) 107

37. What number is 21 less than the product of 12 and 8?
    (A) 1
    (B) 41
    (C) 63
    (D) 75

38. What number multiplied by 9 is equal to the sum of 10 and the product of 4 and 11?
    (A) 6
    (B) 7
    (C) 12
    (D) 15

39. What number is the sum of 63 and the difference of 25 and 11?
    (A) 7
    (B) 27
    (C) 57
    (D) 77

40. What number added to 12 is equal to the difference of 60 and the sum of 12 and 3?
    (A) 13
    (B) 23
    (C) 33
    (D) 63

Mathematics

On the Actual Test

In the Mathematics section of the HSPT, you will encounter two types of questions:

- Concepts
- Problem-Solving

There will be 64 questions on the actual Mathematics section, which you will have 45 minutes to complete.

These questions are more traditional math questions than those in the Quantitative Skills section. You can expect to find straightforward calculation problems and word problems in this section.

Calculators

Students are <u>not</u> permitted to use calculators on the HSPT. To help your study, we recommend <u>not</u> using a calculator as you work through the problems in this book. Your brain is like a muscle, and by doing mental math, you exercise and prepare it for the conditions of the actual test, where you're not allowed to use a calculator without a diagnosed learning disability and special accommodation from your testing site.

In This Practice Book

This book gives you the chance to practice many questions from the areas covered in the Mathematics section. By practicing each question type individually, you will develop the correct reasoning strategies. Repeated practice and exposure to each of these question types is the key to success!

Remember: there are detailed answer explanations available online at www.thetutorverse.com/books. Be sure to obtain permission before going online.

Concepts

Overview

These questions test a student's knowledge of the underlying principles of math problems.

There are four types of math concepts questions in this section:

- Algebraic
- Geometry
- Measurements
- Numbers & Operations

How to Use This Section

As determined by your study plan, including the results of your diagnostic tests, we encourage you to focus on the topics that are most challenging to you. This section will give you exposure to the different types of questions that are presented in mathematics concepts, and give you the practice to finding the path to the correct answer. Are you great at algebra but need more help with geometric concepts? Head to that section for more intensive practice. If you find that you are challenged by this area and need additional help, remember to reach out to a trusted educator. Don't get discouraged! Take the materials to a teacher or tutor if you need additional enrichment in any given topic.

Tutorverse Tips!

Remember that on the HSPT, there is no penalty for guessing. If you don't know an answer to a question, take your best guess.

Looking for a tutor?

Look no further—we're The Tutorverse for a reason! We offer one-one-one tutoring in-home or online. Our tutoring is the ultimate test-prep and supplemental educational service.

TO LEARN MORE, SCAN THE QR CODE OR VISIT:
thetutorverse.com/hspt

QUESTIONS? SEND US AN EMAIL:
hello@thetutorverse.com

Concepts Exercises
Algebraic

Inequalities

1. Solve: $\frac{1}{y} - 7 < 3$.
   (A) $y > \frac{1}{10}$
   (B) $y < \frac{1}{10}$
   (C) $y > 10$
   (D) $y < 10$

2. Solve: $\frac{3}{y} - 28 < -1$.
   (A) $y < \frac{3}{9}$
   (B) $y > 9$
   (C) $y > \frac{1}{9}$
   (D) $y < \frac{1}{9}$

3. Solve: $\frac{2}{3}y + 1 > 2y$
   (A) $y < \frac{4}{3}$
   (B) $y < 3$
   (C) $y < \frac{3}{4}$
   (D) $y > \frac{3}{4}$

Slope

4. What is the slope of the line that contains the points $(2,5)$ and $(-3, 4)$?
   (A) $-\frac{1}{5}$
   (B) $\frac{1}{5}$
   (C) $\frac{2}{5}$
   (D) 5

5. What is the slope of the line that contains the points $(-3, 2)$ and $(-2, -1)$?
   (A) -3
   (B) $-\frac{1}{3}$
   (C) $\frac{3}{5}$
   (D) 3

6. What is the slope of the line that contains the points $(1, 4)$ and $(-1, -2)$?
   (A) $-\frac{1}{3}$
   (B) $\frac{1}{3}$
   (C) $\frac{5}{3}$
   (D) 3

7. What is the slope of the line that contains the points $(-6, 3)$ and $(0, -1)$?
   (A) $-\frac{2}{3}$
   (B) $-\frac{1}{3}$
   (C) $\frac{2}{3}$
   (D) $\frac{3}{2}$

8. If a line has a slope of 1 and includes the points $(2, 6)$ and $(x, 7)$, what is the value of x?
   (A) -3
   (B) -1
   (C) 1
   (D) 3

9. If a line has a slope of 2 and includes the points $(x, 4)$ and $(5, 6)$, what is the value of x?
   (A) -4
   (B) -1
   (C) 1
   (D) 4

10. If a line is expressed as $y = -3x - 6$, what is its slope?
    (A) -6
    (B) -3
    (C) 2
    (D) 3

11. If the equation of a line is $3x - 4y = 8$, what is the slope of the line?
    (A) -2
    (B) $-\frac{4}{4}$
    (C) $\frac{3}{4}$
    (D) 2

12. If the equation of a line is $-2x + 5y = -15$, what is the slope of the line?
    (A) -3
    (B) $-\frac{5}{2}$
    (C) $\frac{2}{5}$
    (D) 2

13. If the equation of a line is $6x - y = \frac{3}{5}$, what is the slope of the line?
    (A) $-\frac{3}{5}$
    (B) $\frac{1}{6}$
    (C) $\frac{3}{5}$
    (D) 6

14. What is the slope of the line shown in the graph?

    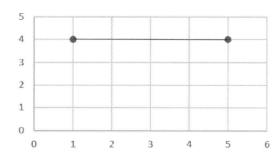

    (A) -1
    (B) 0
    (C) 1
    (D) The slope is undefined.

Geometry

Angles

1. If the measure of ∠AOC is 45° and the circumference of circle O is 48 inches, what is the length of arc AC?

    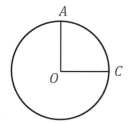

    (A) 4 in.
    (B) 4.5 in.
    (C) 6 in.
    (D) 8 in.

2. What is the value of x?

    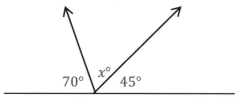

    (A) 25°
    (B) 45°
    (C) 65°
    (D) 115°

3. What is the value of x?

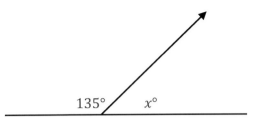

(A) 35°
(B) 45°
(C) 115°
(D) 135°

4. The following circle has been divided into 8 equal sections. What is the measure of the central angle of one section?

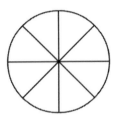

(A) 45°
(B) 60°
(C) 75°
(D) 90°

5. Which of the following statements is FALSE?
(A) A parallelogram has two sets of parallel sides.
(B) The internal angles of equilateral triangles are always the same.
(C) An isosceles triangle has two internal angles of the same measure.
(D) The sum of the internal angles of a quadrilateral depends on the length of its sides.

Area/Perimeter

6. The area of square ABCD is 49 square centimeters. If you increase the width of square ABCD by 20%, what is the area of the new rectangle?
(A) 9.8 square centimeters
(B) 26 square centimeters
(C) 50 square centimeters
(D) 58.8 square centimeter

7. A single gallon of paint can be used to paint a wall measuring 10 square yards. How many gallons of paint are needed to cover a wall measuring 18 ft by 15 ft?
(A) 3
(B) 6
(C) 9
(D) 27

8. Which of the following could be the perimeter of an isosceles triangle if one side measures 3 cm and another side measures 6 cm?
(A) 12 cm
(B) 14 cm
(C) 15 cm
(D) 28 cm

9. A carpet store sells rugs for $3.00 per square foot. Jaime wants to use the rug to perfectly cover a triangular area with a base of 3 yards and a height of 4 yards. How much will it cost her to cover this area with a rug?
(A) $18.00
(B) $36.00
(C) $162.00
(D) $324.00

10. The area of a triangle is twice the area of a square. If the area of the triangle is 72 square ft, what is the perimeter of the square?
(A) 6 ft
(B) 24 ft
(C) 28 ft
(D) 36 ft

11. A square has an area of 144 cm². If we increase each of its sides by 3 cm, what is its new area?
    (A) 150 cm²
    (B) 153 cm²
    (C) 156 cm²
    (D) 225 cm²

12. Jon must paint a wall with a height of 8 feet and a width of 15 feet. Each can of paint can cover an area of 24 square feet. How many cans will he need?
    (A) 2 cans
    (B) 5 cans
    (C) 10 cans
    (D) 96 cans

13. Three congruent squares are shown. Each square has a perimeter of 28 inches. What is the total area of the figure?

    (A) 49 in²
    (B) 140 in²
    (C) 147 in²
    (D) 210 in²

14. A rectangle has an area of 84 square inches, as shown. If the height is 12 inches, what is the width?

    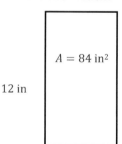

    (A) 4 inches
    (B) 7 inches
    (C) 40 inches
    (D) 62 inches

15. The isosceles right triangle shown has the same area as the rectangle shown. What is the height of the triangle?

    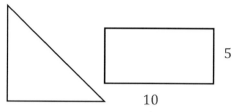

    (A) 10 inches
    (B) 15 inches
    (C) 25 inches
    (D) 50 inches

16. A rectangle with a width that is three times its length has an area of 48 square feet, as shown. What is its perimeter?

    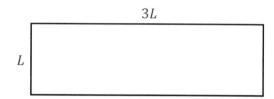

    (A) 12 feet
    (B) 24 feet
    (C) 26 feet
    (D) 32 feet

17. The area of a square is a quarter the area of a triangle. If the triangle has an area of 100 square inches, what is the perimeter of the square?
    (A) 20 inches
    (B) 25 inches
    (C) 30 inches
    (D) 50 inches

18. Julie wants to make a quilt that is 6 feet wide and 8 feet long. The fabric she wants costs $3.00 per square foot. How much will she spend?
    (A) $48
    (B) $51
    (C) $126
    (D) $144

Circles

19. What is the diameter, in centimeters, of a circle with a radius of 1.5 meters?
    (A) 3 cm
    (B) 15 cm
    (C) 150 cm
    (D) 300 cm

20. What is the circumference of a circle with a radius of 4.5?
    (A) 4.5π
    (B) 9π
    (C) 18π
    (D) 20.25π

21. Circle R has a radius of 5 and Circle Y has a radius of 7. What is the difference between the areas of these circles?
    (A) 4π
    (B) 24π
    (C) 25π
    (D) 49π

22. What is the diameter of a circle with an area of 121π square feet?
    (A) 5.5 feet
    (B) 11 feet
    (C) 22 feet
    (D) 60.5 feet

23. Circle Q is inscribed within Square WXYZ. If WX has a length of 12, what is the area of Circle Q?

    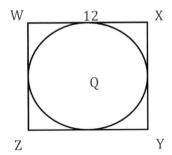

    (A) 12π
    (B) 24π
    (C) 36π
    (D) 48π

24. What is the diameter of a circle with a circumference of 25π feet?
    (A) 5 ft
    (B) 10 ft
    (C) 12.5 ft
    (D) 25 ft

25. Circle R has a radius of 5 cm. Circle O is congruent to Circle R. What is their combined area?
    (A) 10π cm²
    (B) 25π cm²
    (C) 50π cm²
    (D) 100π cm²

26. The circle shown has a radius of 9 inches. What is the circumference of the circle?

    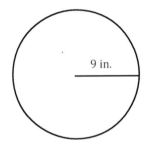

    (A) 9π in
    (B) 18π in
    (C) 27π in
    (D) 81π in

27. What is the radius of a circle with a circumference of 11π centimeters?
    (A) 11 cm
    (B) 5π cm
    (C) 5.5 cm
    (D) 5.5π cm

28. In the figure below, the radius of the circle is 3 inches. What is the area of the shaded region in square inches?

    (A) $9 - 9\pi$
    (B) $24 - 9\pi$
    (C) $36 - 6\pi$
    (D) $36 - 9\pi$

29. What is the area of a circle with a circumference of 14π?
    (A) 28
    (B) 28π
    (C) 49
    (D) 49π

30. What is the circumference of a circle with an area of 144π?
    (A) 12
    (B) 12π
    (C) 24
    (D) 24π

31. What is the radius of a circle with a circumference of 9π inches?
    (A) 3 in.
    (B) 4.5 in.
    (C) 9 in.
    (D) 18 in.

32. What is the circumference of a circle with an area of 49π square feet?
    (A) 7π
    (B) 12π
    (C) 14π
    (D) 49π

33. Circle O is inscribed within square QRST. If the length of TQ =10 in., which of the following represents the area of the shaded region?

    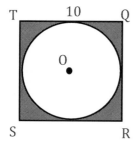

    (A) $10 - 5\pi$ in²
    (B) $100 - 10\pi$ in²
    (C) $100 - 25\pi$ in²
    (D) $100 - 56\pi$ in²

Polygons

34. What type of shape is shown below?

    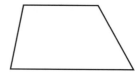

    (A) parallelogram
    (B) pentagon
    (C) rhombus
    (D) trapezoid

35. A decagon has how many sides?
    (A) 6
    (B) 7
    (C) 9
    (D) 10

36. What type of triangle must have all angles less than 90°?
    (A) acute
    (B) scalene
    (C) isosceles
    (D) obtuse

37. Which of the following sets of numbers could be the side lengths of a triangle?
    (A) 3, 3, 9
    (B) 4, 8, 11
    (C) 5, 5, 12
    (D) 6, 7, 14

38. Which of the following sets of numbers could make up the sides of a triangle?
    (A) 1, 5, 2
    (B) 2, 4, 8
    (C) 3, 7, 12
    (D) 6, 5, 4

39. How many sides does a hexagon have?
    (A) 5
    (B) 6
    (C) 7
    (D) 8

40. If a triangle has exactly two congruent angles, what kind of triangle is it?
    (A) isosceles
    (B) equilateral
    (C) scalene
    (D) none of the above

41. How many parallel sides does a trapezoid have?
    (A) 2
    (B) 4
    (C) 6
    (D) 8

Surface Area/Volume

42. What is the volume of this object?

    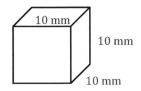

    (A) 30 mm³
    (B) 100 mm³
    (C) 1000 mm³
    (D) 10,000 mm³

43. A rectangular prism has side lengths of 10 mm, 8 mm, and 2 mm. What is its surface area?
    (A) 106 mm²
    (B) 116 mm²
    (C) 160 mm²
    (D) 232 mm²

44. A rectangular planter has a length of 15 inches, a width of 6 inches, and a height of 10 inches. How much soil is needed to fill the planter?
    (A) 60 in³
    (B) 150 in³
    (C) 480 in³
    (D) 900 in³

45. A fish tank measures 10 feet by 4 feet by 4 feet. What is its surface area?
    (A) 40 square feet
    (B) 96 square feet
    (C) 160 square feet
    (D) 192 square feet

46. What is the volume of the following triangular prism?

    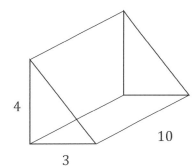

    (A) 30
    (B) 40
    (C) 60
    (D) 120

47. The surface area of a cube is 294 square inches. What is the length of one side?
    (A) 7 in
    (B) 17 in
    (C) 49 in
    (D) 343 in

48. The volume of a cube is 27 cm³. What is its surface area?
    (A) 27 cm²
    (B) 54 cm²
    (C) 162 cm²
    (D) 729 cm²

49. What is the volume of this cylinder?

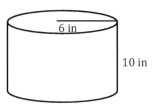

(A) 36π in³
(B) 60π in³
(C) 360π in³
(D) 600π in³

50. The cylinder shown has a volume of 40π. What is the radius of the base?

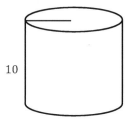

(A) 2 in.
(B) 4 in.
(C) 10 in.
(D) 14 in.

51. A sphere has a radius of 2. What is its volume? ($V = \frac{4}{3}\pi r^3$)
(A) 3π
(B) $\frac{8}{3}\pi$
(C) 8π
(D) $\frac{32}{3}\pi$

Measurements

Appropriate Units

1. Which of the following units would be most appropriate for recording the weight of a book?
   (A) acres
   (B) milligrams
   (C) ounces
   (D) tons

2. Calvin is a fisherman who fishes for tuna off the coast of Alaska. Every day, he catches 300 fish, and each fish weighs approximately 40 pounds. Which of the following would be the most appropriate unit to use to record the total weight of all the fish Calvin will catch in a week?
   (A) cubic meters
   (B) hectares
   (C) tons
   (D) watts

3. Which of the following units would be the best way to rewrite 1 gallon of milk?
   (A) kiloliters
   (B) liters
   (C) microliter
   (D) pounds

Numbers & Operations

Comparing Fractions

1. Which fraction is largest?
   - (A) $\frac{3}{4}$
   - (B) $\frac{3}{5}$
   - (C) $\frac{3}{6}$
   - (D) $\frac{3}{7}$

2. Which fraction is largest?
   - (A) $\frac{6}{10}$
   - (B) $\frac{9}{21}$
   - (C) $\frac{19}{40}$
   - (D) $\frac{24}{51}$

3. Which fraction is smallest?
   - (A) $\frac{3}{5}$
   - (B) $\frac{5}{9}$
   - (C) $\frac{6}{12}$
   - (D) $\frac{7}{15}$

4. Which of the following fractions is closest in value to 1?
   - (A) $\frac{1}{4}$
   - (B) $\frac{1}{5}$
   - (C) $\frac{3}{10}$
   - (D) $\frac{5}{20}$

5. Which of the following fractions does not equal $\frac{1}{5}$?
   - (A) $\frac{4}{20}$
   - (B) $\frac{7}{30}$
   - (C) $\frac{8}{40}$
   - (D) $\frac{11}{55}$

Converting Fractions, Decimals, Percents

6. How would you write 300.05 in word form?
   - (A) Three hundred and five
   - (B) Three hundredths and five
   - (C) Three hundred and five tenths
   - (D) Three hundred and five hundredths.

7. How would you write 4,008.009 in word form?
   - (A) Four thousand eight and nine hundredths
   - (B) Four thousand eight and nine thousandths
   - (C) Four thousand eighty and nine thousandths
   - (D) Four thousand eight ones and nine hundredths

8. Express $\frac{5}{11}$ as a decimal.
   - (A) $0.45\overline{4}$
   - (B) 0.4545
   - (C) $0.45\overline{45}$
   - (D) $0.54\overline{54}$

9. Express 31.7% as a decimal.
   - (A) 0.317
   - (B) 3.17
   - (C) 31.7
   - (D) 3170

10. Express 0.28 as a percent.
    - (A) 0.0028%
    - (B) 0.28%
    - (C) 2.8%
    - (D) 28%

Divisibility

11. What is the remainder when 96,741 is divided by 3?
    - (A) 0
    - (B) 1
    - (C) 2
    - (D) 3

12. If x is an integer, and x^2 is divisible by 2, then x must be:
    (A) even
    (B) odd
    (C) positive
    (D) negative

13. Which of the following numbers is divisible by only 4 distinct integers?
    (A) 12
    (B) 14
    (C) 18
    (D) 20

14. How many distinct integers are divisors of 36?
    (A) 7
    (B) 8
    (C) 9
    (D) 10

15. Which of the following numbers is divisible by 9?
    (A) 1,111,111
    (B) 11,111,111
    (C) 111,111,111
    (D) 1,111,111,111

Exponents

16. What is equivalent to $y \times y \times y \times y \times z \times z$?
    (A) y^2z^2
    (B) y^2z^4
    (C) y^4z^2
    (D) y^4z^4

17. What is equivalent to $a \times a \times b \times c \times c \times c$?
    (A) abc
    (B) ab^2c^3
    (C) a^2bc^2
    (D) a^2bc^3

18. What is equivalent to $(x^3)^2$?
    (A) x^5
    (B) x^6
    (C) x^7
    (D) x^9

Factors

19. What is the prime factorization of 54?
    (A) $2 \times 2 \times 7$
    (B) 2×9
    (C) 2×3^3
    (D) 2×3^4

20. What is the GCF of $45b^3$ and $81a^2$?
    (A) $3b^3$
    (B) $5a^2$
    (C) 9
    (D) $9ab$

21. What is the GCF of $21x^2y^3$ and $7y^5$?
    (A) $3y^3$
    (B) 7
    (C) $7y^3$
    (D) $7xy$

Multiples

22. Assume that a and b are both prime numbers. What is the LCM of $2a^3$ and $13b^3$?
    (A) $26ab$
    (B) $26a^3b$
    (C) $26a^3b^3$
    (D) $29a^3b^3$

23. Find the LCM of 8 and 12.
    (A) 16
    (B) 24
    (C) 36
    (D) 48

24. What is the LCM of $x^2y^3z^6$ and x^5yz^3?
    (A) xyz
    (B) xy^2z^3
    (C) $x^2y^3z^6$
    (D) $x^5y^3z^6$

Scientific Notation

25. Which of the following is equal to $(7 \times 10^2) \times (3 \times 10^4)$?
    (A) 2.1×10^4
    (B) 2.1×10^6
    (C) 2.1×10^7
    (D) 2.1×10^8

26. Which of the following is equal to $(8 \times 10^3) \times (5 \times 10^{-2})$, in scientific notation?
    (A) 4×10^1
    (B) 4×10^2
    (C) 4×10^3
    (D) 40×10^1

27. What is the value of the expression $(2 \times 10^3) + (4 \times 10^2)$?
    (A) 2.4×10^1
    (B) 2.4×10^3
    (C) 2.4×10^5
    (D) 8×10^5

28. What is the value of the expression $(6 \times 10^3) + (9 \times 10^4)$?
    (A) 5.4×10^4
    (B) 6.9×10^3
    (C) 5.4×10^7
    (D) 9.6×10^4

29. What is the value of the expression $(5 \times 10^4) - (3 \times 10^3)$?
    (A) 4.7×10^3
    (B) 4.7×10^4
    (C) 5.3×10^3
    (D) 2×10^1

30. Which of the following is equal to 3.742×10^2?
    (A) 0.03742
    (B) 37.42
    (C) 374.2
    (D) 3742

31. Which of the following is equal to 0.035×10^4?
    (A) 0.0000035
    (B) 3.5
    (C) 35
    (D) 350

32. Which of the following is equal to 70.4×10^3?
    (A) 7,040
    (B) 7,400
    (C) 70,400
    (D) 74,000

33. Which of the following is equal to 500×10^{-3}?
    (A) 0.5
    (B) 5
    (C) 50
    (D) 250

34. Which of the following is equal to 20×10^2?
    (A) 40
    (B) 2,000
    (C) 4,000
    (D) 20,000

35. Which number is in the ten-thousands place after simplifying $(8 \times 10^3) + (9 \times 10^4) + (6 \times 10^2) + (3 \times 10^1)$?
    (A) 3
    (B) 6
    (C) 8
    (D) 9

36. How will the following be written in standard form: $(2 \times 10^4) + (5 \times 10^3) + (9 \times 10^2) + (9 \times 10^1)$?
    (A) 259
    (B) 2,590
    (C) 2,599
    (D) 25,990

37. How will the following be written in standard form: $(5 \times 10^3) + (7 \times 10^4) + (6 \times 10^1) + (2 \times 10^2)$?
    (A) 5,762
    (B) 57,620
    (C) 75,260
    (D) 75,620

38. Which of the following is equivalent to 1,309?
    (A) $(1 \times 10^2) + (3 \times 10^1) + 9$
    (B) $(1 \times 10^3) + (3 \times 10^2) + 9$
    (C) $(1 \times 10^3) + (3 \times 10^2) + (9 \times 10^1)$
    (D) $(1 \times 10^4) + (3 \times 10^2) + (9 \times 10^1)$

Problem-Solving

Overview

These questions test practical math knowledge by asking students to solve mathematical problems.

There are four types of math concepts questions in this section:

- Algebraic Concepts
- Data & Probability
- Measurements
- Numbers & Operations

How to Use This Section

As determined by your study plan, including the results of your diagnostic tests, we encourage you to focus on the topics that are most challenging to you. This section will give you exposure to the different types of questions that are presented in mathematics problem solving, and give you the practice to finding the path to the correct answer. If you find that you are challenged by this area and need additional help, remember to reach out to a trusted educator. Don't get discouraged! Take the materials to a teacher or tutor if you need additional enrichment in any given topic.

Tutorverse Tips!

Remember that on the HSPT, there is no penalty for guessing. If you don't know an answer to a question, take your best guess.

Looking for a tutor?

Look no further—we're The Tutorverse for a reason! We offer one-one-one tutoring in-home or online. Our tutoring is the ultimate test-prep and supplemental educational service.

TO LEARN MORE, SCAN THE QR CODE OR VISIT:
thetutorverse.com/hspt

QUESTIONS? SEND US AN EMAIL:
hello@thetutorverse.com

Problem-Solving Exercises

Algebraic Concepts

Algebra Word Problems

1. Mikaiah and Portia are twins, and their brother Jalen is two years older. Their grandmother is 64 years old. The sum of Mikaiah, Portia, and Jalen's ages is exactly half of their grandmother's age. How old is Jalen?
   (A) 10
   (B) 12
   (C) 31
   (D) 33

2. In the forest, there are four times as many snakes as there are bear. There are twice as many frogs as there are snakes. There are also three owls. If the sum of owls, bear, snakes, and frogs is 68, how many frogs are in the forest?
   (A) 3
   (B) 5
   (C) 20
   (D) 40

3. Teresa is making a treehouse. She is going to cut one piece of wood that is 8 feet long into two separate pieces. One piece will be four times as long as the other. After she cuts it, how long will the shorter piece be?
   (A) $1\frac{1}{4}$ feet
   (B) $1\frac{1}{2}$ feet
   (C) $1\frac{3}{5}$ feet
   (D) 2 feet

4. The sum of the lengths of a parallelogram's sides is 42. If the shorter sides are half the length of the longer sides, what is the length of each longer side?
   (A) 7
   (B) 10.5
   (C) 14
   (D) 21

5. A bird flies three times as many miles on Tuesday as it did on Monday. If the bird flew a total of 36 miles during those two days, how many miles did it fly on Tuesday?
   (A) 9
   (B) 12
   (C) 24
   (D) 27

6. The ratio of miles a bird flies on each of three days is 2:3:5. If the bird flies a total of 200 miles during those three days, what is the shortest number of miles it flew on one day?
   (A) 20
   (B) 40
   (C) 50
   (D) 100

7. Julie has $1.50 in change in her pocket, with just dimes and quarters. She has one more dime than she has quarters. How many dimes does she have in her pocket?
   (A) 3
   (B) 4
   (C) 5
   (D) 6

8. The difference of three times a number and 16 is 24. Which equation could be used to find the number?
   (A) $x + 16 = 24$
   (B) $x - 16 = 24$
   (C) $3x + 16 = 24$
   (D) $3x - 16 = 24$

9. Two times the sum of a number and 8 is 15. Which equation could be used to find the number?
   (A) $2x + 8 = 15$
   (B) $2(x - 8) = 15$
   (C) $2(x + 8) = 15$
   (D) $x + 8 = 2 \times 15$

The Tutorverse
www.thetutorverse.com

10. The difference of three times a number and two times that number is 20. Which equation could be used to find the number?
    (A) $3x + 2x = 20$
    (B) $3x - 2 = 20$
    (C) $3x = 20 - 2x$
    (D) $3x - 2x = 20$

11. If three times the sum of a number and 4 is equal to 7 less than the number, which equation could be used to find the number?
    (A) $3x + 4 = x + 7$
    (B) $3x + 4 = x - 7$
    (C) $3(x + 4) = x - 7$
    (D) $3(x + 4) = 7 - x$

12. If the sum of five times a number and 6 is equal to the difference of 8 and the number, which equation could be used to find the number?
    (A) $5x + 6 = x - 8$
    (B) $5x + 6 = 8 - x$
    (C) $5(x + 6) = x - 8$
    (D) $5(x + 6) = 8 - x$

13. Sofia read 6 more books than Maya. Maya read half as many books as Sebastian. Together they read 26 books. How many books did Sofia read?
    (A) 5
    (B) 6
    (C) 10
    (D) 11

14. Felix read four books. Naomi read four more books than Tarun read. The total number of books all three read was three times the number Tarun read. How many books did Naomi read?
    (A) 4
    (B) 8
    (C) 12
    (D) 24

15. The relationship of distance, rate, and time is given in the formula $d = rt$. If Tomas drove 100 miles at a rate of 40 miles per hour, how long did it take him?
    (A) 2 hours
    (B) 2 hours 15 minutes
    (C) 2 hours 30 minutes
    (D) 2 hours 50 minutes

Proportions

16. On a map of a hiking trail, the distance from the beginning to the end of the trail is 4.5 inches. If the scale is 1 inch is equal to 3 miles, how long is the trail?
    (A) 1.5 miles
    (B) 7.5 miles
    (C) 12.5 miles
    (D) 13.5 miles

17. A class is creating a diorama of the solar system in its classroom. They plan to have the scale be 1 foot is equal to 100 million miles. If the distance from Earth to Jupiter is 430 million miles, approximately how far will Jupiter be from Earth in the classroom?
    (A) 4 feet
    (B) 13 feet
    (C) 23 feet
    (D) 43 feet

18. Talia can make $\frac{2}{5}$ of a model car in one hour. How many model cars can she make in 20 hours?
    (A) 8
    (B) 12
    (C) 40
    (D) 50

19. One gallon of liquid is equal to 8 pints. If a coffeemaker has a capacity of 4 gallons, how many pints can it hold?
    (A) 2
    (B) 8
    (C) 16
    (D) 32

20. One quart is equal to 32 ounces. If a chef orders 112 ounces of olive oil, how many quarts of olive oil does she order?
    (A) 3.2 quarts
    (B) 3.5 quarts
    (C) 3,584 quarts
    (D) 3,904 quarts

21. The ratio of ducks to geese on a pond is 5 to 2. If there are 10 geese, how many ducks are there?
    (A) 4
    (B) 15
    (C) 25
    (D) 30

22. A bag contains only blue, red, and gold marbles. The ratio of blue to red to gold marbles is 4:5:2. If there are 20 blue marbles in the bag, what is the total number of marbles in the bag?
    (A) 8
    (B) 11
    (C) 44
    (D) 55

23. In a high school, the ratio of 9th graders to 10th graders to 11th graders to 12th graders is 10:9:7:5. If there are 270 9th graders, what is the total number of students in the school?
    (A) 752
    (B) 819
    (C) 837
    (D) 930

24. The two figures below are similar triangles. What is the length of side x?

    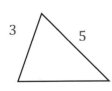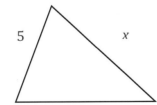

    (A) 3
    (B) 3.6
    (C) $8.\overline{3}$
    (D) 10

25. The two figures below are similar shapes. What is the length of side x?

    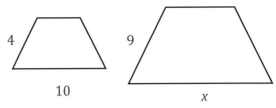

    (A) 3.6
    (B) $4.\overline{4}$
    (C) 22.5
    (D) $25.\overline{5}$

Solving Algebraic Equations

26. Solve for x: $\frac{3}{4} \times 10 = 2x$
    (A) $2\frac{5}{8}$
    (B) $3\frac{3}{8}$
    (C) $3\frac{3}{4}$
    (D) $4\frac{1}{8}$

27. Solve for x: $5x = \frac{1}{3} + \frac{5}{2} + \frac{5}{6}$
    (A) $-1\frac{1}{3}$
    (B) $\frac{11}{15}$
    (C) $\frac{23}{30}$
    (D) $3\frac{1}{3}$

28. Solve for x: $\frac{9}{-0.3} = \frac{x}{1.2}$
    (A) -36
    (B) 12
    (C) 25
    (D) 36

29. Solve for y: $-6 - 2y = -4.2$
    (A) -5.1
    (B) -0.9
    (C) 0.9
    (D) 5.1

30. Solve for n: $4 - 0.6n = -7.4$
    (A) -19
    (B) -1.9
    (C) 1.9
    (D) 19

31. Solve for x: $\frac{-2.4}{1.2} = \frac{x}{5}$
    (A) -10
    (B) -3.6
    (C) 4.8
    (D) 10

32. Solve for x: $3x + 5 = -2x - 10$
    (A) -15
    (B) -3
    (C) 3
    (D) 15

33. Solve for y: $-\frac{1}{2}y + \frac{2}{3} = \frac{3}{2}y - \frac{7}{3}$
    (A) $-\frac{3}{2}$
    (B) $-\frac{1}{3}$
    (C) $\frac{2}{3}$
    (D) $\frac{3}{2}$

34. Solve for a: $-3.5 - 1.2a = -0.8a + 1.7$
    (A) -13
    (B) 0.9
    (C) 2.6
    (D) 13

35. Solve for k: $\frac{-3}{k} = \frac{0.5}{-1.5}$
    (A) -4.5
    (B) 1
    (C) 4.5
    (D) 9

36. Solve for x: $-9 + 7 - 4 = 5x - 8x$
    (A) -4
    (B) -2
    (C) 2
    (D) 4

37. Solve for x: $-4 - x + 3x = -5 - 3$
    (A) -8
    (B) -6
    (C) -2
    (D) 6

38. Solve for y: $\frac{y}{-0.4} = \frac{2.4}{0.8}$
    (A) -2.4
    (B) -1.2
    (C) 1.2
    (D) 2.4

39. Solve for p: $\frac{1}{2}p - 4 - \frac{1}{3}p = 2$
    (A) -6
    (B) 1
    (C) 6
    (D) 36

40. Solve for k: $3k - (-2k) - 7k = 4.8$
    (A) -2.4
    (B) -0.8
    (C) 0.8
    (D) 2.4

Variable Exponents

41. If $2^x = 16$, then $x =$?
    (A) 3
    (B) 4
    (C) 6
    (D) 8

42. If $19^x = 361$, then $x =$?
    (A) 2
    (B) 3
    (C) 4
    (D) 5

43. If $2^x \times 10^x = 8{,}000$, then $x =$?
    (A) 2
    (B) 3
    (C) 4
    (D) 16

44. If $5^x \times 10^x = 2{,}500$, then $x =$?
    (A) -2
    (B) -1
    (C) 2
    (D) 5

45. If $4^x = \frac{1}{64}$, then $x =$?
    (A) -3
    (B) -2
    (C) 3
    (D) 6

46. If $7^x = \frac{1}{49}$, then $x =$?
    (A) -2
    (B) -1
    (C) $\frac{1}{2}$
    (D) 7

47. If $(3^4)^x = 1$, then $x =$?
    (A) -1
    (B) 0
    (C) $\frac{1}{2}$
    (D) 1

48. If the prime factorization of 175 is $7^x \times 5^y$, then what does $x - y$ equal?
    (A) -1
    (B) 0
    (C) 1
    (D) 2

49. If the prime factorization of 216 is $2^x \times 3^y$, then what does $x \times y$ equal?
    (A) 3
    (B) 6
    (C) 8
    (D) 9

50. If the prime factorization of 1,400 is $2^x \times 5^y \times 7^z$, then what does x equal?
    (A) 3
    (B) 4
    (C) 5
    (D) 9

Data & Probability

Averages

1. Alicia has taken four tests and has received scores of 80, 90, 70, and 92. What score does she need on her fifth test to get an average of 84?
    (A) 84
    (B) 85
    (C) 88
    (D) 90

2. The five starters on a basketball team had the following number of points in a game: 12, 2, 9, 20, and 7. What was the range of points for those five players?
    (A) 5
    (B) 10
    (C) 13
    (D) 18

3. A group of nine students surveyed their parents to find out how far each drives to work. What is the mode of this set of data: 5 miles, 3 miles, 1 mile, 2 miles, 1 mile, 3 miles, 4 mile, 10 miles, 1 mile?
    (A) 1 mile
    (B) 2 miles
    (C) 3 miles
    (D) 9 miles

4. Jordan, Chris, and Dominic are competing in a javelin throwing competition, and they each get three throws. The data is included in the chart below. What was the approximate average of Dominic's three throws?

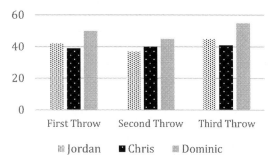

Javelin Throw (in meters)

(A) 10m
(B) 40m
(C) 45m
(D) 50m

5. A group of students surveyed a parent to find out how far each drives to work. What was the median of this set of data: 5 miles, 3 miles, 1 mile, 2 miles, 1 mile, 3 miles, 4 mile, 10 miles, 1 mile?
(A) 1 mile
(B) 2 miles
(C) 3 miles
(D) 9 miles

6. A group of students kept track of how many minutes a week they played video games. What is the median of this set of data: 28, 120, 57, 145, 95?
(A) 57
(B) 89
(C) 95
(D) 117

7. A group of students kept track of how many minutes a week they played video games. What is the mean of this set of data: 28, 120, 57, 145, 95?
(A) 82.6
(B) 89
(C) 95
(D) 117

8. A group of students created a set of data based on how many siblings each one had. The data set they created was: 0, 1, 1, 1, 2, 0, 2, 3, 4, 3, 2, 1. What is the median number of siblings each student had?
(A) 0
(B) 1
(C) 1.5
(D) 2

9. A group of students created a set of data based on how many siblings each one had. The data set they created was: 0, 1, 1, 1, 2, 0, 2, 3, 4, 3, 2, 1. What is the mean number of siblings each student had?
(A) 1
(B) $1.\overline{3}$
(C) 1.5
(D) $1.\overline{6}$

10. A group of students received the following scores on their English test: 98, 75, 78, 84, 67, 99, 93, 89, 77, 82, 79. If one of the following pairs of scores were added to the set, which pair would NOT change the range of the scores?
(A) 73 and 100
(B) 65 and 93
(C) 67 and 96
(D) 64 and 88

11. If there is a set of data, and one value is added that is lower than all the other values, what will happen to the mean of the set?
    (A) It will increase.
    (B) It will decrease.
    (C) It will stay the same.
    (D) There is not enough information to answer the question.

12. If there is a set of data, and one value is added that is lower than all the other values, what will happen to the range of the set?
    (A) It will increase.
    (B) It will decrease.
    (C) It will stay the same.
    (D) There is not enough information to answer the question.

13. If there is a set of data, and one value is added that is lower than all the other values, what will happen to the median of the set?
    (A) It will increase.
    (B) It will decrease.
    (C) It will stay the same.
    (D) There is not enough information to answer the question.

14. Ronaldo is throwing a dart at a target and measuring how far away each dart is from the center of the target. His throws so far have been 5 cm, 9 cm, and 12 cm away from the target. If he wants the mean distance to be less than or equal to 7.5 cm from the target after his next throw, which of these throws will meet his goal?

    I. 4 cm
    II. 5 cm
    III. 5.5 cm
    IV. 6 cm

    (A) I only
    (B) I and II
    (C) I, II, and III
    (D) I, II, III, and IV

15. Jason takes a spelling test every week, and the data for the first five weeks is included in the chart below. What is the mean of the data? (*Note: Tests are in order from 1-5 from left to right in the graph as the key indicates*)

    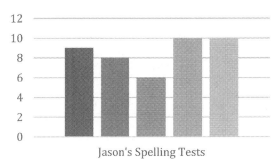

    (A) 4
    (B) 8.6
    (C) 8.8
    (D) 9

Graphs

16. The pie chart shows the most-liked school meal of 2,100 students. How many liked pizza the most?

    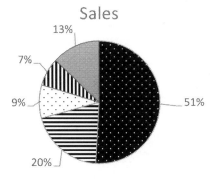

    (A) 1029
    (B) 1050
    (C) 1071
    (D) 2049

17. What kind of graph would better illustrate following information?

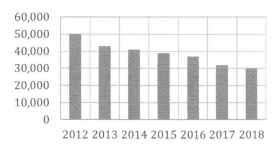

(A) pie chart
(B) line graph
(C) histogram
(D) box-and-whisker plot

18. What type of graph is this?

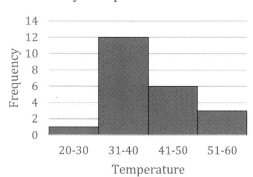

(A) pictogram
(B) histogram
(C) line chart
(D) pie chart

19. 300 people responded to a survey about their favorite sea animal. How many more people chose penguins than sharks as their favorite animal?

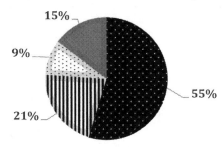

(A) 27
(B) 46
(C) 138
(D) 192

20. What kind of graph is best for showing data over time?
(A) line graph
(B) bar graph
(C) histogram
(D) pie chart

21. The following graph shows the average daily temperature in a city over the course of 10 months. Which month in the graph had the lowest temperature?

    Use the following graph for questions 21, 22, and 23.

    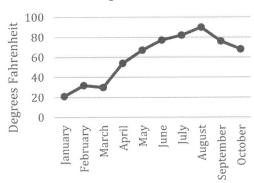

    (A) April
    (B) August
    (C) March
    (D) January

22. Which month had the highest temperature?
    (A) October
    (B) May
    (C) July
    (D) August

23. Between which two consecutive months do we see the greatest difference in temperature?
    (A) September and October
    (B) March and April
    (C) July and August
    (D) August and September

24. How many students received a grade of over 80% on the test?

    Use the following graph for questions 24, 25, and 26.

    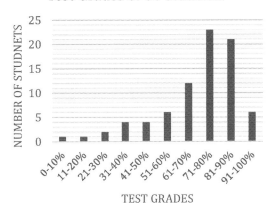

    (A) 6 students
    (B) 21 students
    (C) 27 students
    (D) 50 students

25. How many students received grades from 21% to 60% on the test?
    (A) 8 students
    (B) 16 students
    (C) 18 students
    (D) 24 students

26. What percent of the class received a grade below 41%?
    (A) 7%
    (B) 9%
    (C) 10%
    (D) 12%

27. A class has 50 students. According to the circle graph shown, how many students did not study for the test?

Use the following graph for questions 27 and 28

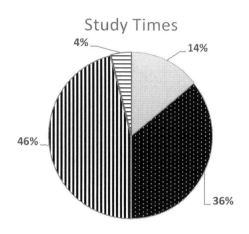

- Did not study
- Studied 15-30 minutes
- Studied 30-60 minutes
- Studied over an hour

(A) 2
(B) 7
(C) 11
(D) 14

28. How many students studied for at least 30 minutes?
(A) 20
(B) 25
(C) 33
(D) 50

29. Thirty-six students in Ms. Meyers class have one sibling. How many students are in her class?

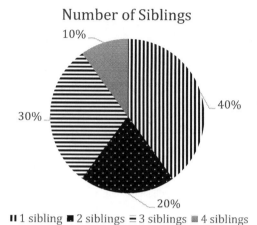

- 1 sibling
- 2 siblings
- 3 siblings
- 4 siblings

(A) 72 students
(B) 90 students
(C) 144 students
(D) 360 students

30. How many students have 4 siblings? [see fig. from q. 29]
(A) 9 students
(B) 18 students
(C) 27 students
(D) 36 students

Probability

31. A bag is filled with 4 blue marbles, 7 green marbles, and 3 red marbles. What is the probability of choosing a blue marble at random?
(A) $\frac{3}{14}$
(B) $\frac{2}{7}$
(C) $\frac{5}{14}$
(D) $\frac{1}{2}$

32. Ms. Simmons is renting a car and is hoping for a black car. There are 3 red cars, 4 gray cars, and 2 black cars. If the cars are assigned at random, what is the probability that Ms. Simmons gets the color that she wants?
   (A) $\frac{2}{9}$
   (B) $\frac{3}{9}$
   (C) $\frac{5}{9}$
   (D) 1

33. A bag of marbles has 4 clear marbles, 3 blue marbles, 2 purple marbles, and 1 red marble. Tara randomly selects a marble from the bag, replaces it, and then chooses a second marble. What is the probability that she will choose a purple marble both times?
   (A) $\frac{1}{25}$
   (B) $\frac{1}{5}$
   (C) $\frac{1}{4}$
   (D) $\frac{4}{10}$

34. Jonathan is playing a game with cards that have animals on them. There are 8 cards with dogs, 6 cards with cats, and 6 cards with birds. If Jonathan randomly chooses a card and then replaces it back into the deck before randomly choosing a second card, what is the probability that he will choose a cat card the first time and a bird card the second?
   (A) $\frac{1}{36}$
   (B) $\frac{9}{100}$
   (C) $\frac{3}{10}$
   (D) $\frac{12}{20}$

35. Britney flips a coin three times. What is the probability that she gets heads all three times?
   (A) $\frac{1}{8}$
   (B) $\frac{1}{6}$
   (C) $\frac{3}{8}$
   (D) $\frac{1}{2}$

36. There are three kinds of candy in a jar: 4 strawberry, 2 grape, and 3 cherry. If Katie randomly selects two candies and keeps them both, what is the probability that her first is a cherry and her second is a strawberry?
   (A) $\frac{1}{6}$
   (B) $\frac{1}{3}$
   (C) $\frac{4}{9}$
   (D) $\frac{5}{6}$

37. A survey is taken of the boys and girls at a local middle school about whether they prefer basketball or soccer. The data is recorded in the table below. If a student is selected at random from the students who prefer soccer, what is the probability that it is a boy?

	Basketball	Soccer	Total
Boys	18	32	50
Girls	23	16	39
Total	41	48	89

   (A) $\frac{32}{89}$
   (B) $\frac{16}{48}$
   (C) $\frac{39}{48}$
   (D) $\frac{2}{3}$

38. Felicia has 20 cousins. Seven are boys, and the rest are girls. If one cousin is selected at random for her to buy a gift for, what is the probability that the present will be for a girl?
    (A) $\frac{7}{20}$
    (B) $\frac{7}{13}$
    (C) $\frac{3}{5}$
    (D) $\frac{13}{20}$

39. Kenji has 11 pairs of tennis shoes. Five are red, two are yellow, and the rest are black. If he chooses a pair at random, what is the probability that it will be black?
    (A) $\frac{2}{11}$
    (B) $\frac{4}{11}$
    (C) $\frac{2}{5}$
    (D) $\frac{5}{11}$

40. Traci has a bowl full of candy and nuts. There are 8 walnuts, 5 cashews, 10 pieces of licorice, and 7 gumdrops. If she chooses one of those at random, what is the probability that she will choose a cashew?
    (A) $\frac{1}{6}$
    (B) $\frac{1}{5}$
    (C) $\frac{7}{30}$
    (D) $\frac{1}{3}$

41. A store gives a free gift to anyone who spends $100 in the store. If the gift is chosen at random from a bag that contains 7 baseball hats, 4 earrings, and 9 bracelets, what is the probability that a customer will get a bracelet?
    (A) $\frac{9}{100}$
    (B) $\frac{4}{9}$
    (C) $\frac{9}{20}$
    (D) $\frac{1}{2}$

42. Ellen is choosing an outfit for school. She has 3 red shirts, 2 white shirts, and a black shirt in her closet, as well as 5 pairs of jeans and 2 pairs of dress pants. If she chooses a shirt and a pair of pants at random, what is the probability that she will choose a white shirt and a pair of dress pants?
    (A) $\frac{2}{21}$
    (B) $\frac{2}{7}$
    (C) $\frac{1}{3}$
    (D) $\frac{5}{7}$

43. Von gets to randomly pick a number out of two different bags. If the numbers in one bag are 1 through 6 and the numbers in the other bag are 7 through 12, what is the probability that he will pick a 3 and a 10?
    (A) $\frac{1}{36}$
    (B) $\frac{1}{12}$
    (C) $\frac{1}{6}$
    (D) $\frac{1}{3}$

44. Jin is randomly choosing two marbles out of a jar, and he will keep both. Before he makes his choice, there are 4 blue marbles, 2 red marbles, and 1 yellow marble. What is the probability that he will choose a blue marble and a red marble?
    (A) $\frac{4}{49}$
    (B) $\frac{8}{49}$
    (C) $\frac{8}{42}$
    (D) $\frac{4}{21}$

45. Yuna's teacher has put 6 math problems in a hat. Two are fraction problems, two are decimal problems, one is a percent problem, and one is an integer problem. If Yuna has to randomly select two problems to solve (without putting the first one back), what is the probability that they will both be decimal problems?

   (A) $\frac{1}{15}$
   (B) $\frac{1}{5}$
   (C) $\frac{1}{3}$
   (D) $\frac{1}{2}$

Venn Diagrams

46. The following Venn diagram represents the choice students made as to what sport they enjoy. What does the area marked "A" represent?

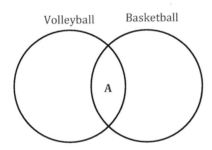

   (A) students who prefer playing volleyball
   (B) students who prefer playing basketball
   (C) students who enjoy playing both basketball and volleyball
   (D) students who do not enjoy playing either basketball or volleyball

47. The following Venn diagram indicates the states where students have lived. What does the region where the "B" is placed represent?

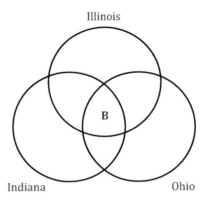

   (A) students who have lived only in Ohio
   (B) students who have lived in Indiana and Ohio
   (C) students who have lived in Illinois and Indiana
   (D) students who have lived in Illinois, Indiana, and Ohio

48. 24 students were surveyed to see how many enjoy French fries, onion rings, or both. Every student indicated liking at least one of the choices. If 16 students enjoy French fries and 14 students enjoy onion rings, how many students enjoy both?

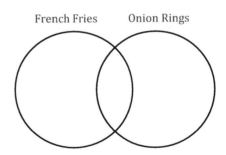

   (A) 6
   (B) 8
   (C) 10
   (D) 12

49. The following Venn diagram represents how many students enjoy comedy movies and/or scary movies. If 40 students replied to the survey and 9 said they enjoy neither, how many students enjoy comedy movies?

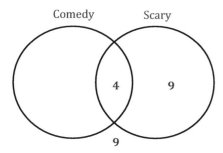

(A) 13
(B) 18
(C) 22
(D) 31

50. The following Venn diagram represents how many people enjoy listening to music or watching television. If 80 people replied to the survey and 12 said they enjoy neither, how many people enjoy listening to music?

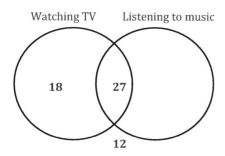

(A) 23
(B) 42
(C) 50
(D) 68

51. 27 teachers were surveyed about whether they drink coffee or tea. Twelve teachers drink neither, 8 teachers drink only coffee, and 4 teachers drink only tea. How many teachers drink tea?
(A) 3
(B) 7
(C) 10
(D) 15

52. A group of 120 adults are surveyed about how they get their news. Forty-five said that they watch television news, 73 said that they read the internet, and 44 said that they do not follow the news at all. How many adults use both television and the internet to get their news?
(A) 3
(B) 29
(C) 31
(D) 42

53. In a group of 50 music students, 28 play piano, 15 play trumpet, and 18 play guitar. Ten students play piano and guitar, 8 play piano and trumpet, 3 play trumpet and guitar, and 2 play all three instruments. How many music students play only piano?
(A) 6
(B) 8
(C) 12
(D) 15

54. In a group of music students, 200 play piano, 120 play trumpet, and 80 play guitar. Forty play piano and guitar, 30 play piano and trumpet, 20 play trumpet and guitar, and 10 play all three instruments. How many music students play only trumpet?
(A) 20
(B) 40
(C) 60
(D) 80

55. In a group of 250 music students, 140 play piano, 70 play trumpet, and 90 play guitar. Fifty play piano and guitar, 40 play piano and trumpet, 30 play trumpet and guitar, and 20 play all three instruments. How many music students do not play piano, guitar, or trumpet?
    (A) 40
    (B) 50
    (C) 60
    (D) 80

Measurements

Speed

1. Sandra biked for 60 minutes at a 10 miles per hour pace. What is the equation for the distance she traveled?
   (A) $D = 60 \times 10$
   (B) $D = 6 \times 10$
   (C) $D = 1 \times 10$
   (D) $D = 60 \times 6$

2. Ilana drove for 30 minutes at a 40 mile per hour pace. How far did she drive?
   (A) 20 miles
   (B) 22 miles
   (C) 32 miles
   (D) 40 miles

3. Miles's flight to Chicago will fly for two and a half hours at an average pace of 400 mile per hour. How far away is Chicago?
   (A) 425 miles
   (B) 750 miles
   (C) 1,000 miles
   (D) 1,500 miles

4. Federico wants to run a 24-mile race in two hours. How fast does he have to run to achieve his goal?
   (A) 11 miles per hour
   (B) 12 miles per hour
   (C) 12.5 miles per hour
   (D) 20 miles per hour

5. Geoff biked 30 miles at 6 miles per hour. How long did it take him?
   (A) 3 hours
   (B) 4.5 hours
   (C) 5 hours
   (D) 6 hours

6. Luisa ran half a mile in 6 minutes. How fast did she run?
   (A) 3 miles per hour
   (B) 3.5 miles per hour
   (C) 5 miles per hour
   (D) 6 miles per hour

7. Tara must drive 20 miles in the fast lane at 60 miles per hour, while Reid has to drive 15 miles, but can only reach a speed of 45 miles per hour. What is the difference between their travel times?
   (A) 0 minutes
   (B) 2 minutes
   (C) 5 minutes
   (D) 10 minutes

8. It is 4:30 pm, and Lola is walking to the post office to drop off a letter before they close at 5 pm. If she is 3.2 miles away and is walking at a speed of 4 miles per hour, when will she arrive?
   (A) 4:58 pm
   (B) 5:00 pm
   (C) 5:02 pm
   (D) 5:18 pm

9. Yolanda biked for 30 minutes at a 15 miles per hour pace. What is the equation for the distance she traveled?
   (A) $D = 15 \times 30$
   (B) $D = .25 \times .5$
   (C) $D = 15 \times 3$
   (D) $D = 15 \times .5$

10. Meeka drove 40 miles in 45 minutes. What is the equation for her speed?
    (A) $S = \frac{.75}{40}$
    (B) $S = \frac{40}{.45}$
    (C) $S = \frac{45}{.40}$
    (D) $S = \frac{40}{.75}$

Units

11. How many quarts of orange juice are there in a gallon?
    (A) 4 quarts
    (B) 8 quarts
    (C) 16 quarts
    (D) 32 quarts

12. How many pints fit in a gallon?
    (A) 4 pints
    (B) 8 pints
    (C) 16 pints
    (D) 32 pints

13. 20 minutes is equivalent to what fraction of two hours?
    (A) $\frac{1}{6}$
    (B) $\frac{1}{3}$
    (C) $\frac{2}{5}$
    (D) $\frac{2}{3}$

14. Two nickels make up what fraction of one dollar?
    (A) $\frac{1}{10}$
    (B) $\frac{1}{5}$
    (C) $\frac{2}{5}$
    (D) $\frac{2}{3}$

15. 45 minutes makes up what fraction of three hours?
    (A) $\frac{1}{5}$
    (B) $\frac{1}{4}$
    (C) $\frac{1}{3}$
    (D) $\frac{2}{5}$

16. Three dimes make up what fraction of one dollar?
    (A) $\frac{1}{3}$
    (B) $\frac{3}{10}$
    (C) $\frac{3}{5}$
    (D) $\frac{1}{5}$

17. 46 oz. equals:
    (A) 2 lb. 4 oz.
    (B) 2 lb. 14 oz.
    (C) 3 lb.
    (D) 3 lb. 1 oz.

18. How many inches are in 52 yards?
    (A) 520 inches
    (B) 5200 inches
    (C) 1430 inches
    (D) 1872 inches

19. 10 lbs. 11 oz. equals:
    (A) 111 oz
    (B) 101 oz
    (C) 109 oz
    (D) 171 oz

20. 1.424 km equals:
    (A) 14.24 meters
    (B) 142.4 meters
    (C) 1424 meters
    (D) 14240 meters

21. 3.25 gallons equals:
    (A) 26 pints
    (B) 32.5 pints
    (C) 40.25 pints
    (D) 42 pints

22. What is 5 miles per hour in feet per minute?
    (A) 50 feet per minute
    (B) 250 feet per minute
    (C) 440 feet per minute
    (D) 500 feet per minute

23. 913 millimeters equals:
    (A) .913 meters
    (B) 91.3 meters
    (C) .913 centimeters
    (D) 9.13 centimeters

24. How many feet are in 90 inches?
    (A) 7.5 feet
    (B) 9 feet
    (C) 10.25 feet
    (D) 12 feet

25. 4 hours makes up what fraction of a day?
    (A) $\frac{1}{8}$
    (B) $\frac{1}{6}$
    (C) $\frac{2}{5}$
    (D) $\frac{1}{7}$

Numbers & Operations

Arithmetic

1. Solve: $14 + (-4) - (-6) =$
   (A) 4
   (B) 8
   (C) 16
   (D) 24

2. Solve: $-180 \div -12 =$
   (A) -15
   (B) -14
   (C) $\frac{1}{15}$
   (D) 15

3. Solve: $152 \div (-4 \times -2) =$
   (A) -76
   (B) -19
   (C) 19
   (D) 76

4. Solve: $(-12) + 8 - (-3) - 20 =$
   (A) -27
   (B) -21
   (C) -20
   (D) 3

5. Solve: $(-3) + (-2) \times 4 - 1 =$
   (A) -21
   (B) -19
   (C) -12
   (D) -9

6. Solve: $24 \div (-3) - (-2) \times 3 =$
   (A) -18
   (B) -16
   (C) -2
   (D) 8

7. Solve: $(-200) \div (-25) =$
   (A) -9
   (B) -8
   (C) 8
   (D) 9

8. Solve: $957 \div 25 =$
   (A) 37 R7
   (B) 37 R32
   (C) 38
   (D) 38 R7

9. Solve: $6351 \div 8 =$
   (A) 793
   (B) 793 R7
   (C) 806 R3
   (D) 907 R2

10. Solve: $659 \div 6 =$
    (A) 19 R4
    (B) 19 R5
    (C) 109 R4
    (D) 109 R5

11. Solve: $823 \div 45 =$
    (A) 13 R18
    (B) 16 R3
    (C) 18 R13
    (D) 19 R 3

12. Solve: $254 \times 25 =$
    (A) 1,778
    (B) 6,305
    (C) 6,350
    (D) 63,500

13. Solve: $3,083 \times 100 =$
    (A) 38,300
    (B) 308,300
    (C) 383,000
    (D) 3,083,000

14. Solve: $2,000 \times 53 =$
    (A) 10,600
    (B) 16,000
    (C) 106,000
    (D) 107,000

15. Solve:
    $1,021 + 101,210 + 10,002 + 202,021 =$
    (A) 134,245
    (B) 224,245
    (C) 305,245
    (D) 314,254

Operations with Fractions and Decimals

16. Solve: $\frac{2}{3} + \frac{1}{6} =$
    (A) $\frac{3}{9}$
    (B) $\frac{5}{6}$
    (C) $\frac{14}{18}$
    (D) $\frac{15}{9}$

17. Solve: $\frac{7}{8} - \frac{1}{2} =$
    (A) $\frac{3}{8}$
    (B) $\frac{6}{16}$
    (C) $\frac{6}{6}$
    (D) $\frac{11}{8}$

18. Solve: $\frac{\frac{2}{3}}{\frac{3}{4}} =$
    (A) $\frac{1}{2}$
    (B) $\frac{6}{12}$
    (C) $\frac{7}{8}$
    (D) $\frac{8}{9}$

19. Solve: $\frac{\frac{3}{4}}{\frac{9}{8}} =$
    (A) $\frac{2}{3}$
    (B) $\frac{3}{4}$
    (C) $\frac{24}{36}$
    (D) $\frac{27}{32}$

20. Solve: $\frac{5}{8} \div 2 =$
    (A) $\frac{3}{8}$
    (B) $\frac{5}{16}$
    (C) $\frac{5}{4}$
    (D) $\frac{10}{8}$

21. Solve: $2.1201 + 0.212 =$
    (A) 2.3321
    (B) 2.333
    (C) 4.2401
    (D) 4.333

22. Solve: $4.5 - 2.37 =$
    (A) 2.13
    (B) 2.17
    (C) 2.27
    (D) 6.87

23. Solve: $0.07 \times 0.04 =$
    (A) 0.0028
    (B) 0.028
    (C) 0.28
    (D) 28

24. Solve: $\frac{8}{0.2} =$
    (A) 2.5
    (B) 4
    (C) 16
    (D) 40

25. Solve: $9\frac{15}{25} \div 5\frac{1}{5} =$
    (A) $1\frac{11}{13}$
    (B) $1\frac{110}{130}$
    (C) $2\frac{3}{25}$
    (D) $3\frac{1}{5}$

26. Solve: $5 \div 1.6 =$
    (A) 0.32
    (B) 3.125
    (C) 3.2
    (D) 3.5

27. Solve: $8.1 - (-1.5) =$
    (A) 6.6
    (B) 7.6
    (C) 9.6
    (D) 10.6

28. Solve: $(-1.7) \times (-0.3) =$
    (A) −5.1
    (B) −0.51
    (C) 0.51
    (D) 5.1

29. Solve: $\frac{0.86}{-4}$
    (A) −0.215
    (B) 2.15
    (C) 2.5
    (D) 25

30. Solve: $4 + 0.04 + 1.4 + 0.014 =$
    (A) 0.854
    (B) 1.494
    (C) 5.094
    (D) 5.454

Percent Word Problems

31. In 2020, a city museum attracted 3,200 visitors to its traditional art exhibit. In 2021, the number of visitors to the exhibit increased by 15%. How many visitors did the exhibit attract in 2021?
    (A) 3,215
    (B) 3,248
    (C) 3,520
    (D) 3,680

32. A department store is having a 40% sale on all sports items. What is the sale price of a set of golf clubs that originally cost $320?
    (A) $128
    (B) $148
    (C) $192
    (D) $232

33. A basket at the farmers' market is filled with apples, oranges, bananas, and peaches. There are 50% more oranges than apples and 10% fewer peaches than oranges. If there are 20 apples, how many peaches are in the basket?
    (A) 20
    (B) 27
    (C) 20
    (D) 33

34. Marguerite borrows $15,000 from the bank at an annual interest rate of 10%. After two years, Marguerite paid back the loan plus the interest to the bank. How much total money did Marguerite pay back to the bank?
    (A) $16,000
    (B) $17,500
    (C) $18,000
    (D) $18,500

35. If x is 50% larger than z, and y is 20% larger than z, then x is what percent greater than y?
    (A) 25%
    (B) 30%
    (C) 35%
    (D) 40%

36. Dennis paid $30 for a pair of baseball cards which he received at a 40% discount. What was the original price of the baseball cards before the discount?
    (A) $34.00
    (B) $38.00
    (C) $49.00
    (D) $50.00

37. The discounted price of a video game is 20% less than the original price. Calvin has a coupon that allows him to buy the game for an additional 30% off the discount price. What percent of the original price did Calvin pay?
    (A) 42%
    (B) 48%
    (C) 50%
    (D) 56%

38. A 20,000-gallon tank at an aquarium houses three different types of fish: tuna, seabass, and parrot fish. If there are a total of 680 fish in the aquarium, and tuna and seabass make up 510 fish, what percentage of the fish in the aquarium are parrot fish?
    (A) 20%
    (B) 25%
    (C) 75%
    (D) 80%

39. A boxed set of movies that originally cost $200 was on sale for 40% off. Timothy purchased the boxed set for $120. He also had to pay an 8% sales tax. How much did Timothy pay in sales tax on his purchase?
    (A) $9.60
    (B) $10.35
    (C) $11.50
    (D) $11.65

40. Mrs. Williams took out a $9,000 loan from the bank. After one year, she paid $720 in interest on her loan. What is Mrs. Williams annual interest rate in percentage?
    (A) 3%
    (B) 3.5%
    (C) 4%
    (D) 8%

Percents

41. Which of the following has the same value as $2\frac{1}{4}\%$?
    (A) $\frac{9}{40}$
    (B) $\frac{9}{4}$
    (C) 0.0225
    (D) 2.25

42. If $K\%$ of 50 is 10, then $K =$
    (A) 2
    (B) 5
    (C) 20
    (D) 500

43. $0.42\% =$
    (A) 0.0042
    (B) 0.042
    (C) 4.2
    (D) 42

44. 75% of 20 is the same as what percent of 60?
    (A) 25
    (B) 50
    (C) 65
    (D) 70

45. What percentage of 110 is 44?
    (A) 10%
    (B) 40%
    (C) 80%
    (D) 400%

46. Which of the following has the same value as 2.5%?
    (A) 0.025
    (B) 0.25
    (C) 2.5
    (D) $\frac{2}{5}$

47. What percentage of the figure below is shaded?

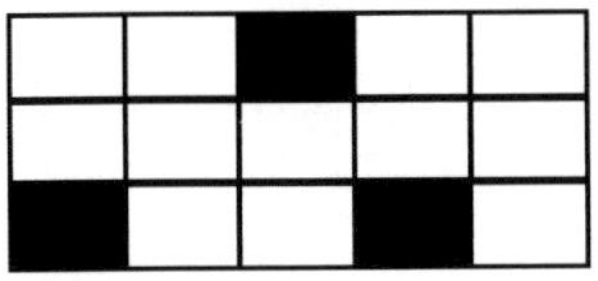

    (A) 2%
    (B) 3%
    (C) 20%
    (D) 30%

48. 0.12% =
    (A) 120
    (B) 1.2
    (C) 0.012
    (D) 0.0012

49. What is 130% of 60?
    (A) 18
    (B) 42
    (C) 78
    (D) 180

50. Which of the following has the same value as $10\frac{1}{2}$%?
    (A) 0.105
    (B) 0.150
    (C) 1.50
    (D) 10.5

Roots

51. The square root of 42 is between which two numbers?
    (A) 5 and 6
    (B) 6 and 7
    (C) 7 and 8
    (D) 8 and 9

52. What is the value of $\sqrt{169-144}$?
    (A) 1
    (B) 5
    (C) 7
    (D) 25

53. What is the value of $\sqrt{9\sqrt{4}}$?
    (A) $3\sqrt{2}$
    (B) $\sqrt{6}$
    (C) $\sqrt{12}$
    (D) 6

54. The square root of 159 is between which two numbers?
    (A) 10 and 11
    (B) 11 and 12
    (C) 12 and 13
    (D) 13 and 14

55. What is the value of $\frac{\sqrt{18}}{3}$?
    (A) $\sqrt{2}$
    (B) 3
    (C) $\sqrt{6}$
    (D) $\frac{9}{2}$

56. If $\sqrt{121} + x = 34$, what is the value of x?
    (A) 13
    (B) 23
    (C) 33
    (D) 43

57. If $x = \sqrt{81}$, then what is the value of $2x^2 - 21$?
    (A) 101
    (B) 121
    (C) 131
    (D) 141

58. Which of the following is equivalent to $\sqrt{4ab^2} \cdot \sqrt{a}$?
    (A) $2b$
    (B) $2ab$
    (C) $2b\sqrt{a}$
    (D) $ab\sqrt{a}$

59. What is the value of $\sqrt[3]{27} - \sqrt[3]{8}$?
    (A) 1
    (B) 4
    (C) 9
    (D) 11

60. Which of the following is equivalent to $\sqrt[3]{125x^3} - \sqrt[3]{8x^3}$?
    (A) $3x$
    (B) $5x$
    (C) $17x$
    (D) $35x$

Rounding

61. What is 2.37 + 1.436 rounded to the nearest hundredth?
    (A) 3.8
    (B) 3.805
    (C) 3.81
    (D) 3.82

62. Which of the following would equal 0.9 when rounded to the tenths place?
    (A) 10.23 − 6.875
    (B) 4.351 − 3.527
    (C) 8.054 − 4.146
    (D) 7.571 − 6.679

63. What is 2.6 × 0.48 rounded to the nearest tenth?
    (A) 1.1
    (B) 1.2
    (C) 1.3
    (D) 1.4

64. Which of the following can be approximated to 40?
    (A) 9.7 × 5.3
    (B) 7.9 × 5.8
    (C) 8.2 × 4.8
    (D) 6.9 × 5.1

65. What is the product of 1.499 and 4 rounded to the nearest hundredth?
    (A) 5.5
    (B) 5.996
    (C) 6
    (D) 6.99

66. What is $\frac{0.006}{0.12}$ rounded to the nearest tenth?
    (A) 0.05
    (B) 0.1
    (C) 0.2
    (D) 20

67. What results from rounding the quotient of 1980 and 12 to the nearest hundred?
    (A) 100
    (B) 165
    (C) 170
    (D) 200

68. Which of the following can be approximated to 30?
    (A) 821 ÷ 22
    (B) 396 ÷ 18
    (C) 587 ÷ 19
    (D) 985 ÷ 22

69. Which of the following can be approximated to 200?
    (A) 308 − 95
    (B) 614 − 278
    (C) 793 − 515
    (D) 887 − 605

70. What is 0.189 + 0.12 + 0.9251 + 0.0008 rounded to the nearest hundredth?
    (A) 1.23
    (B) 1.235
    (C) 1.24
    (D) 1.25

Vocabulary

71. Which of the following figures describes the shape of a soup can?
    (A) cone
    (B) cube
    (C) cylinder
    (D) pyramid

72. What type of triangle is shown?

    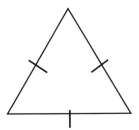

    (A) scalene
    (B) equilateral
    (C) obtuse
    (D) right

73. What is the name of this polygon?

    (A) heptagon
    (B) hexagon
    (C) octagon
    (D) pentagon

74. Which of the following is an irrational number?
    (A) -29
    (B) $\frac{11}{3}$
    (C) $\sqrt{6}$
    (D) $7.\overline{3}$

75. What is the best description for line segment AB?

    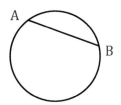

    (A) chord
    (B) diameter
    (C) secant
    (D) tangent

76. What is the name that best describes this polygon?

    (A) kite
    (B) pentagon
    (C) square
    (D) trapezoid

77. Which of the following is NOT a parallelogram?
    (A) rectangle
    (B) rhombus
    (C) square
    (D) trapezoid

78. Which of the following statements are true?
    I. A trapezoid has no parallel sides.
    II. A rhombus has exactly one pair of parallel sides.
    III. A parallelogram always has two pairs of parallel sides.

    (A) Only III is true
    (B) II and III are true
    (C) I, II, and III are true
    (D) None of the statements are true

79. The number 0 is which of the following?
    I. counting number (also known as natural number)
    II. integer
    III. whole number

    (A) I
    (B) I and II
    (C) II and III
    (D) I, II, and III

80. Which of the following shapes is always symmetrical?
    (A) pentagon
    (B) quadrilateral
    (C) square
    (D) triangle

Word Problems

81. A teacher purchases supplies for her classroom. She buys five more pencils than pens. In total, she purchases 47 items. How many pencils did she buy?
    (A) 21
    (B) 26
    (C) 28
    (D) 42

82. Mr. Gonzalez paid $530.40 for his electricity bills last year. How much did he pay, on average, per month?
    (A) $55.20
    (B) $54.40
    (C) $46.30
    (D) $44.20

83. A city had a $39,600 annual budget in 2022. On average, how much was the MONTHLY budget for the city in 2022?
    (A) $3,000
    (B) $3,300
    (C) $3,800
    (D) $3,900

84. The number of viruses in a bacterial culture double every 12 hours. If there are 70 viruses in the culture on Monday morning at 9am, how many viruses will be in the culture on Wednesday at 9pm?
    (A) 2,240
    (B) 1,120
    (C) 560
    (D) 280

85. Henrietta buys cookies for an office party. She purchases 7 boxes of cookies, and each box contains 8 cookies. If the nine people at the party each eat 5 cookies, how many cookies are left at the end of the party?
    (A) 11
    (B) 19
    (C) 47
    (D) 51

86. A bus begins a trip with 11 people on board. At the first stop, 5 people get off the bus, and twice as many as that get on the bus. At the second stop, half of the passengers get off the bus and one person gets on. How many passengers are on the bus at the end of the second stop?
    (A) 8
    (B) 9
    (C) 17
    (D) 18

87. Buckley is saving up money to buy a present for her mother. If the present costs $30, and Buckley saves 70 cents a day, how many whole days will it take for her to save up enough money to afford the gift?
    (A) 21 days
    (B) 22 days
    (C) 42 days
    (D) 43 days

88. Vanessa is making decorations for the formal dance at school. She needs to cover four identical walls with dimensions of 9 feet by 12 feet with velvet fabric. If the fabric is $20 per square yard, how much money does she need?
    (A) $720
    (B) $960
    (C) $2,160
    (D) $8,640

89. Alesha is raising money for her class to go on a field trip. Her parents agree to contribute $2 for every $1 that she earns from selling candy. If she earns $37 from candy sales, how much total did she raise for the field trip?
    (A) $39.00
    (B) $74.00
    (C) $94.00
    (D) $111.00

90. Henry buys a 2 comic books each day of the week, except for Wednesdays and Thursdays, when he buys only 1 comic book. If a comic book costs $6, how much money does Henry spend on comic books in two weeks?
    (A) $36
    (B) $72
    (C) $108
    (D) $144

91. Mary earns 65 cents for every envelope she seals and mails for a fundraiser. She wants to earn enough money to purchase a scooter for $78. How many envelopes does she have to seal and mail to earn enough to afford the scooter?
    (A) 90
    (B) 100
    (C) 120
    (D) 240

92. At the grocery store, 3 bananas and 4 oranges cost $7.39. If 3 oranges cost $3.27, how much does a single banana cost?
    (A) $1.01
    (B) $3.03
    (C) $4.12
    (D) $4.36

93. The amount of money in an account doubles every 3 days. If there is $20 in the account on January 13, on what date will there be $160 in the account?
    (A) January 16
    (B) January 19
    (C) January 22
    (D) February 1

94. Jason currently has $10 in his savings account. He takes a job that earns $30 per week. If he only gets paid for full weeks worked, how many weeks will it take Jason to have enough money to buy a stereo that costs $115?
    (A) 2 weeks
    (B) 3 weeks
    (C) 4 weeks
    (D) 5 weeks

95. Erin and Jessica are selling necklaces to raise money for a school trip. Erin sold 4 more than twice the number of necklaces that Jessica sold. If Jessica sold 5 necklaces, and the necklaces sell for $12 each, how much money did they earn in total?
    (A) $96
    (B) $108
    (C) $180
    (D) $228

Practice Test 1

Overview

The practice test is designed to assess your understanding of key skills and concepts. It is important to take the final practice test after completing the diagnostic tests and after you have spent time studying and practicing.

The main difference between the practice tests and the actual test is that the practice tests are scored differently from how the actual exam is scored. On the actual exam, your score will be determined by how well you did compared to other students in your grade. On the practice tests, however, we will score every question in order to gauge your mastery over skills and concepts.

Format

The format of the practice test is similar to that of the actual test. The number of questions included in each section mirror those of the actual test, *even though the actual test includes questions that will not be scored*. This is done by design, in order to help familiarize you with the actual length of the test.

The diagnostic includes the following sections:

In addition to the math concepts reviewed in this workbook, the practice tests also include English Language Arts material, similar to what will be on the actual exam. If you feel you need more practice on the English Language Arts concepts covered in this test, consider consulting "HSPT Reading Comprehension, Verbal, and Language: 1,700+ Practice Questions," which is available for purchase at www.thetutorverse.com/books.

Diagnostic Test Section	Questions	Time Limit
Verbal Skills	60	16 minutes
Quantitative Skills	52	30 minutes
Reading Comprehension	62	25 minutes
Mathematics	64	45 minutes
Language	60	25 minutes
Total	**298**	**2h 21 minutes**

Generally, 2 brief breaks are given between sections of the test; however, the timing and duration of the breaks are determined by the individual school that is administering the exam.

Calculators

Students are not permitted to use calculators on the HSPT. **To ensure the results of the practice test are as accurate as possible, do not use a calculator on this exam**. If you have a diagnosed learning disability which requires the use of a calculator, contact your testing site to organize special accommodations and continue to practice with a calculator as needed.

Answering

Use the answer sheet provided on the next several pages to record your answers. You may wish to tear these pages out of the workbook.

Practice Test Answer Sheet

[Carefully tear or cut out this page.]

Section 1: Verbal Skills

1 ABCD	13 ABC	25 ABCD	37 ABCD	49 ABCD
2 ABCD	14 ABCD	26 ABCD	38 ABC	50 ABC
3 ABCD	15 ABCD	27 ABCD	39 ABCD	51 ABCD
4 ABC	16 ABCD	28 ABCD	40 ABCD	52 ABCD
5 ABCD	17 ABCD	29 ABCD	41 ABCD	53 ABCD
6 ABCD	18 ABCD	30 ABCD	42 ABC	54 ABC
7 ABC	19 ABCD	31 ABCD	43 ABCD	55 ABCD
8 ABCD	20 ABCD	32 ABCD	44 ABCD	56 ABCD
9 ABCD	21 ABCD	33 ABCD	45 ABC	57 ABCD
10 ABCD	22 ABCD	34 ABCD	46 ABCD	58 ABCD
11 ABC	23 ABCD	35 ABCD	47 ABCD	59 ABCD
12 ABCD	24 ABCD	36 ABCD	48 ABC	60 ABCD

Section 2: Quantitative Skills

61 ABCD	72 ABCD	83 ABCD	94 ABCD	105 ABCD
62 ABCD	73 ABCD	84 ABCD	95 ABCD	106 ABCD
63 ABCD	74 ABCD	85 ABCD	96 ABCD	107 ABCD
64 ABCD	75 ABCD	86 ABCD	97 ABCD	108 ABCD
65 ABCD	76 ABCD	87 ABCD	98 ABCD	109 ABCD
66 ABCD	77 ABCD	88 ABCD	99 ABCD	110 ABCD
67 ABCD	78 ABCD	89 ABCD	100 ABCD	111 ABCD
68 ABCD	79 ABCD	90 ABCD	101 ABCD	112 ABCD
69 ABCD	80 ABCD	91 ABCD	102 ABCD	
70 ABCD	81 ABCD	92 ABCD	103 ABCD	
71 ABCD	82 ABCD	93 ABCD	104 ABCD	

Section 3: Reading

113 ABCD	121 ABCD	129 ABCD	137 ABCD	145 ABCD
114 ABCD	122 ABCD	130 ABCD	138 ABCD	146 ABCD
115 ABCD	123 ABCD	131 ABCD	139 ABCD	147 ABCD
116 ABCD	124 ABCD	132 ABCD	140 ABCD	148 ABCD
117 ABCD	125 ABCD	133 ABCD	141 ABCD	149 ABCD
118 ABCD	126 ABCD	134 ABCD	142 ABCD	150 ABCD
119 ABCD	127 ABCD	135 ABCD	143 ABCD	151 ABCD
120 ABCD	128 ABCD	136 ABCD	144 ABCD	152 ABCD

The Tutorverse
www.thetutorverse.com

153 Ⓐ Ⓑ Ⓒ Ⓓ	158 Ⓐ Ⓑ Ⓒ Ⓓ	163 Ⓐ Ⓑ Ⓒ Ⓓ	168 Ⓐ Ⓑ Ⓒ Ⓓ	173 Ⓐ Ⓑ Ⓒ Ⓓ
154 Ⓐ Ⓑ Ⓒ Ⓓ	159 Ⓐ Ⓑ Ⓒ Ⓓ	164 Ⓐ Ⓑ Ⓒ Ⓓ	169 Ⓐ Ⓑ Ⓒ Ⓓ	174 Ⓐ Ⓑ Ⓒ Ⓓ
155 Ⓐ Ⓑ Ⓒ Ⓓ	160 Ⓐ Ⓑ Ⓒ Ⓓ	165 Ⓐ Ⓑ Ⓒ Ⓓ	170 Ⓐ Ⓑ Ⓒ Ⓓ	
156 Ⓐ Ⓑ Ⓒ Ⓓ	161 Ⓐ Ⓑ Ⓒ Ⓓ	166 Ⓐ Ⓑ Ⓒ Ⓓ	171 Ⓐ Ⓑ Ⓒ Ⓓ	
157 Ⓐ Ⓑ Ⓒ Ⓓ	162 Ⓐ Ⓑ Ⓒ Ⓓ	167 Ⓐ Ⓑ Ⓒ Ⓓ	172 Ⓐ Ⓑ Ⓒ Ⓓ	

Section 4: Mathematics

175 Ⓐ Ⓑ Ⓒ Ⓓ	188 Ⓐ Ⓑ Ⓒ Ⓓ	201 Ⓐ Ⓑ Ⓒ Ⓓ	214 Ⓐ Ⓑ Ⓒ Ⓓ	227 Ⓐ Ⓑ Ⓒ Ⓓ
176 Ⓐ Ⓑ Ⓒ Ⓓ	189 Ⓐ Ⓑ Ⓒ Ⓓ	202 Ⓐ Ⓑ Ⓒ Ⓓ	215 Ⓐ Ⓑ Ⓒ Ⓓ	228 Ⓐ Ⓑ Ⓒ Ⓓ
177 Ⓐ Ⓑ Ⓒ Ⓓ	190 Ⓐ Ⓑ Ⓒ Ⓓ	203 Ⓐ Ⓑ Ⓒ Ⓓ	216 Ⓐ Ⓑ Ⓒ Ⓓ	229 Ⓐ Ⓑ Ⓒ Ⓓ
178 Ⓐ Ⓑ Ⓒ Ⓓ	191 Ⓐ Ⓑ Ⓒ Ⓓ	204 Ⓐ Ⓑ Ⓒ Ⓓ	217 Ⓐ Ⓑ Ⓒ Ⓓ	230 Ⓐ Ⓑ Ⓒ Ⓓ
179 Ⓐ Ⓑ Ⓒ Ⓓ	192 Ⓐ Ⓑ Ⓒ Ⓓ	205 Ⓐ Ⓑ Ⓒ Ⓓ	218 Ⓐ Ⓑ Ⓒ Ⓓ	231 Ⓐ Ⓑ Ⓒ Ⓓ
180 Ⓐ Ⓑ Ⓒ Ⓓ	193 Ⓐ Ⓑ Ⓒ Ⓓ	206 Ⓐ Ⓑ Ⓒ Ⓓ	219 Ⓐ Ⓑ Ⓒ Ⓓ	232 Ⓐ Ⓑ Ⓒ Ⓓ
181 Ⓐ Ⓑ Ⓒ Ⓓ	194 Ⓐ Ⓑ Ⓒ Ⓓ	207 Ⓐ Ⓑ Ⓒ Ⓓ	220 Ⓐ Ⓑ Ⓒ Ⓓ	233 Ⓐ Ⓑ Ⓒ Ⓓ
182 Ⓐ Ⓑ Ⓒ Ⓓ	195 Ⓐ Ⓑ Ⓒ Ⓓ	208 Ⓐ Ⓑ Ⓒ Ⓓ	221 Ⓐ Ⓑ Ⓒ Ⓓ	234 Ⓐ Ⓑ Ⓒ Ⓓ
183 Ⓐ Ⓑ Ⓒ Ⓓ	196 Ⓐ Ⓑ Ⓒ Ⓓ	209 Ⓐ Ⓑ Ⓒ Ⓓ	222 Ⓐ Ⓑ Ⓒ Ⓓ	235 Ⓐ Ⓑ Ⓒ Ⓓ
184 Ⓐ Ⓑ Ⓒ Ⓓ	197 Ⓐ Ⓑ Ⓒ Ⓓ	210 Ⓐ Ⓑ Ⓒ Ⓓ	223 Ⓐ Ⓑ Ⓒ Ⓓ	236 Ⓐ Ⓑ Ⓒ Ⓓ
185 Ⓐ Ⓑ Ⓒ Ⓓ	198 Ⓐ Ⓑ Ⓒ Ⓓ	211 Ⓐ Ⓑ Ⓒ Ⓓ	224 Ⓐ Ⓑ Ⓒ Ⓓ	237 Ⓐ Ⓑ Ⓒ Ⓓ
186 Ⓐ Ⓑ Ⓒ Ⓓ	199 Ⓐ Ⓑ Ⓒ Ⓓ	212 Ⓐ Ⓑ Ⓒ Ⓓ	225 Ⓐ Ⓑ Ⓒ Ⓓ	238 Ⓐ Ⓑ Ⓒ Ⓓ
187 Ⓐ Ⓑ Ⓒ Ⓓ	200 Ⓐ Ⓑ Ⓒ Ⓓ	213 Ⓐ Ⓑ Ⓒ Ⓓ	226 Ⓐ Ⓑ Ⓒ Ⓓ	

Section 5: Language Skills

239 Ⓐ Ⓑ Ⓒ Ⓓ	251 Ⓐ Ⓑ Ⓒ Ⓓ	263 Ⓐ Ⓑ Ⓒ Ⓓ	275 Ⓐ Ⓑ Ⓒ Ⓓ	287 Ⓐ Ⓑ Ⓒ Ⓓ
240 Ⓐ Ⓑ Ⓒ Ⓓ	252 Ⓐ Ⓑ Ⓒ Ⓓ	264 Ⓐ Ⓑ Ⓒ Ⓓ	276 Ⓐ Ⓑ Ⓒ Ⓓ	288 Ⓐ Ⓑ Ⓒ Ⓓ
241 Ⓐ Ⓑ Ⓒ Ⓓ	253 Ⓐ Ⓑ Ⓒ Ⓓ	265 Ⓐ Ⓑ Ⓒ Ⓓ	277 Ⓐ Ⓑ Ⓒ Ⓓ	289 Ⓐ Ⓑ Ⓒ Ⓓ
242 Ⓐ Ⓑ Ⓒ Ⓓ	254 Ⓐ Ⓑ Ⓒ Ⓓ	266 Ⓐ Ⓑ Ⓒ Ⓓ	278 Ⓐ Ⓑ Ⓒ Ⓓ	290 Ⓐ Ⓑ Ⓒ Ⓓ
243 Ⓐ Ⓑ Ⓒ Ⓓ	255 Ⓐ Ⓑ Ⓒ Ⓓ	267 Ⓐ Ⓑ Ⓒ Ⓓ	279 Ⓐ Ⓑ Ⓒ Ⓓ	291 Ⓐ Ⓑ Ⓒ Ⓓ
244 Ⓐ Ⓑ Ⓒ Ⓓ	256 Ⓐ Ⓑ Ⓒ Ⓓ	268 Ⓐ Ⓑ Ⓒ Ⓓ	280 Ⓐ Ⓑ Ⓒ Ⓓ	292 Ⓐ Ⓑ Ⓒ Ⓓ
245 Ⓐ Ⓑ Ⓒ Ⓓ	257 Ⓐ Ⓑ Ⓒ Ⓓ	269 Ⓐ Ⓑ Ⓒ Ⓓ	281 Ⓐ Ⓑ Ⓒ Ⓓ	293 Ⓐ Ⓑ Ⓒ Ⓓ
246 Ⓐ Ⓑ Ⓒ Ⓓ	258 Ⓐ Ⓑ Ⓒ Ⓓ	270 Ⓐ Ⓑ Ⓒ Ⓓ	282 Ⓐ Ⓑ Ⓒ Ⓓ	294 Ⓐ Ⓑ Ⓒ Ⓓ
247 Ⓐ Ⓑ Ⓒ Ⓓ	259 Ⓐ Ⓑ Ⓒ Ⓓ	271 Ⓐ Ⓑ Ⓒ Ⓓ	283 Ⓐ Ⓑ Ⓒ Ⓓ	295 Ⓐ Ⓑ Ⓒ Ⓓ
248 Ⓐ Ⓑ Ⓒ Ⓓ	260 Ⓐ Ⓑ Ⓒ Ⓓ	272 Ⓐ Ⓑ Ⓒ Ⓓ	284 Ⓐ Ⓑ Ⓒ Ⓓ	296 Ⓐ Ⓑ Ⓒ Ⓓ
249 Ⓐ Ⓑ Ⓒ Ⓓ	261 Ⓐ Ⓑ Ⓒ Ⓓ	273 Ⓐ Ⓑ Ⓒ Ⓓ	285 Ⓐ Ⓑ Ⓒ Ⓓ	297 Ⓐ Ⓑ Ⓒ Ⓓ
250 Ⓐ Ⓑ Ⓒ Ⓓ	262 Ⓐ Ⓑ Ⓒ Ⓓ	274 Ⓐ Ⓑ Ⓒ Ⓓ	286 Ⓐ Ⓑ Ⓒ Ⓓ	298 Ⓐ Ⓑ Ⓒ Ⓓ

The Tutorverse
www.thetutorverse.com

Verbal Skills

Questions 1-60, 16 Minutes

1. Which word does *not* belong with the others?
   (A) broom
   (B) chores
   (C) mop
   (D) soap

2. Elegance most nearly means
   (A) difficulty
   (B) grace
   (C) ease
   (D) wealth

3. Spacious means the opposite of
   (A) cramped
   (B) land
   (C) open
   (D) rural

4. Apples grow on trees. Apples are sweet. All fruit that grows on trees is sweet. If the first two statements are true, then the third is
   (A) True
   (B) False
   (C) Uncertain

5. Surpass most nearly means
   (A) charge
   (B) excel
   (C) ignore
   (D) struggle

6. Which word does *not* belong with the others?
   (A) eyes
   (B) fingers
   (C) lips
   (D) nose

7. Presidents must be at least 35 years old. Barack Obama was a president. Barack Obama was at least 35 years old when he became president. If the first two statements are true, then the third is
   (A) True
   (B) False
   (C) Uncertain

8. Which word does *not* belong with the others?
   (A) depressed
   (B) emotion
   (C) joyful
   (D) worried

9. Rose is to garden as tree is to
   (A) bird
   (B) daisy
   (C) forest
   (D) squirrel

10. Serious means the opposite of
    (A) conversation
    (B) intense
    (C) meaningful
    (D) silly

11. Some socks are made of wool. Some socks are very warm. Wool socks are very warm. If the first two statements are true, then the third is
    (A) True
    (B) False
    (C) Uncertain

12. Which word does *not* belong with the others?
    (A) engineer
    (B) fisherman
    (C) sailor
    (D) ship

13. Tim is taller than Jessica. Abraham is taller than Tim. Abraham is taller than Jessica. If the first two statements are true, then the third is
    (A) True
    (B) False
    (C) Uncertain

14. Filthy means the opposite of
    (A) dirty
    (B) murky
    (C) pristine
    (D) sudden

15. Wave is to ocean as rapids is to
    (A) danger
    (B) nature
    (C) raft
    (D) river

16. Which word does *not* belong with the others?
    (A) dairy
    (B) groceries
    (C) meat
    (D) produce

17. Which word does *not* belong with the others?
    (A) daisy
    (B) fern
    (C) growth
    (D) tulip

18. Reduce means the opposite of
    (A) alleviate
    (B) increase
    (C) produce
    (D) signify

19. Lively most nearly means
    (A) active
    (B) dull
    (C) sleepy
    (D) vital

20. Stove is to appliance as hammer is to
    (A) building
    (B) screwdriver
    (C) tool
    (D) wood

21. Essential most nearly means
    (A) necessary
    (B) real
    (C) special
    (D) unimportant

22. Desire most nearly means
    (A) disinterest
    (B) longing
    (C) relationship
    (D) success

23. Sanitize is to safety as teach is to
    (A) education
    (B) professor
    (C) school
    (D) student

24. Erode most nearly means
    (A) build
    (B) burn
    (C) crumble
    (D) strengthen

25. Which word does *not* belong with the others?
    (A) book
    (B) movie
    (C) read
    (D) show

26. Absence most nearly means
    (A) lack
    (B) penalty
    (C) tardy
    (D) trouble

27. Eliminate means the opposite of
    (A) compete
    (B) delete
    (C) include
    (D) obstruct

28. Impartial is to biased as failure is to
    (A) achievement
    (B) complete
    (C) disappointment
    (D) equality

29. Introduction most nearly means
    (A) beginning
    (B) closing
    (C) conclusion
    (D) description

30. Calmly most nearly means
    (A) carefully
    (B) creatively
    (C) peacefully
    (D) slowly

31. Cryptic means the opposite of
    (A) clear
    (B) magnified
    (C) scientific
    (D) terrific

32. Extract most nearly means
    (A) add
    (B) identify
    (C) sample
    (D) uproot

33. Suspect most nearly means
    (A) charge
    (B) punish
    (C) shame
    (D) speculate

34. Esteemed means the opposite of
    (A) estimated
    (B) prestigious
    (C) respected
    (D) unknown

35. Day is to night as summer is to
    (A) season
    (B) spring
    (C) time
    (D) winter

36. Which word does *not* belong with the others?
    (A) celebration
    (B) dinner
    (C) feast
    (D) meal

37. City is to state as region is to
    (A) country
    (B) town
    (C) travel
    (D) village

38. Sharks are a species of fish. Some fish need to live in salt water. All sharks must live in salt water. If the first two statements are true, then the third is
    (A) True
    (B) False
    (C) Uncertain

39. Which word does *not* belong with the others?
    (A) destruction
    (B) earthquake
    (C) tornado
    (D) tsunami

40. Which word does *not* belong with the others?
    (A) decorations
    (B) food
    (C) music
    (D) party

41. Climax most nearly means
    (A) author
    (B) end
    (C) height
    (D) story

42. Lions are carnivores. Carnivores only eat meat. Lions only eat meat. If the first two statements are true, then the third is
    (A) True
    (B) False
    (C) Uncertain

43. Which word does *not* belong with the others?
    (A) lizard
    (B) reptile
    (C) snake
    (D) turtle

44. Apathy is to enthusiasm as melancholy is to
    (A) feeling
    (B) joy
    (C) music
    (D) sadness

45. Most horror movies have a rating of PG-13 or higher. Melissa isn't allowed to watch movies with a rating of PG-13 or higher. Melissa isn't allowed to watch any horror movies. If the first two statements are true, then the third is
    (A) True
    (B) False
    (C) Uncertain

46. Impede means the opposite of
    (A) allow
    (B) delay
    (C) generate
    (D) halt

47. Ornate most nearly means
    (A) flamboyant
    (B) humble
    (C) irritable
    (D) ordinary

48. Roger loves to read books. Books can be checked out for free at the library. Roger loves to hang out at the library. If the first two statements are true, then the third is
    (A) True
    (B) False
    (C) Uncertain

49. Scorch most nearly means
    (A) burn
    (B) lift
    (C) rest
    (D) soothe

50. Sage is a type of herb. Herbs are often added to pasta. Pasta always contains sage. If the first two statements are true, then the third is
    (A) True
    (B) False
    (C) Uncertain

51. Which word does *not* belong with the others?
    (A) pastry
    (B) muffin
    (C) croissant
    (D) strudel

52. Discord most nearly means
    (A) agreement
    (B) conflict
    (C) harmony
    (D) interest

53. Which word does *not* belong with the others?
    (A) adjective
    (B) definition
    (C) noun
    (D) verb

54. The blue fish can swim faster than the green fish. The red fish can swim faster than the green fish. The red fish can swim faster than the blue fish. If the first two statements are true, then the third is
    (A) True
    (B) False
    (C) Uncertain

55. Which word does *not* belong with the others?
    (A) cardigan
    (B) jacket
    (C) sweater
    (D) t-shirt

56. Obscure means the opposite of
    (A) beneath
    (B) invisible
    (C) jealous
    (D) ubiquitous

57. Category is to group as community is to
    (A) house
    (B) member
    (C) neighborhood
    (D) service

58. Which word does *not* belong with the others?
    (A) dressing
    (B) lettuce
    (C) salad
    (D) tomatoes

59. Which word does *not* belong with the others?
    (A) dream
    (B) hope
    (C) imagine
    (D) succeed

60. Rabid is to wild as calm is to
    (A) animal
    (B) loose
    (C) tame
    (D) violent

Quantitative Skills

Questions 61-112, 30 Minutes

61. In the sequence 5, 12, −12, −5..., what should come next?
    (A) −12
    (B) −5
    (C) 0
    (D) 5

62. Examine I, II, and III and find the *best* answer:

    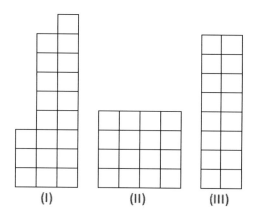

    (A) I = II > III
    (B) I > II = III
    (C) II > I > III
    (D) III < II < I

63. What number is 8 less than $\frac{1}{2}$ of 100?
    (A) 42
    (B) 48
    (C) 52
    (D) 54

64. In the sequence 68, 57, 46, 35..., what number should come next?
    (A) 22
    (B) 23
    (C) 24
    (D) 25

65. Examine the following and find the best answer.

    I. The degree measure of an acute angle
    II. The degree measure of an obtuse angle
    III. The degree measure of a right angle

    (A) I < II < III
    (B) II < III = I
    (C) II > I > III
    (D) I < III < II

66. Examine the line graph and find the *best* answer.

    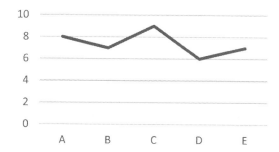

    (A) A equals E
    (B) B equals D
    (C) C is greater than D plus E
    (D) A plus B equals C plus D

67. Examine I, II, and III and find the *best* answer.

    I. 2 yards
    II. 6 feet
    III. 8 inches

    (A) I + III < II
    (B) I < II < III
    (C) I > II + III
    (D) I = II

68. In the sequence 2.2, 6.6, 19.8..., which number should come next?
    (A) 26.4
    (B) 39.6
    (C) 44.4
    (D) 59.4

69. Examine I, II, and III, and find the *best* answer.

    I. $\frac{3}{7}$
    II. $\frac{3}{4}$
    III. $\frac{3}{11}$

    (A) I > III > II
    (B) I < III < II
    (C) II > I > III
    (D) III > I > II

70. What number subtracted from 22 leaves you 5 more than the difference of 18 and 5?
    (A) 4
    (B) 9
    (C) 14
    (D) 19

71. Which should fill the blank in the following sequence: $\frac{21}{6}$, 7, ___, 28?
    (A) $\frac{42}{6}$
    (B) $\frac{21}{6}$
    (C) 12
    (D) 14

72. In the sequence 15, 12, 9, 6..., what number should come next?
    (A) 3
    (B) 4
    (C) 5
    (D) 8

73. The following circle graph shows the value of four variables. Find the *best* answer.

    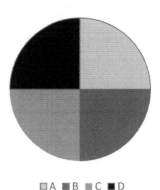

    □ A ■ B ■ C ■ D

    (A) The sum of A and B is greater than the sum of C and D
    (B) The sum of A and D is equal to the sum of B and C
    (C) The sum of C and D is less than B
    (D) The sum of A and C is less than the sum of B and D

74. Examine I, II, and III, and find the *best* answer.

    I. 0.07
    II. 0.70
    III. 0.070

    (A) II > I = III
    (B) II > I > III
    (C) II = III > I
    (D) II = I > III

75. Examine I, II, and III, and find the *best* answer.

    I. 1.013
    II. 2.013
    III. 1.103

    (A) I < II < III
    (B) I < III < II
    (C) I = III < II
    (D) III < I < II

76. What number multiplied by 5 is $\frac{1}{2}$ of 100?

    (A) 5
    (B) 10
    (C) 20
    (D) 40

77. Examine I, II, and III and find the *best* answer when *x* and *y* are both positive.

    I. $-(y - x)$
    II. $x + y - 2y$
    III. $x - y$

    (A) II and III are equal, and both are greater than I
    (B) II and III are equal, and both are less than I
    (C) I, II, and III are all equal
    (D) I is less than II, and II is less than III

78. Examine I, II, and III and find the *best* answer when *x* and *y* are both positive.

    I. $\frac{2x+4y}{2}$
    II. $2(x + y) - y$
    III. $x + y$

    (A) III is less than both I and II
    (B) III is more than I
    (C) I and III are equal
    (D) II is less than III

79. Examine I, II, and III and find the *best* answer.

    I. (1 dime) (1 dime)
    II. (1 quarter) (1 quarter) (1 quarter) (1 quarter)
    III. One Dollar

    (A) I and II are equal
    (B) III is less than I
    (C) II and III are equal
    (D) III is less than II

80. What number subtracted from $\frac{1}{3}$ of 60 is 10% of 50?

    (A) 10
    (B) 12
    (C) 15
    (D) 25

81. Examine the following and find the best answer.

    I. The area of a square with a side of 2
    II. The area of a right triangle with legs of length 3 and 2
    III. The circumference of a circle with diameter 2

    (A) I > II > III
    (B) III > I > II
    (C) I > III > II
    (D) I = III < II

82. Examine the angles and find the *best* answer.

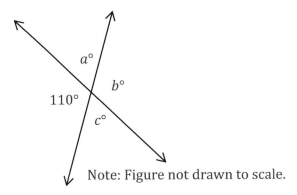

Note: Figure not drawn to scale.

(A) $a + b = c$
(B) $a = 110$
(C) $a - b = 110$
(D) $b > a$

83. What number is 10 more than the product of 3^2 and 5?
(A) 40
(B) 45
(C) 50
(D) 55

84. Examine the following and find the best answer:

   I. $-3(4 \times 3)$
   II. $3(-4 \times 3)$
   III. $-3(-4 \times -3)$

(A) I is greater than II, which is greater than III
(B) I, II, and III are equal
(C) III is smaller than II and I, which are equal
(D) I is greater than III, which is greater than II

85. What number added to 5^2 is $\frac{1}{3}$ of 90?
(A) 5
(B) 10
(C) 20
(D) 55

86. Examine the following and find the best answer:

   I. 23,400
   II. 23.4×10^3
   III. 0.234×10^5

(A) I is greater than II, which is greater than III
(B) I, II, and III are equal
(C) II is smaller than III and I, which are equal
(D) I is greater than III, which is greater than II

87. What number subtracted from 62 leaves you 12 less than twice the sum of 8 and 7?
(A) 6
(B) 18
(C) 35
(D) 44

88. Examine I, II, and III and find the *best* answer.

I.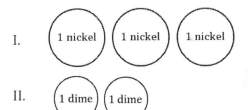

II.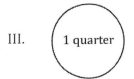

III. 1 quarter

(A) I > II
(B) II > III
(C) II = III
(D) I + II > III

89. Examine I, II, and III and find the *best* answer when *x* and *y* are both positive.

   I. $4x - y$
   II. $2(2x - y)$
   III. $2(2x + y)$

   (A) III is greater than II, and II is greater than I
   (B) I and II are equal, and both are less than III
   (C) I is less than II, and II is less than III
   (D) III is greater than II, and I is greater than II

90. Examine I, II, and III and find the best answer.

   I. the slope of the line shown
   II. the slope of $2x + 4y = 10$
   III. the slope of $y = 2x - 10$

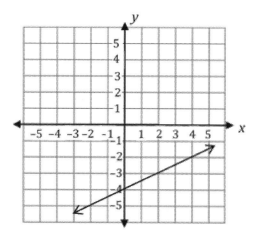

   (A) I > II
   (B) I = III
   (C) I > III
   (D) II > III

91. What number should fill in the blank in this series: 13, 9, ___, 14, 28, 24?
   (A) 5
   (B) 12
   (C) 16
   (D) 18

92. Below are two rectangles, with a diagonal dividing one of them. Compare angles *a, b, c,*

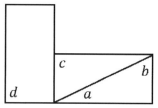

   and *d*. Find the *best* answer.

   (A) $c = d$
   (B) $a > b$
   (C) $c < b$
   (D) $a + b > d$

93. Examine I, II, and III and find the best answer.

   I. the slope of $x + y = 5$
   II. the slope of $y = 2x - 5$
   III. the slope of the line shown

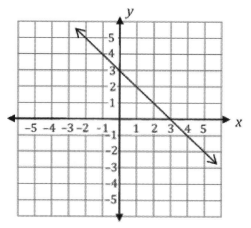

   (A) I is equal to II
   (B) I is equal to III
   (C) II is equal to III
   (D) II is greater than I

94. In the sequence 110, 104, 98, 92..., what number should come next?
   (A) 84
   (B) 86
   (C) 87
   (D) 88

95. Examine the following and find the best answer:

   I. 1.09×10^2
   II. 109×10^1
   III. 0.0109×10^3

   (A) II is greater than I, which is greater than III
   (B) I, II, and III are equal
   (C) II is smaller than III and I, which are equal
   (D) I is greater than III, which is greater than II

96. The following graph records how many points Jonathan and Teddy scored in the first five games of the basketball season. Find the *best* answer.

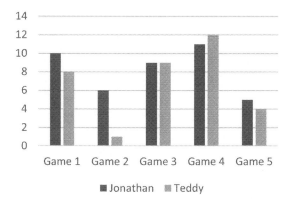

   (A) Jonathan outscored Teddy in two games
   (B) Jonathan outscored Teddy in three games
   (C) Jonathan and Teddy had the same number of points in two games
   (D) Teddy never had more points than Jonathan had

97. Examine I, II, and III and find the *best* answer.

   I. 6 inches
   II. 1 foot
   III. 4 inches

   (A) II > I + III
   (B) II + III < I
   (C) III < II < I
   (D) I > II

98. Examine I, II, and III and find the *best* answer when *x* and *y* are both positive.

   I. $x + 2y$
   II. $x - y$
   III. $2(x + y)$

   (A) II is less than III, and III is less than I
   (B) III and II are both greater than I
   (C) III is greater than I, and I is greater than II
   (D) I and III are equal

99. Examine I, II, and III and find the best answer.

   I. the slope of $6x + 2y = 4$
   II. the slope of the line shown
   III. the slope of $y = 3x - 8$

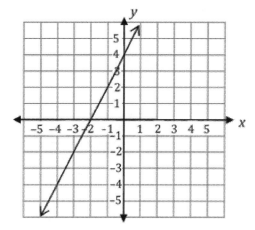

   (A) I is greater than II
   (B) I is less than III
   (C) II is greater than III
   (D) III is less than I

100. In the sequence 87, 78, 69, 60..., what number should come next?
    (A) 49
    (B) 50
    (C) 51
    (D) 52

101. Examine I, II, and III, and find the *best* answer.
    I. $\frac{1}{5}$
    II. $\frac{1}{6}$
    III. $\frac{1}{8}$

    (A) I > II > III
    (B) I > II = III
    (C) III > I = II
    (D) III > II > I

102. Examine the angles below and find the *best* answer.

    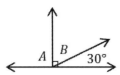
    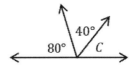

    (A) ∠A + ∠B = ∠C
    (B) ∠A = ∠C
    (C) ∠B < ∠C
    (D) ∠B = ∠C

103. What number should come next in this series: 9, 18, 6, 15 , __?
    (A) 2
    (B) 5
    (C) 9
    (D) 24

104. What number subtracted from 56 leaves the sum of 15, 12, and 8?
    (A) 11
    (B) 16
    (C) 21
    (D) 91

105. Examine I, II, and III and find the *best* answer:

    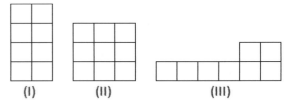

    (A) I = III < II
    (B) II < III < I
    (C) III = I > II
    (D) II > III > I

106. In the sequence $110, \frac{55}{2}, \frac{55}{8}$..., which number should come next?
    (A) $\frac{55}{64}$
    (B) $\frac{55}{32}$
    (C) $\frac{55}{16}$
    (D) $\frac{55}{10}$

107. Examine the following and find the best answer.

    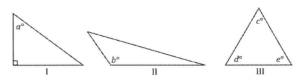

    I. measure of ∠a
    II. measure of ∠b
    III. The sum of the measure of angles ∠c, ∠d, and ∠e

    (A) III is greater than II, and II is greater than I
    (B) II is greater than III, and III is greater than I
    (C) I and II are equal, and both are less than III
    (D) Not enough information is provided to choose an answer.

108. What number added to 86 gives you twice the sum of 20 and 30?
    (A) 6
    (B) 12
    (C) 14
    (D) 36

109. What number subtracted from 77 leaves you 4 more than the product of 12 and 4?
    (A) 18
    (B) 25
    (C) 34
    (D) 70

110. Examine I, II, and III and find the *best* answer:

    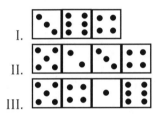

    (A) III is greater than II which is greater than I
    (B) I and II are equal, and both are less than III
    (C) III is less than II which is less than I
    (D) I is less than II which is greater than III

111. In the sequence 3, 5, −10, −8, 16..., what term should come next?
    (A) −32
    (B) −16
    (C) 18
    (D) 32

112. Which number should fill the blank in the following sequence: 84, __, 21, $\frac{21}{2}$, $\frac{21}{4}$?
    (A) 40
    (B) 42
    (C) 50
    (D) 63

Reading
Questions 113-174, 25 Minutes

Swirling rain; ferocious winds; giant waves: these are the makings of one of the world's most dangerous types of natural disaster—the hurricane. The damage caused by a hurricane can be so <u>catastrophic</u> that it impacts a community for years and years after a storm has hit, forever altering the lives of the people affected.

Hurricanes are large, powerful tropical storms that develop in coastal areas. They form over the ocean and sometimes make their way to land, bringing with them waves of ocean water called "surges" which can cause massive flooding and destruction. Hurricanes can also cause <u>immense</u> damage with their powerful winds, at speeds of 74 miles per hour or more, faster than a cheetah. Some especially intense hurricanes have clocked in at speeds as high as 215 miles per hour. These strong winds have the power to knock down trees, powerlines, and buildings—even people's homes!

Meteorologists (scientists who study weather) believe that hurricanes need two things to form. The first is warm water. Warm ocean water heats the air above it, causing it to rise and create creating pressure and momentum that makes the tropical storm clouds higher and more powerful. The second thing a forming hurricane needs is ideal wind conditions. When winds change direction a lot, it can cause a storm to break apart, but if winds remain consistent, hurricanes have an easier time forming. Meteorologists track hurricanes in order to predict how strong they will become and whether they will hit land. This information can help people prepare for a storm, telling them if they need to take shelter or even evacuate their homes, if necessary.

One unique aspect of hurricanes is their naming. Beginning in June of each year, tropical storms (which can become hurricanes) are named in alphabetical order from a list of pre-chosen names. For example, the first four tropical storms of 2023 were named Arlene, Bret, Cindy, and Don. Names are typically reused after six years, unless a storm was particularly damaging—for instance, the name "Hurricane Katrina" will never be used again, after a particularly destructive hurricane bearing that name hit the Gulf Coast and New Orleans in 2005, leaving over 1,300 people dead. This naming system makes it easier for meteorologists to communicate about storms, both current and historic, with each other and the public.

113. What would be the most appropriate title for this passage?
    (A) All About a Dangerous Type of Storm
    (B) Famous Hurricanes
    (C) Hurricane Katrina
    (D) Hurricanes & Tornadoes

114. This passage is mostly about
    (A) a specifically destructive natural phenomenon.
    (B) the most devastating hurricanes in history.
    (C) different types of tropical storms.
    (D) how to help people who have lost their homes because of hurricanes.

115. According to the facts of the passage,
    (A) hurricanes mainly happen in cold water.
    (B) scientists are unable to track hurricanes.
    (C) uneven winds can disrupt a hurricane's forming.
    (D) hurricanes only take place out in the middle of the ocean.

116. The author says that hurricane winds
    (A) can knock down trees, buildings, and homes.
    (B) are strong, but slow.
    (C) are the least dangerous part of the storm.
    (D) usually stop the second a storm makes it to land.

117. Based on the details of the passage, tropical storms are named according to
    (A) the name of the meteorologist who discovered the storm.
    (B) an alphabetical list of pre-chosen names.
    (C) the name of the town where the storm is projected to hit.
    (D) a community vote in which people vote for their favorite name.

118. Which of the following can be inferred from the passage?
    (A) Only a few hurricanes have ever actually touched land.
    (B) Hurricanes are easy to survive.
    (C) Preparing for a storm does not help you to be safe.
    (D) People living in coastal areas should be aware of the dangers of hurricanes.

119. You would probably find this passage in
    (A) a newspaper.
    (B) a young adult novel.
    (C) a science magazine.
    (D) a fantasy book.

120. The author would most likely agree with which of the following statements?
    (A) No one should live near the coast because the risk of hurricanes is too high.
    (B) Because hurricanes are rare, there is no reason to study them.
    (C) Learning about something helps you be more prepared if it happens to you.
    (D) Hurricanes are the least interesting type of storm because the effects of them are so mild.

121. The word "catastrophic", as it is used in the passage, most nearly means
    (A) basic.
    (B) disastrous.
    (C) minor.
    (D) tropical.

122. The word "immense," as it is used in the passage, most nearly means
    (A) comfortable.
    (B) extensive.
    (C) infinite.
    (D) limited.

Living on the Philippine islands, the Philippine tarsier is one of the smallest species of primate, usually weighing less than half a pound. Their name comes from their unusually long tarsal bones in their ankles, which allow them to jump up to three meters—an impressive distance, considering their diminutive size. The Philippine tarsier has short brown fur and large, soft ears. One of their most noticeable features is their extremely large eyes, which can be as large as their brains! As a result of this size, their eyes cannot move the way humans' eyes can. If they want to look around, they have to turn their entire head. Because of this, they can turn their heads farther than other mammals: a full 180 degrees in both directions!

Philippine tarsiers are shy, nocturnal animals. They sleep high in trees during the day and hunt insects and small lizards during the night. Philippine tarsiers are also solitary and territorial. Male tarsiers will even fight to the death if one wanders into another's space. These animals have a unique way of conversing with each other, making sounds to signal all kinds of emotions, including distress, happiness, surprise, and more. Scientists have noted up to eight distinct sounds the tarsiers make that each have their own meanings. It's like they're speaking their own language!

The Philippine tarsier lives in forests and has a lifespan of up to 24 years in the wild, and lower in captivity, where the tarsier can be stressed by the loud noises, confined space, and presence of humans. These primates are considered a threatened species, meaning their populations are declining in the wild. Habitat loss is the main reason for this. Philippine tarsiers only live in the Philippine islands and have very specific environmental needs—as the forests are demolished by humans, so are the Philippine tarsier's habitats. In addition to this, these animals are hunted and sometimes even kidnapped by humans. If Philippine tarsiers are not protected, they could soon face extinction.

123. This passage is mostly about
    (A) the last living Philippine tarsier.
    (B) how Philippine tarsiers care for their babies.
    (C) endangered animals in the Philippines.
    (D) a specific threatened species and the dangers that they face.

124. What would be the most appropriate title for this passage?
    (A) Unique Primates
    (B) The Philippine Islands
    (C) A Tiny Type of Primate
    (D) Endangered Animals of the Philippines

125. The author says that Philippine tarsiers
    (A) are nocturnal.
    (B) hibernate in the winter.
    (C) are closely related to koalas.
    (D) live in large groups called colonies.

126. Based on the details in the passage, Philippine tarsiers got their name from
    (A) their uniquely large eyes.
    (B) being the only animal to live in the Philippines.
    (C) the name of the scientist who discovered them.
    (D) a large bone in their ankles.

127. According to the facts of the passage, Philippine tarsiers
    (A) have soft, black fur.
    (B) live in Asia as well as the Philippines.
    (C) are decreasing in number in the wild.
    (D) are one of the largest species of primates.

128. You would probably find this passage in
    (A) a diary.
    (B) a nature journal.
    (C) a sports magazine.
    (D) a school newsletter.

129. The author would most likely agree with which of the following statements?
    (A) Philippine tarsier populations will soon increase.
    (B) Humans have a negative impact on animals and the environment.
    (C) Philippine tarsiers would be endangered even without the presence of humans.
    (D) Philippine tarsiers are not affected by habitats destruction because they are highly adaptable.

130. Which of the following can be inferred from the passage?
    (A) Philippine tarsiers are intelligent in their ability to communicate.
    (B) Philippine tarsiers are picky eaters.
    (C) Philippine tarsiers sleep too much.
    (D) Philippine tarsiers do not take care of their babies.

131. The word "diminutive", as it is used in the passage, most nearly means
    (A) awe-inspiring.
    (B) incredible.
    (C) impressive.
    (D) tiny.

132. The word "conversing", as it is used in the passage, most nearly means
    (A) arguing.
    (B) disagreeing.
    (C) communicating.
    (D) reversing.

Imagine being completely isolated from the outside world, with none of the conveniences of modern civilization, alone on an island about 40 miles from the nearest land—this is the lifestyle of the people of North Sentinel Island. Located in the northeastern Indian Ocean, North Sentinel Island is one of the few civilizations in the world still truly off-limits to outsiders. Researchers believe the Sentinelese people who occupy the island have lived there for over 55,000 years—over ten times as far back from modern day as ancient Egypt! The Sentinelese have their own way of life, <u>secluded</u> from the rest of the world. and are assumed to be in good health. Though many attempts have been made to contact the Sentinelese people, these attempts have often ended poorly for both sides. The Sentinelese people want to be left alone and will defend their island with violence when necessary.

Anthropologists (researchers who study human cultural development) have tried to gather information about the Sentinelese people since sailors first noticed fires on the beach of North Sentinel Island in 1771. Still, all these years later, very little is known about them. According to the little data we do have, roughly 80 to 150 people live on North Sentinel Island. The Sentinelese people make their homes in lean-tos (huts with slanted roofs and one open wall), which surround a communal firepit. They weave baskets and wear woven strings around their waists, necks, and heads. They also build canoes which they use to fish in the shallow waters around the island. Some Sentinelese people carry weapons such as spears, knives, and bows, which they use to hunt for food and defend their island from unwelcome visitors.

Anthropologists believe that the Sentinelese people have their own language. However, this language is not known to outsiders. We do not even know what the Sentinelese people call themselves. Though anthropologists prefer to call communities by the name they call themselves, they refer to the people on North Sentinel Island as the Sentinelese, due to their location; they likely have a different name for themselves. Contacting the Sentinelese people has proven near impossible due to their <u>aversion</u> to outsiders and the language barrier between them and the outside world. There are also now government orders that prevent people from attempting to visit North Sentinel Island for the protection of visitors and for the Sentinelese people alike. The Sentinelese people have demonstrated their desire to be left alone—their wishes are finally being respected.

133. This passage is mostly about
    (A) islands off the coast of North America.
    (B) the world's smallest and largest islands.
    (C) why North Sentinel Island is a great travel destination.
    (D) an isolated population in the Indian Ocean.

134. What would be the most appropriate title for this passage?
    (A) Tropical Places
    (B) Islands of India
    (C) Top Tourist Spots on North Sentinel Island
    (D) Leaving North Sentinel Island Alone!

135. The author states that the Sentinelese people
    (A) do not have a language of their own.
    (B) eat mainly fruits and berries found on the island.
    (C) use canoes that they build to fish in the island's surrounding waters
    (D) used to be more welcoming to outsiders.

136. North Sentinel Island is
    (A) the largest island on earth.
    (B) located in the middle of the Pacific Ocean.
    (C) one of the only places on earth where coconuts are grown.
    (D) one of the few places on earth where people live in isolation.

137. According to the facts of the passage,
    (A) when outsiders have visited North Sentinel Island in the past, it's ended poorly.
    (B) outsiders have never stepped foot on North Sentinel Island.
    (C) outsiders are welcomed on North Sentinel Island as long as they follow certain procedures.
    (D) anthropologists are unsure how the Sentinelese people would respond to an outsider stepping foot on their island.

138. The author would most likely agree with which of the following statements?
    (A) North Sentinel Island does not need to be protected.
    (B) It is perfectly safe to visit North Sentinel Island.
    (C) The Sentinelese people should be left alone.
    (D) Curious travelers should consider going to North Sentinel Island.

139. It can be inferred from the passage that
    (A) the Sentinelese people have access to advanced technologies.
    (B) anthropologists have some understanding of the Sentinelese people's homes.
    (C) North Sentinel Island will likely be explored more in the future.
    (D) the Sentinelese people trade regularly with India.

140. Which of the following can be inferred from the passage?
    (A) The Sentinelese people want to protect their island from outsiders.
    (B) The Sentinelese people fought in World War Two.
    (C) North Sentinel Island is easy to access by airplane.
    (D) North Sentinel Island has a diverse population of people.

141. The word "secluded", as is used in the passage, most nearly means
    (A) appreciated.
    (B) beloved.
    (C) isolated.
    (D) trusted.

142. The word "aversion", as it is used in the passage, most nearly means
    (A) curiosity.
    (B) desire.
    (C) dislike.
    (D) trade.

It was her first day as a small business owner, and Lara already had an impressive list of clients: eight fuzzy and friendly dogs! The excitement of walking and feeding dogs as part of her own pet-care business kept her awake kept her awake at night, excited to meet each client on her list. This small business had been a long time coming!

Lara had always loved dogs, but this was a whole new level of devotion. Sure, this time last year, she would sometimes help Mrs. Grayson walk her aging miniature pinscher and dog-sit the Bronsons' yellow Lab, Sandy. But now, she'd dedicate her time to eight little dogs, each different from the last! The business was also entirely hers—at the age of thirteen, she was already becoming a young <u>entrepreneur</u>!

When her parents urged her to find work during her summer break, Lara wondered why she should have to fill out application after application for boring jobs like cashier or waitress when what she really enjoyed was spending time with animals. When she thought of this, she immediately logged onto her computer and made an eye-catching flyer to advertise her services: "Lara the Pet Nanny: I will walk, play with, and love your furry friends as much as you do!" She spent a few hours on the graphic design, then hung the bright, <u>engaging</u> ads all around her neighborhood. She started getting phone calls that very first day! By the end of the week, she was telling people that she'd have to get back to them. So many pet owners were interested in her services!

She had to admit; setting up the "business" part of things was a little difficult—licenses, permits, tax documents. It was all overwhelming! Fortunately, her dad was an accountant and helped her apply for a permit and register her company with the state. Now, she could say she was the proud owner of Pet Heaven, Inc. She had a website, a Venmo account, business cards—it was all so exciting! She felt grown up. But the part she was most excited for was spending every day of the summer with such lovely animals. As far as she was concerned, it wasn't even work!

143. This passage is mostly about
    (A) one student's love of animals.
    (B) a frustrating summer job experience.
    (C) the challenges of running a business.
    (D) a young girl's first business.

144. According to the passage, Mrs. Grayson and the Bronsons
    (A) are Pet Heaven's first official customers.
    (B) convince Lara that she should start her own pet-care business.
    (C) gave Lara her earlier experience caring for pets.
    (D) no longer need Lara's help taking care of their dogs

145. The word "<u>entrepreneur</u>", as it is used in the passage, most nearly means
    (A) veterinarian.
    (B) business person.
    (C) interpreter.
    (D) employee.

146. The author would most likely agree with which of the following statements?
    (A) a young person opening a business is a unique and impressive thing.
    (B) Lara is being selfish for not working as a waitress.
    (C) people should never hire dogsitters.
    (D) by opening a small business, Lara is betraying Mrs. Grayson and the Bronsons.

147. Based on the passage, what can the reader infer that Lara thinks about typical summer jobs for young people?
    (A) They are hard to find.
    (B) Most students open their own businesses.
    (C) They are not that interesting.
    (D) Most temporary summer jobs lead to full-time jobs during the school year.

148. According to the passage, what was one problem that Lara faced after she posted her pet-care flyers?
    (A) Too many people needed her help.
    (B) She didn't get any interest in the services she was offering.
    (C) She decided that pet-care was not for her, after all.
    (D) The job was much harder than she thought it would be.

149. Based on the passage, Lara would be best described as
    (A) lazy and undisciplined.
    (B) timid and studious.
    (C) ambitious and selfish.
    (D) creative and hardworking.

150. The Word "engaging", as it is used in the passage, most nearly means
    (A) appealing.
    (B) expensive.
    (C) fighting.
    (D) marrying.

151. Based on the details of the passage, it can be inferred that Lara
    (A) hates cats.
    (B) has opened a business before.
    (C) is good at graphic design.
    (D) doesn't take good care of her own dogs.

152. What is the most appropriate title for this passage?
    (A) Animal Rescue 101
    (B) Lara's Pet Heaven
    (C) Summer Job Blues
    (D) How to Start Your Own Business

Vocabulary

153. Trying to preserve the peace
    (A) depict
    (B) monetize
    (C) obliviate
    (D) uphold

154. A pleasant exchange
    (A) enjoyable
    (B) forgettable
    (C) ignorant
    (D) limited

155. A torrential storm
    (A) appropriate
    (B) bizarre
    (C) relentless
    (D) unveiled

156. The creative painter
    (A) artistic
    (B) decisive
    (C) eventual
    (D) fellow

157. An exuberant celebration
    (A) exciting
    (B) dreadful
    (C) regular
    (D) unpleasant

158. An unwelcome intruder
    (A) delightful
    (B) invited
    (C) lost
    (D) unwanted

159. His grievous error in judgment
    (A) adorable
    (B) boring
    (C) grave
    (D) rushed

160. The professor's expert opinion
    (A) amateur
    (B) caught
    (C) skilled
    (D) unveiled

161. The scientist's hypothesis
    (A) aim
    (B) boast
    (C) idea
    (D) joke

162. A fraught dynamic
    (A) humble
    (B) knowable
    (C) tense
    (D) unusual

163. Tension spread through the room
    (A) anxiety
    (B) decision
    (C) profit
    (D) query

164. An approximate estimation
    (A) exact
    (B) fine
    (C) imprecise
    (D) perfect

165. A temperate climate
    (A) appropriate
    (B) foolish
    (C) mild
    (D) popular

166. The stealthy attack
    (A) evident
    (B) generalized
    (C) obvious
    (D) surreptitious

167. The army's shameful retreat
    (A) disgraceful
    (B) fearsome
    (C) sensitive
    (D) respectable

168. Her excruciating injury
    (A) comforting
    (B) painful
    (C) harmless
    (D) mediocre

169. To disclose important information
    (A) determine
    (B) moderate
    (C) share
    (D) tear

170. The inevitable outcome
    (A) binding
    (B) grave
    (C) irritable
    (D) unavoidable

171. To address a crowd
    (A) avoid
    (B) hide
    (C) reveal
    (D) speak

172. To dismiss another's opinion
    (A) disregard
    (B) flounder
    (C) hinder
    (D) kindle

173. An acceptable answer
    (A) abject
    (B) egregious
    (C) impossible
    (D) suitable

174. A perfect resolution
    (A) awful
    (B) flawless
    (C) helpless
    (D) roundabout

Mathematics
Questions 175-238, 45 Minutes

175. What is the sum of the exterior angles of a rectangle?
    (A) 345°
    (B) 360°
    (C) 540°
    (D) 720°

176. Circle A and Circle B are congruent. If the combined area of both circles is 50π yards, what is the length of AB?

    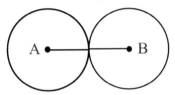

    (A) 5 yd
    (B) 10 yd
    (C) 15 yd
    (D) 20 yd

177. A right triangle has legs of 7 feet and 24 feet, and a hypotenuse of 25 feet. What is the area of the triangle?
    (A) 84 square feet
    (B) 87.5 square feet
    (C) 168 square feet
    (D) 175 square feet

178. What is the area of a circle with a circumference of 16π feet?
    (A) 8π sq. ft.
    (B) 64π sq. ft.
    (C) 128π sq. ft.
    (D) 256π sq. ft.

179. If a, b, and c are prime numbers, what is the LCM of a, b, and c?
    (A) ab
    (B) abc
    (C) a^2bc
    (D) ab^2c^2

180. What is equivalent to $(a^2b) \times (ab) \times (a^2b^3)$?
    (A) a^4b^3
    (B) a^4b^4
    (C) a^5b^4
    (D) a^5b^5

181. Which of the following is equal to $(2 \times 10^{-2}) \times (9 \times 10^{-3})$?
    (A) 1.8×10^{-6}
    (B) 1.8×10^{-5}
    (C) 1.8×10^{-4}
    (D) 1.8×10^{5}

182. If the volume of a cube is 216 cubic inches, what is its surface area?
    (A) 18 in²
    (B) 36 in²
    (C) 108 in²
    (D) 216 in²

183. What is equivalent to $\frac{m^5n^7}{m^2n^4}$?
    (A) m^3n^3
    (B) m^3n^4
    (C) m^7n^3
    (D) m^7n^{11}

184. What is the perimeter of a square that has an area of 144 square inches?
    (A) 12 in.
    (B) 24 in.
    (C) 36 in.
    (D) 48 in.

185. How many positive integers from 1 to 20, inclusive, are divisible by 2?
    (A) 9
    (B) 10
    (C) 11
    (D) 12

186. What is the GCF of 12 of 18?
    (A) 2
    (B) 4
    (C) 6
    (D) 9

187. Find the LCM of 5, 9, and 15.
    (A) 15
    (B) 30
    (C) 45
    (D) 60

188. A right triangle has a perimeter of 24 centimeters, one side length of 8, and another side length of 10, as shown in the figure. What is its area?

    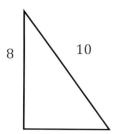

    (A) 24 cm²
    (B) 40 cm²
    (C) 48 cm²
    (D) 80 cm²

189. Eighteen thousandths can be written as
    (A) 0.018
    (B) 0.18
    (C) 1,800
    (D) 18,000

190. If the surface area of a cube is 96 square inches, what is its side length?
    (A) 2 inches
    (B) 4 inches
    (C) 6 inches
    (D) 16 inches

191. Express $\frac{1}{12}$ as a decimal.
    (A) 0.083
    (B) 0.08$\overline{3}$
    (C) 0.833
    (D) 0.83$\overline{3}$

192. Which fraction is smallest?
    (A) $\frac{4}{7}$
    (B) $\frac{5}{10}$
    (C) $\frac{6}{11}$
    (D) $\frac{7}{13}$

193. What is the prime factorization of 27?
    (A) 3^2
    (B) 3^3
    (C) $2^2 \times 3$
    (D) $9^2 \times 3$

194. All of the following fractions are equal EXCEPT:
    (A) $\frac{18}{24}$
    (B) $\frac{21}{28}$
    (C) $\frac{24}{36}$
    (D) $\frac{30}{40}$

195. Solve: $\frac{5}{6}x + 9 > 7$.
    (A) $x < 2$
    (B) $x > \frac{12}{5}$
    (C) $x > -\frac{12}{5}$
    (D) $x < -2$

196. If $x > -5$, which of the following is true?
    (A) $5x \leq -20$
    (B) $-x > -5$
    (C) $20x < 136$
    (D) $7x > -35$

197. What is the slope of a line perpendicular to the line $2x + 3y = 6$?
    (A) $-\frac{3}{2}$
    (B) $-\frac{2}{3}$
    (C) $\frac{3}{2}$
    (D) 2

198. Mark is building a scale model of the Brooklyn Bridge out of popsicle sticks that will cover his dinner table. Which unit of length would be most appropriate for his scale model?
(A) centimeters
(B) kilometers
(C) micrometers
(D) miles

199. Which of the following is equal to $\frac{4 \times 10^3}{8 \times 10^1}$?
(A) 5×10^1
(B) 5×10^2
(C) 5×10^3
(D) 5×10^4

200. Which of the following units would be the most appropriate for measuring the height of a flag pole?
(A) cubic feet
(B) feet
(C) millimeters
(D) square feet

201. What is the total degree measure when the three internal angles of a triangle are added together?
(A) 100°
(B) 180°
(C) 300°
(D) 360°

202. What is the slope of the line shown in the graph?

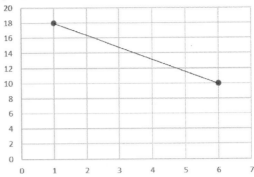

(A) $-\frac{8}{5}$
(B) $-\frac{5}{8}$
(C) $\frac{5}{8}$
(D) $\frac{8}{5}$

Problem Solving

203. How many cups fit in a gallon?
(A) 4 cups
(B) 8 cups
(C) 16 cups
(D) 32 cups

204. Krystal's teacher is three times as old as Krystal. The difference of their two ages is 20. How old is Krystal's teacher?
(A) 20
(B) 24
(C) 30
(D) 36

205. On a map, the scale is 1 inch is equal to 250 miles. If the distance between two cities is 10 inches on the map, how far apart are the cities?
(A) 0.04 miles
(B) 25 miles
(C) 250 miles
(D) 2,500 miles

206. What is 10.1 + 101.1 + .11 + 13 rounded to the nearest tens place?
    (A) 20
    (B) 120
    (C) 124.3
    (D) 124.31

207. What is the value of $\sqrt{\frac{9}{64}}$?
    (A) $\frac{1}{2}$
    (B) $\frac{3}{8}$
    (C) $\sqrt{\frac{3}{8}}$
    (D) $\frac{3}{32}$

208. Which of the following line segments are congruent?

    m _____

    n _____

    p _____

    q _____

    (A) m and n
    (B) m and p
    (C) n and p
    (D) n and q

209. Susan gets paid for pet sitting at a rate of $15 per hour. Last week, she worked for 3 hours on Monday and Tuesday each, 4 hours on Wednesday, and 5 hours on Thursday and Friday combined. How much money, in dollars, did she earn last week?
    (A) $180
    (B) $225
    (C) $255
    (D) $300

210. Franny is meeting her friend 10 miles away in 15 minutes. How fast does she have to drive to get there on time?
    (A) 15 miles per hour
    (B) 20 miles per hour
    (C) 35 miles per hour
    (D) 40 miles per hour

211. Solve: $(-5) - (-2) + 3 =$
    (A) -6
    (B) -4
    (C) 0
    (D) 10

212. Solve: $\frac{3}{4} + \frac{3}{8} =$
    (A) $\frac{6}{12}$
    (B) $\frac{9}{8}$
    (C) $\frac{36}{32}$
    (D) $1\frac{1}{8}$

213. A class of eleven students had the following scores on their history test: 87, 99, 95, 68, 73, 99, 94, 85, 77, 80, 99. What was the median score on this test?
    (A) 31
    (B) 85
    (C) 87
    (D) 99

214. A group of 80 office workers were surveyed about whether they've driven to work, taken the bus, or done both. Five said that they had other ways of getting to work, 58 had driven to work, and 30 had taken the bus. How many workers have done both?
    (A) 8
    (B) 10
    (C) 13
    (D) 15

215. The following Venn diagram indicates the states where students have lived. What does the region where the "B" is placed represent?

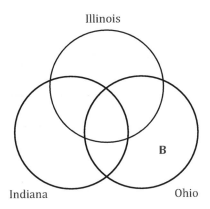

(A) students who have lived only in Ohio
(B) students who have lived in Indiana and Ohio
(C) students who have lived in Illinois and Indiana
(D) students who have lived in Illinois, Indiana, and Ohio

216. What is the sum of 6.72 and 2.02 rounded to the nearest tenth?
(A) 8.7
(B) 8.74
(C) 8.8
(D) 13.6

217. Increased by 100%, the number 20 becomes:
(A) 20
(B) 40
(C) 120
(D) 200

218. 2 lb. 2 oz. equals:
(A) 30 oz.
(B) 34 oz.
(C) 40 oz.
(D) 44 oz.

219. A survey is taken of the boys and girls at a local middle school about whether they prefer basketball or soccer. The data is recorded in the table below. If a student is selected at random from all of the students, what is the probability that it is a girl who prefers basketball?

	Basketball	Soccer	Total
Boys	18	32	50
Girls	23	16	39
Total	41	48	89

(A) $\frac{23}{89}$
(B) $\frac{16}{39}$
(C) $\frac{23}{41}$
(D) $\frac{23}{39}$

220. In 2010, the number of houses built in Town A was 25% greater than the number of houses built in Town B. If 70 houses were built in Town A during 2010, how many were built in Town B?
(A) 56
(B) 88
(C) 97
(D) 105

221. Solve for q: $(-\frac{2}{5})(6) = -\frac{1}{4}q$
(A) $-\frac{3}{5}$
(B) $\frac{3}{5}$
(C) 8
(D) $9\frac{3}{5}$

222. What is the percent represented by the decimal 1.3?
(A) 0.013%
(B) 1.3%
(C) 13%
(D) 130%

223. The following graph shows the percent of people who watch specific sports from different regions. Which sport has the greatest following in Latin America?

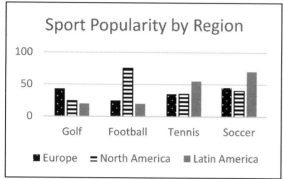

(A) football
(B) golf
(C) soccer
(D) tennis

224. Jamie's ferry ride lasts for 1 hour and 30 minutes. If the ferry is going 15 miles an hour, how many miles is the trip?
(A) 22.5 miles
(B) 25 miles
(C) 33.5 miles
(D) 35 miles

225. Solve: $\frac{1.2+3+0.7+2.3}{9} =$
(A) 0.5
(B) 0.6
(C) 0.8
(D) 1.2

226. What is the value of $\sqrt{2} \times \sqrt{4} \times \sqrt{8}$?
(A) 2
(B) 4
(C) 6
(D) 8

227. How much more does the average Ford cost than the average Toyota?

(A) $7,000
(B) $10,000
(C) $40,000
(D) $50,000

228. Martin has 50 cents in change in his pocket, with just nickels and dimes. He has one more nickel than he has dimes. How many dimes does he have in his pocket?
(A) 3
(B) 4
(C) 15
(D) 20

229. In a gym class, students are being randomly assigned to one of three different games. A basketball game needs 10 players, a soccer game needs 14 players, and a tennis game needs 4 players. What is the probability that Billy will be assigned to the soccer game?
(A) $\frac{4}{28}$
(B) $\frac{10}{28}$
(C) $\frac{1}{2}$
(D) $\frac{16}{28}$

230. Solve for x: $\frac{1}{2} - \frac{7}{8} = -\frac{1}{8}x$
    (A) −5
    (B) −3
    (C) $\frac{5}{8}$
    (D) 3

231. If $(2^x)^2 = 16$, then $x =$?
    (A) 1
    (B) 2
    (C) 3
    (D) 4

232. Solve: $(-5{,}895) + (-4{,}207) =$
    (A) −10,102
    (B) −10,012
    (C) −1,688
    (D) 1,688

233. In his last four baseball games, Frankie scored 3 runs, 2 runs, 2 runs, and 0 runs. How many runs does he need to score in the next game if he wants to have a mean of 2 runs in all of these games?
    (A) 1
    (B) 2
    (C) 3
    (D) 4

234. The two figures below are similar triangles. What is the length of side x?

    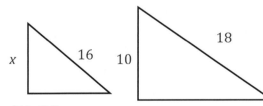

    (A) 3.5
    (B) $8.\overline{8}$
    (C) $12.1\overline{6}$
    (D) 28.8

235. Which of the following is a rational number?
    (A) π
    (B) $\sqrt{49}$
    (C) $\sqrt{61}$
    (D) $\sqrt{80}$

236. If $5^x = 625$, then $x =$?
    (A) 2
    (B) 3
    (C) 4
    (D) 5

237. Darrelle purchased a pair of jeans from a department store. The store had a sale for 20% off. If Darrelle paid $20 for the jeans, what was the original price?
    (A) $16.00
    (B) $24.00
    (C) $25.00
    (D) $27.00

238. At Johnny's Coffee Shop, 2 hamburgers and 1 order of fries costs $10.00. If 3 hamburgers cost $12.90, how much is a single order of fries?
    (A) $1.40
    (B) $2.90
    (C) $4.30
    (D) $5.70

Language Skills

Questions 239-298, 25 Minutes

For questions 239–278, choose the sentence that contains an error in punctuation, capitalization, or usage. If there is no error, select choice (D).

239. (A) Summer days are more longer than winter days.
(B) Her nails were longer than his.
(C) She completed the test faster than her peers.
(D) No mistake.

240. (A) There's a great view from the top of the Empire State Building.
(B) She walked all the way across the Brooklyn bridge.
(C) The senator came to town to inspect the new construction.
(D) No mistake.

241. (A) She had barely made it into the show on time.
(B) Maria never eats no dairy.
(C) Everything has fallen to pieces.
(D) No mistake.

242. (A) She preferred pens to pencils.
(B) Made everyone a delicious feast.
(C) The alligator crept out of the pond.
(D) No mistake.

243. (A) They couldn't verify the information.
(B) All the cars stopped on the highway.
(C) Her turtle was found.
(D) No mistake.

244. (A) She cried and then went home.
(B) They decorated every part of the house.
(C) They watched movies, listened to music, and playing games.
(D) No mistake.

245. (A) They couldn't live on a planet that was his.
(B) She lost her backpack at school.
(C) Seth was grateful to have his dog returned to them.
(D) No mistake.

246. (A) The movie coming out today.
(B) He is the coolest guy in school.
(C) John went to the store yesterday.
(D) No mistake.

247. (A) The jungle is more humid than the desert.
(B) The mountain was the most highest in the land.
(C) The ocean is deeper than a lake.
(D) No mistake.

248. (A) She studied all week for the algebra test.
(B) Her favorite movie was The Wizard of Oz.
(C) It was the longest Bridge in the United States.
(D) No mistake.

249. (A) The US. is a very large country.
(B) The first, and last, time they went to the beach was a disaster.
(C) The tennis match was the most exciting game I had ever seen!
(D) No mistake.

250. (A) "You can't do this to me!" Walt shouted at Jessie.
(B) He really shouldnt have lied to his mom.
(C) There was a problem: she couldn't answer the question.
(D) No mistake.

251. (A) December is the last month of the year.
     (B) They endeavored to reach the north pole.
     (C) She named her child after the planet Jupiter.
     (D) No mistake.

252. (A) She always finished her sentences.
     (B) Never able to cook a real meal.
     (C) The movie's ending was fabulous.
     (D) No mistake.

253. (A) Cedric couldn't stand the color yellow.
     (B) Fleur was excited to see the Eiffel tower.
     (C) Victor was leaving town on Tuesday.
     (D) No mistake.

254. (A) He expressed disappointment upon finding out his brother will lie.
     (B) Loretta drives down the same highway every morning.
     (C) This month, the student with the highest grade will receive a prize.
     (D) No mistake.

255. (A) He decided to merge both companies into one.
     (B) My mentor and close friend request that he be invited.
     (C) Honestly, she isn't the first person who made that mistake.
     (D) No mistake.

256. (A) It was me, Paul and Laurie.
     (B) It's not over.
     (C) There's so much more left.
     (D) No mistake.

257. (A) She canned her jams for winter.
     (B) Jeff broke his ankle walking downstairs.
     (C) Julia's markers leaked all over his bag.
     (D) No mistake.

258. (A) The phone number wasn't working.
     (B) Jordan always said he only needed two things to be happy, friends and family.
     (C) She needed milk, flour, sugar, and oil to finish the recipe.
     (D) No mistake.

259. (A) The hospital will have to fire the doctor after the scandal broke out.
     (B) The church bells ring every Monday, Wednesday, and Friday.
     (C) He wanted to go to the movies after band practice was over.
     (D) No mistake.

260. (A) The friends shared a burger.
     (B) Marcel opened the blinds on the window.
     (C) Katherine and her mother shops early in the morning.
     (D) No mistake.

261. (A) The Great Barrier Reef contains countless marine species.
     (B) Tourists come from all over to see the Grand Canyon.
     (C) The only sight Mark hadn't seen on the trip was mount Rushmore.
     (D) No mistake.

262. (A) He baked, iced, and decorating the cake.
     (B) Every kid cried and ran.
     (C) The movie was horrifying and scary.
     (D) No mistake.

263. (A) Rachel's friend Rebecca had three cousins.
     (B) Ali asked his Dad for a bigger allowance.
     (C) Joe's great aunt had a house in Florida.
     (D) No mistake.

264. (A) The store was sold out so she could not buy what she needed.
(B) She is not expected to make it to the wedding.
(C) Lucy forgot that she needs to buy groceries yesterday.
(D) No mistake.

265. (A) Her dog was smarter than her cat.
(B) She was more hungrier than she'd ever been.
(C) The sharpest knife was perfect for chopping onions.
(D) No mistake.

266. (A) Steve's two cats' toys are everywhere.
(B) My dog is barking, so I should feed him.
(C) I want to go to a movie; Devin wants to go home.
(D) No mistake.

267. (A) April still hasn't told her mom.
(B) Jake's sister was late.
(C) The debt was her's alone.
(D) No mistake.

268. (A) She is both kind and intelligently.
(B) Everyone thought the event had been boring.
(C) She eventually made it to the party.
(D) No mistake.

269. (A) She couldn't wait to see Mount Rushmore in person.
(B) The Mountains are so beautiful in the winter.
(C) She learned about President Lincoln in class.
(D) No mistake.

270. (A) The farthest planet from earth is Neptune.
(B) They traveled to the desert to observe the Milky Way.
(C) A solar eclipse is a rare astronomical occurrence.
(D) No mistake.

271. (A) She wasn't ready to leave.
(B) Already, she had to stop playing.
(C) She was tired but, she kept going.
(D) No mistake.

272. (A) Amanda's favorite genre of books is Mystery novels.
(B) She should have realized it was a prank since it was April Fool's Day.
(C) Fireworks became a hot commodity around Fourth of July.
(D) No mistake.

273. (A) The psychic couldn't predict the future.
(B) The sun had hardly breached the horizon.
(C) There wasn't no gas in the tank.
(D) No mistake.

274. (A) The tea's temperature was too hot.
(B) Her favorite actresses restaurant was incredibly expensive.
(C) The artist's income was too little for her to live on.
(D) No mistake.

275. (A) The crowd was exuberant.
(B) They cheered loudly.
(C) The band played energetically.
(D) No mistake.

276. (A) He was wiser than his grandfather.
(B) She was the most fastest runner on the team.
(C) Mars is smaller than Jupiter.
(D) No mistake.

277. (A) I'm less concerned about the storm than Gerald.
(B) Every day that week was cloudy; on Friday, it rained all day.
(C) The calendar's pages were falling to the floor.
(D) No mistake.

278. (A) They imagined they would celebrate after they won the game.
(B) The mayor has a vision for changes to this town this year.
(C) She is hurrying to catch the bus so she won't miss her class.
(D) No mistake.

Spelling

For questions 279-288, choose the sentence that contains an error in spelling. If there is no error, select choice (D).

279. (A) Only the best can win the competition.
(B) The teacher assigned her students homework.
(C) Her excercise routine was rather simple.
(D) No mistake.

280. (A) The viscosity of the liquid is unpleasant.
(B) His curiousity got the best of him.
(C) He wanted to help save the environment.
(D) No mistake.

281. (A) She reached her arms up to the sky.
(B) Katherine was definitely going to be late for the bus.
(C) She was not conscious of anything being wrong.
(D) No mistake.

282. (A) She wished she could disappear in that moment.
(B) Leo didn't believe in the existance of ghosts.
(C) Her father's business was in trouble.
(D) No mistake.

283. (A) Stephen trembled in the cold.
(B) The sugar in the candy was addicting.
(C) She definately afraid of making any mistakes.
(D) No mistake.

284. (A) She felt betrayed by her best freind.
(B) The story had an unfortunate ending.
(C) He tried to get tickets to the concert on Friday.
(D) No mistake.

285. (A) He forwarded the email to his client.
(B) The forrest was filled with noisy birds.
(C) Her skin itched after she touched the poison oak.
(D) No mistake.

286. (A) Her manicure took less than fifteen minutes.
(B) The movie garnered excellent reviews.
(C) He was so dissapointed that the game was sold out.
(D) No mistake.

287. (A) She was a skilled gardener.
(B) He was nervous to travel to a foriegn country.
(C) She was grateful for all her birthday gifts.
(D) No mistake.

288. (A) Marissa's favorite color was violet.
(B) They knew a storm was coming when they saw the lightening.
(C) Every evening brought a chorus of chirping.
(D) No mistake.

Composition

289. Which of these sentences expresses the idea most clearly?

(A) Maria had never planted a vegetable garden and was excited to see her hard work pay off.
(B) Maria was excited to see if her hard work would pay off because she had never planted a vegetable garden.
(C) Never a gardener, excited Maria waited for her hard work to pay off.
(D) Having never planted a vegetable garden, Maria waited for her hard work to pay off excitedly.

290. Choose the best word or words to join the thoughts together.

I usually ride my bike to my friend's house; _____ my bike is broken.

(A) therefore,
(B) however,
(C) nonetheless,
(D) none of these

291. Choose the best word or words to join the thoughts together.

Cats are playful animals; _____ they love to chase feather toys.

(A) surprisingly,
(B) for example,
(C) unfortunately,
(D) none of these

292. Which of the following sentences offers the *least* support for the topic "Please Shovel the Snow"?

(A) When snow melts, it turns to ice, which is slippery and dangerous.
(B) Deep snow is difficult to walk through.
(C) It is fun to play outside in the snow.
(D) Snow makes a mess when it is tracked inside the house.

293. Which of these sentences expresses the idea most clearly?

(A) Every day was when Thomas loved to read horoscopes.
(B) Reading horoscopes every day, Thomas loved to.
(C) Reading horoscopes was what Thomas loved to do every day.
(D) Thomas loved to read horoscopes every day.

294. Which of these best fits under the topic "Bird Migration"?

(A) There are many species of birds.
(B) Many birds fly to warmer climates during the winter.
(C) Birds eat a variety of different foods.
(D) none of these

295. Which of these best fits under the topic "Home Remodeling"?

(A) There are homes in urban, suburban, and rural places.
(B) Making modern updates to your home can increase its value.
(C) Some people prefer to stay at home.
(D) none of these

296. Choose the word that best completes the sentence.

Tanya, who was nervous for her ballet tryouts, _____ paced the room.

(A) curiously
(B) anxiously
(C) confidently
(D) surprisingly

297. Which of the following expresses the idea most clearly?

(A) She went to the refrigerator to get a snack.
(B) The refrigerator she went to in order to get a snack.
(C) To get a snack, she went to the refrigerator.
(D) By going to the refrigerator, she got a snack.

298. Choose the word that is a clear connective to complete the sentence.

The blizzard snowed us in; _____ we were unable to make it to the show.

(A) excitedly,
(B) sadly,
(C) hopefully,
(D) none of these

Scoring Practice Test 1

Using your answer sheet and referring to the answer key at the back of the book, calculate the percentage of questions you answered correctly in each section by taking the number of questions you answered correctly in that section and dividing it by the number of questions in that section. Multiply this number by 100 to determine your percentage score. The higher the percentage, the stronger your performance in that section. The lower the percentage, the more time you should spend practicing that section.

Note that the actual test will not evaluate your score based on percentage correct or incorrect. Instead, it will evaluate your performance relative to all other students in your grade who took the test.

Record your results here:

Section	Questions Correct	Total Questions	Percent Questions Correct
Verbal Skills	___	60	___%
Quantitative Skills	___	52	___%
Reading Comprehension	___	62	___%
Mathematics Achievement	___	64	___%
Language	___	60	___%

Remember that, depending on the curriculum at your school, there may be material on this test that you have not yet been taught. If this is the case, and you would like to improve your score beyond what is expected of your grade, consider outside help from an adult—such as a tutor or teacher – who can help you learn more about the topics that are new to you.

Answer Key

The keys are organized by section, and each question has an answer associated with it. Remember: there are detailed answer explanations available online at www.thetutorverse.com/books. Be sure to obtain permission before going online.

Practice Test 2

Overview

The practice test is designed to assess your understanding of key skills and concepts. It is important to take the final practice test after completing the diagnostic tests and after you have spent time studying and practicing.

The main difference between the practice tests and the actual test is that the practice tests are scored differently from how the actual exam is scored. On the actual exam, your score will be determined by how well you did compared to other students in your grade. On the practice tests, however, we will score every question in order to gauge your mastery over skills and concepts.

Format

The format of the practice test is similar to that of the actual test. The number of questions included in each section mirror those of the actual test. This is done by design, in order to help familiarize you with the actual length of the test.

In addition to the math concepts reviewed in this workbook, the practice tests also include English Language Arts material, similar to what will be on the actual exam. If you feel you need more practice on the English Language Arts concepts covered in this test, consider consulting "HSPT Reading Comprehension, Verbal, and Language: 1,700+ Practice Questions," which is available for purchase at www.thetutorverse.com/books.

The practice test includes the following sections:

Practice Test Section	Questions	Time Limit
Verbal Skills	60	16 minutes
Quantitative Skills	52	30 minutes
Reading Comprehension	62	25 minutes
Mathematics	64	45 minutes
Language	60	25 minutes
Total	**298**	**2h 21 minutes**

Generally, 2 brief breaks are given between sections of the test; however, the timing and duration of the breaks are determined by the individual school that is administering the exam.

Calculators

Students are not permitted to use calculators on the HSPT. **To ensure the results of the practice test are as accurate as possible, do not use a calculator on this exam**. If you have a diagnosed learning disability which requires the use of a calculator, contact your testing site to organize special accommodations and continue to practice with a calculator as needed.

Answering

Use the answer sheet provided on the next several pages to record your answers. You may wish to tear these pages out of the workbook.

Practice Test Answer Sheet

[Carefully tear or cut out this page.]

Section 1: Verbal Skills

1. Ⓐ Ⓑ Ⓒ Ⓓ
2. Ⓐ Ⓑ Ⓒ Ⓓ
3. Ⓐ Ⓑ Ⓒ Ⓓ
4. Ⓐ Ⓑ Ⓒ
5. Ⓐ Ⓑ Ⓒ Ⓓ
6. Ⓐ Ⓑ Ⓒ Ⓓ
7. Ⓐ Ⓑ Ⓒ Ⓓ
8. Ⓐ Ⓑ Ⓒ Ⓓ
9. Ⓐ Ⓑ Ⓒ
10. Ⓐ Ⓑ Ⓒ Ⓓ
11. Ⓐ Ⓑ Ⓒ Ⓓ
12. Ⓐ Ⓑ Ⓒ Ⓓ
13. Ⓐ Ⓑ Ⓒ Ⓓ
14. Ⓐ Ⓑ Ⓒ Ⓓ
15. Ⓐ Ⓑ Ⓒ Ⓓ
16. Ⓐ Ⓑ Ⓒ Ⓓ
17. Ⓐ Ⓑ Ⓒ Ⓓ
18. Ⓐ Ⓑ Ⓒ
19. Ⓐ Ⓑ Ⓒ Ⓓ
20. Ⓐ Ⓑ Ⓒ Ⓓ
21. Ⓐ Ⓑ Ⓒ Ⓓ
22. Ⓐ Ⓑ Ⓒ Ⓓ
23. Ⓐ Ⓑ Ⓒ
24. Ⓐ Ⓑ Ⓒ Ⓓ
25. Ⓐ Ⓑ Ⓒ Ⓓ
26. Ⓐ Ⓑ Ⓒ Ⓓ
27. Ⓐ Ⓑ Ⓒ Ⓓ
28. Ⓐ Ⓑ Ⓒ
29. Ⓐ Ⓑ Ⓒ Ⓓ
30. Ⓐ Ⓑ Ⓒ Ⓓ
31. Ⓐ Ⓑ Ⓒ Ⓓ
32. Ⓐ Ⓑ Ⓒ Ⓓ
33. Ⓐ Ⓑ Ⓒ Ⓓ
34. Ⓐ Ⓑ Ⓒ Ⓓ
35. Ⓐ Ⓑ Ⓒ
36. Ⓐ Ⓑ Ⓒ Ⓓ
37. Ⓐ Ⓑ Ⓒ Ⓓ
38. Ⓐ Ⓑ Ⓒ Ⓓ
39. Ⓐ Ⓑ Ⓒ
40. Ⓐ Ⓑ Ⓒ Ⓓ
41. Ⓐ Ⓑ Ⓒ Ⓓ
42. Ⓐ Ⓑ Ⓒ
43. Ⓐ Ⓑ Ⓒ Ⓓ
44. Ⓐ Ⓑ Ⓒ Ⓓ
45. Ⓐ Ⓑ Ⓒ Ⓓ
46. Ⓐ Ⓑ Ⓒ Ⓓ
47. Ⓐ Ⓑ Ⓒ Ⓓ
48. Ⓐ Ⓑ Ⓒ Ⓓ
49. Ⓐ Ⓑ Ⓒ Ⓓ
50. Ⓐ Ⓑ Ⓒ Ⓓ
51. Ⓐ Ⓑ Ⓒ
52. Ⓐ Ⓑ Ⓒ Ⓓ
53. Ⓐ Ⓑ Ⓒ Ⓓ
54. Ⓐ Ⓑ Ⓒ Ⓓ
55. Ⓐ Ⓑ Ⓒ Ⓓ
56. Ⓐ Ⓑ Ⓒ
57. Ⓐ Ⓑ Ⓒ Ⓓ
58. Ⓐ Ⓑ Ⓒ Ⓓ
59. Ⓐ Ⓑ Ⓒ Ⓓ
60. Ⓐ Ⓑ Ⓒ Ⓓ

Section 2: Quantitative Skills

61. Ⓐ Ⓑ Ⓒ Ⓓ
62. Ⓐ Ⓑ Ⓒ Ⓓ
63. Ⓐ Ⓑ Ⓒ Ⓓ
64. Ⓐ Ⓑ Ⓒ Ⓓ
65. Ⓐ Ⓑ Ⓒ Ⓓ
66. Ⓐ Ⓑ Ⓒ Ⓓ
67. Ⓐ Ⓑ Ⓒ Ⓓ
68. Ⓐ Ⓑ Ⓒ Ⓓ
69. Ⓐ Ⓑ Ⓒ Ⓓ
70. Ⓐ Ⓑ Ⓒ Ⓓ
71. Ⓐ Ⓑ Ⓒ Ⓓ
72. Ⓐ Ⓑ Ⓒ Ⓓ
73. Ⓐ Ⓑ Ⓒ Ⓓ
74. Ⓐ Ⓑ Ⓒ Ⓓ
75. Ⓐ Ⓑ Ⓒ Ⓓ
76. Ⓐ Ⓑ Ⓒ Ⓓ
77. Ⓐ Ⓑ Ⓒ Ⓓ
78. Ⓐ Ⓑ Ⓒ Ⓓ
79. Ⓐ Ⓑ Ⓒ Ⓓ
80. Ⓐ Ⓑ Ⓒ Ⓓ
81. Ⓐ Ⓑ Ⓒ Ⓓ
82. Ⓐ Ⓑ Ⓒ Ⓓ
83. Ⓐ Ⓑ Ⓒ Ⓓ
84. Ⓐ Ⓑ Ⓒ Ⓓ
85. Ⓐ Ⓑ Ⓒ Ⓓ
86. Ⓐ Ⓑ Ⓒ Ⓓ
87. Ⓐ Ⓑ Ⓒ Ⓓ
88. Ⓐ Ⓑ Ⓒ Ⓓ
89. Ⓐ Ⓑ Ⓒ Ⓓ
90. Ⓐ Ⓑ Ⓒ Ⓓ
91. Ⓐ Ⓑ Ⓒ Ⓓ
92. Ⓐ Ⓑ Ⓒ Ⓓ
93. Ⓐ Ⓑ Ⓒ Ⓓ
94. Ⓐ Ⓑ Ⓒ Ⓓ
95. Ⓐ Ⓑ Ⓒ Ⓓ
96. Ⓐ Ⓑ Ⓒ Ⓓ
97. Ⓐ Ⓑ Ⓒ Ⓓ
98. Ⓐ Ⓑ Ⓒ Ⓓ
99. Ⓐ Ⓑ Ⓒ Ⓓ
100. Ⓐ Ⓑ Ⓒ Ⓓ
101. Ⓐ Ⓑ Ⓒ Ⓓ
102. Ⓐ Ⓑ Ⓒ Ⓓ
103. Ⓐ Ⓑ Ⓒ Ⓓ
104. Ⓐ Ⓑ Ⓒ Ⓓ
105. Ⓐ Ⓑ Ⓒ Ⓓ
106. Ⓐ Ⓑ Ⓒ Ⓓ
107. Ⓐ Ⓑ Ⓒ Ⓓ
108. Ⓐ Ⓑ Ⓒ Ⓓ
109. Ⓐ Ⓑ Ⓒ Ⓓ
110. Ⓐ Ⓑ Ⓒ Ⓓ
111. Ⓐ Ⓑ Ⓒ Ⓓ
112. Ⓐ Ⓑ Ⓒ Ⓓ

Section 3: Reading

113. Ⓐ Ⓑ Ⓒ Ⓓ
114. Ⓐ Ⓑ Ⓒ Ⓓ
115. Ⓐ Ⓑ Ⓒ Ⓓ
116. Ⓐ Ⓑ Ⓒ Ⓓ
117. Ⓐ Ⓑ Ⓒ Ⓓ
118. Ⓐ Ⓑ Ⓒ Ⓓ
119. Ⓐ Ⓑ Ⓒ Ⓓ
120. Ⓐ Ⓑ Ⓒ Ⓓ
121. Ⓐ Ⓑ Ⓒ Ⓓ
122. Ⓐ Ⓑ Ⓒ Ⓓ
123. Ⓐ Ⓑ Ⓒ Ⓓ
124. Ⓐ Ⓑ Ⓒ Ⓓ
125. Ⓐ Ⓑ Ⓒ Ⓓ
126. Ⓐ Ⓑ Ⓒ Ⓓ
127. Ⓐ Ⓑ Ⓒ Ⓓ
128. Ⓐ Ⓑ Ⓒ Ⓓ
129. Ⓐ Ⓑ Ⓒ Ⓓ
130. Ⓐ Ⓑ Ⓒ Ⓓ
131. Ⓐ Ⓑ Ⓒ Ⓓ
132. Ⓐ Ⓑ Ⓒ Ⓓ
133. Ⓐ Ⓑ Ⓒ Ⓓ
134. Ⓐ Ⓑ Ⓒ Ⓓ
135. Ⓐ Ⓑ Ⓒ Ⓓ
136. Ⓐ Ⓑ Ⓒ Ⓓ
137. Ⓐ Ⓑ Ⓒ Ⓓ
138. Ⓐ Ⓑ Ⓒ Ⓓ
139. Ⓐ Ⓑ Ⓒ Ⓓ
140. Ⓐ Ⓑ Ⓒ Ⓓ
141. Ⓐ Ⓑ Ⓒ Ⓓ
142. Ⓐ Ⓑ Ⓒ Ⓓ
143. Ⓐ Ⓑ Ⓒ Ⓓ
144. Ⓐ Ⓑ Ⓒ Ⓓ
145. Ⓐ Ⓑ Ⓒ Ⓓ
146. Ⓐ Ⓑ Ⓒ Ⓓ
147. Ⓐ Ⓑ Ⓒ Ⓓ
148. Ⓐ Ⓑ Ⓒ Ⓓ
149. Ⓐ Ⓑ Ⓒ Ⓓ
150. Ⓐ Ⓑ Ⓒ Ⓓ
151. Ⓐ Ⓑ Ⓒ Ⓓ
152. Ⓐ Ⓑ Ⓒ Ⓓ

(Section 3: Reading continued on reverse)

153 Ⓐ Ⓑ Ⓒ Ⓓ	158 Ⓐ Ⓑ Ⓒ Ⓓ	163 Ⓐ Ⓑ Ⓒ Ⓓ	168 Ⓐ Ⓑ Ⓒ Ⓓ	173 Ⓐ Ⓑ Ⓒ Ⓓ
154 Ⓐ Ⓑ Ⓒ Ⓓ	159 Ⓐ Ⓑ Ⓒ Ⓓ	164 Ⓐ Ⓑ Ⓒ Ⓓ	169 Ⓐ Ⓑ Ⓒ Ⓓ	174 Ⓐ Ⓑ Ⓒ Ⓓ
155 Ⓐ Ⓑ Ⓒ Ⓓ	160 Ⓐ Ⓑ Ⓒ Ⓓ	165 Ⓐ Ⓑ Ⓒ Ⓓ	170 Ⓐ Ⓑ Ⓒ Ⓓ	
156 Ⓐ Ⓑ Ⓒ Ⓓ	161 Ⓐ Ⓑ Ⓒ Ⓓ	166 Ⓐ Ⓑ Ⓒ Ⓓ	171 Ⓐ Ⓑ Ⓒ Ⓓ	
157 Ⓐ Ⓑ Ⓒ Ⓓ	162 Ⓐ Ⓑ Ⓒ Ⓓ	167 Ⓐ Ⓑ Ⓒ Ⓓ	172 Ⓐ Ⓑ Ⓒ Ⓓ	

Section 4: Mathematics

175 Ⓐ Ⓑ Ⓒ Ⓓ	188 Ⓐ Ⓑ Ⓒ Ⓓ	201 Ⓐ Ⓑ Ⓒ Ⓓ	214 Ⓐ Ⓑ Ⓒ Ⓓ	227 Ⓐ Ⓑ Ⓒ Ⓓ
176 Ⓐ Ⓑ Ⓒ Ⓓ	189 Ⓐ Ⓑ Ⓒ Ⓓ	202 Ⓐ Ⓑ Ⓒ Ⓓ	215 Ⓐ Ⓑ Ⓒ Ⓓ	228 Ⓐ Ⓑ Ⓒ Ⓓ
177 Ⓐ Ⓑ Ⓒ Ⓓ	190 Ⓐ Ⓑ Ⓒ Ⓓ	203 Ⓐ Ⓑ Ⓒ Ⓓ	216 Ⓐ Ⓑ Ⓒ Ⓓ	229 Ⓐ Ⓑ Ⓒ Ⓓ
178 Ⓐ Ⓑ Ⓒ Ⓓ	191 Ⓐ Ⓑ Ⓒ Ⓓ	204 Ⓐ Ⓑ Ⓒ Ⓓ	217 Ⓐ Ⓑ Ⓒ Ⓓ	230 Ⓐ Ⓑ Ⓒ Ⓓ
179 Ⓐ Ⓑ Ⓒ Ⓓ	192 Ⓐ Ⓑ Ⓒ Ⓓ	205 Ⓐ Ⓑ Ⓒ Ⓓ	218 Ⓐ Ⓑ Ⓒ Ⓓ	231 Ⓐ Ⓑ Ⓒ Ⓓ
180 Ⓐ Ⓑ Ⓒ Ⓓ	193 Ⓐ Ⓑ Ⓒ Ⓓ	206 Ⓐ Ⓑ Ⓒ Ⓓ	219 Ⓐ Ⓑ Ⓒ Ⓓ	232 Ⓐ Ⓑ Ⓒ Ⓓ
181 Ⓐ Ⓑ Ⓒ Ⓓ	194 Ⓐ Ⓑ Ⓒ Ⓓ	207 Ⓐ Ⓑ Ⓒ Ⓓ	220 Ⓐ Ⓑ Ⓒ Ⓓ	233 Ⓐ Ⓑ Ⓒ Ⓓ
182 Ⓐ Ⓑ Ⓒ Ⓓ	195 Ⓐ Ⓑ Ⓒ Ⓓ	208 Ⓐ Ⓑ Ⓒ Ⓓ	221 Ⓐ Ⓑ Ⓒ Ⓓ	234 Ⓐ Ⓑ Ⓒ Ⓓ
183 Ⓐ Ⓑ Ⓒ Ⓓ	196 Ⓐ Ⓑ Ⓒ Ⓓ	209 Ⓐ Ⓑ Ⓒ Ⓓ	222 Ⓐ Ⓑ Ⓒ Ⓓ	235 Ⓐ Ⓑ Ⓒ Ⓓ
184 Ⓐ Ⓑ Ⓒ Ⓓ	197 Ⓐ Ⓑ Ⓒ Ⓓ	210 Ⓐ Ⓑ Ⓒ Ⓓ	223 Ⓐ Ⓑ Ⓒ Ⓓ	236 Ⓐ Ⓑ Ⓒ Ⓓ
185 Ⓐ Ⓑ Ⓒ Ⓓ	198 Ⓐ Ⓑ Ⓒ Ⓓ	211 Ⓐ Ⓑ Ⓒ Ⓓ	224 Ⓐ Ⓑ Ⓒ Ⓓ	237 Ⓐ Ⓑ Ⓒ Ⓓ
186 Ⓐ Ⓑ Ⓒ Ⓓ	199 Ⓐ Ⓑ Ⓒ Ⓓ	212 Ⓐ Ⓑ Ⓒ Ⓓ	225 Ⓐ Ⓑ Ⓒ Ⓓ	238 Ⓐ Ⓑ Ⓒ Ⓓ
187 Ⓐ Ⓑ Ⓒ Ⓓ	200 Ⓐ Ⓑ Ⓒ Ⓓ	213 Ⓐ Ⓑ Ⓒ Ⓓ	226 Ⓐ Ⓑ Ⓒ Ⓓ	

Section 5: Language Skills

239 Ⓐ Ⓑ Ⓒ Ⓓ	251 Ⓐ Ⓑ Ⓒ Ⓓ	263 Ⓐ Ⓑ Ⓒ Ⓓ	275 Ⓐ Ⓑ Ⓒ Ⓓ	287 Ⓐ Ⓑ Ⓒ Ⓓ
240 Ⓐ Ⓑ Ⓒ Ⓓ	252 Ⓐ Ⓑ Ⓒ Ⓓ	264 Ⓐ Ⓑ Ⓒ Ⓓ	276 Ⓐ Ⓑ Ⓒ Ⓓ	288 Ⓐ Ⓑ Ⓒ Ⓓ
241 Ⓐ Ⓑ Ⓒ Ⓓ	253 Ⓐ Ⓑ Ⓒ Ⓓ	265 Ⓐ Ⓑ Ⓒ Ⓓ	277 Ⓐ Ⓑ Ⓒ Ⓓ	289 Ⓐ Ⓑ Ⓒ Ⓓ
242 Ⓐ Ⓑ Ⓒ Ⓓ	254 Ⓐ Ⓑ Ⓒ Ⓓ	266 Ⓐ Ⓑ Ⓒ Ⓓ	278 Ⓐ Ⓑ Ⓒ Ⓓ	290 Ⓐ Ⓑ Ⓒ Ⓓ
243 Ⓐ Ⓑ Ⓒ Ⓓ	255 Ⓐ Ⓑ Ⓒ Ⓓ	267 Ⓐ Ⓑ Ⓒ Ⓓ	279 Ⓐ Ⓑ Ⓒ Ⓓ	291 Ⓐ Ⓑ Ⓒ Ⓓ
244 Ⓐ Ⓑ Ⓒ Ⓓ	256 Ⓐ Ⓑ Ⓒ Ⓓ	268 Ⓐ Ⓑ Ⓒ Ⓓ	280 Ⓐ Ⓑ Ⓒ Ⓓ	292 Ⓐ Ⓑ Ⓒ Ⓓ
245 Ⓐ Ⓑ Ⓒ Ⓓ	257 Ⓐ Ⓑ Ⓒ Ⓓ	269 Ⓐ Ⓑ Ⓒ Ⓓ	281 Ⓐ Ⓑ Ⓒ Ⓓ	293 Ⓐ Ⓑ Ⓒ Ⓓ
246 Ⓐ Ⓑ Ⓒ Ⓓ	258 Ⓐ Ⓑ Ⓒ Ⓓ	270 Ⓐ Ⓑ Ⓒ Ⓓ	282 Ⓐ Ⓑ Ⓒ Ⓓ	294 Ⓐ Ⓑ Ⓒ Ⓓ
247 Ⓐ Ⓑ Ⓒ Ⓓ	259 Ⓐ Ⓑ Ⓒ Ⓓ	271 Ⓐ Ⓑ Ⓒ Ⓓ	283 Ⓐ Ⓑ Ⓒ Ⓓ	295 Ⓐ Ⓑ Ⓒ Ⓓ
248 Ⓐ Ⓑ Ⓒ Ⓓ	260 Ⓐ Ⓑ Ⓒ Ⓓ	272 Ⓐ Ⓑ Ⓒ Ⓓ	284 Ⓐ Ⓑ Ⓒ Ⓓ	296 Ⓐ Ⓑ Ⓒ Ⓓ
249 Ⓐ Ⓑ Ⓒ Ⓓ	261 Ⓐ Ⓑ Ⓒ Ⓓ	273 Ⓐ Ⓑ Ⓒ Ⓓ	285 Ⓐ Ⓑ Ⓒ Ⓓ	297 Ⓐ Ⓑ Ⓒ Ⓓ
250 Ⓐ Ⓑ Ⓒ Ⓓ	262 Ⓐ Ⓑ Ⓒ Ⓓ	274 Ⓐ Ⓑ Ⓒ Ⓓ	286 Ⓐ Ⓑ Ⓒ Ⓓ	298 Ⓐ Ⓑ Ⓒ Ⓓ

The Tutorverse
www.thetutorverse.com

Verbal Skills

Questions 1-60, 16 Minutes

1. Complex most nearly means
   - (A) comfortable
   - (B) complicated
   - (C) crowded
   - (D) easy

2. Which word does *not* belong with the others?
   - (A) classical
   - (B) jazz
   - (C) music
   - (D) pop

3. Tedious means the opposite of
   - (A) challenging
   - (B) expedited
   - (C) tiresome
   - (D) weary

4. Most amusement parks have roller coasters. Roller coasters are too scary for young children to ride. Amusement parks are too scary for young children. If the first two statements are true, then the third is
   - (A) True
   - (B) False
   - (C) Uncertain

5. Strawberry is to jam as tomato is to
   - (A) blackberry
   - (B) jar
   - (C) ketchup
   - (D) vegetable

6. Which word does *not* belong with the others?
   - (A) duke
   - (B) prince
   - (C) queen
   - (D) royalty

7. Agitate most nearly means
   - (A) appreciate
   - (B) assist
   - (C) bother
   - (D) hate

8. Dispute means the opposite of
   - (A) affirm
   - (B) disagree
   - (C) disprove
   - (D) forget

9. Skiing is an expensive sport. Skiing is fun. All expensive sports are fun. If the first two statements are true, then the third is
   - (A) True
   - (B) False
   - (C) Uncertain

10. Town is to city as creek is to
    - (A) pond
    - (B) river
    - (C) village
    - (D) woods

11. Irrelevant most nearly means
    - (A) detailed
    - (B) related
    - (C) unimportant
    - (D) useful

12. Which word does *not* belong with the others?
    - (A) cuff
    - (B) collar
    - (C) suit
    - (D) tie

13. Infinite most nearly means
    - (A) incredible
    - (B) limitless
    - (C) magical
    - (D) unbelievable

14. Dog is to puppy as cat is to
    (A) feline
    (B) kitten
    (C) mouse
    (D) pet

15. Which word does *not* belong with the others?
    (A) contain
    (B) grip
    (C) hold
    (D) yield

16. Quarrel most nearly means
    (A) confuse
    (B) fight
    (C) please
    (D) split

17. Complicate means the opposite of
    (A) berate
    (B) simplify
    (C) tread
    (D) uncover

18. Some writers are clever people. All clever people are good at making jokes. Writers are good at making jokes. If the first two statements are true, then the third is
    (A) True
    (B) False
    (C) Uncertain

19. Which word does *not* belong with the others?
    (A) bowl
    (B) cup
    (C) plate
    (D) table

20. Patient most nearly means
    (A) kind
    (B) medical
    (C) passive
    (D) sick

21. Library is to books as aquarium is to
    (A) fish
    (B) kids
    (C) learning
    (D) science

22. Complex means the opposite of
    (A) concrete
    (B) intelligent
    (C) invisible
    (D) simple

23. The gray mouse's tail is longer than the white mouse's tail. The brown mouse's tail is longer than the white mouse's tail. The brown mouse's tail is longer than the gray mouse's tail. If the first two statements are true, then the third is
    (A) True
    (B) False
    (C) Uncertain

24. Correct is to error as cure is to
    (A) doctor
    (B) fix
    (C) illness
    (D) pill

25. Prevention most nearly means
    (A) assistance
    (B) deterrence
    (C) imagination
    (D) promotion

26. Which word does *not* belong with the others?
    (A) average
    (B) original
    (C) special
    (D) unique

27. Frigid means the opposite of
    (A) friendly
    (B) icy
    (C) tundra
    (D) warm

28. Red is Caroline's favorite color. Ruby is a gem that is the color red. Caroline loves rubies. If the first two statements are true, then the third is
    (A) True
    (B) False
    (C) Uncertain

29. Extinguish is to ignite as disgrace is to
    (A) disrespect
    (B) fire
    (C) honor
    (D) reputation

30. Which word does *not* belong with the others?
    (A) magician
    (B) spell
    (C) witch
    (D) wizard

31. Scowl most nearly means
    (A) frown
    (B) hunt
    (C) learn
    (D) smile

32. Conquer means the opposite of
    (A) achieve
    (B) dominate
    (C) liberate
    (D) seal

33. Orderly most nearly means
    (A) bossy
    (B) decorative
    (C) intelligent
    (D) tidy

34. Which word does *not* belong with the others?
    (A) flowers
    (B) leaves
    (C) plants
    (D) roots

35. Some lawyers are good at arguing. Some lawyers make large salaries. People who are good at arguing make large salaries. If the first two statements are true, then the third is
    (A) True
    (B) False
    (C) Uncertain

36. Inform is to explain as idle is to
    (A) learn
    (B) question
    (C) wait
    (D) worship

37. Durable most nearly means
    (A) capable
    (B) impossible
    (C) lasting
    (D) likely

38. Which word does *not* belong with the others?
    (A) hail
    (B) rain
    (C) snow
    (D) weather

39. Katherine is smarter than Elena. Bonnie is smarter than Katherine. Elena is smarter than Bonnie. If the first two statements are true, then the third is
    (A) True
    (B) False
    (C) Uncertain

40. Murmur is to shout as stumble is to
    (A) collapse
    (B) rise
    (C) run
    (D) speak

41. Rehearsed means the opposite of
    (A) performed
    (B) practiced
    (C) redone
    (D) spontaneous

42. Some people believe black cats are bad luck. Some people have black cats as pets. Some people believe having pets is bad luck. If the first two statements are true, then the third is
    (A) True
    (B) False
    (C) Uncertain

43. Which word does *not* belong with the others?
    (A) dream
    (B) fantasy
    (C) strategy
    (D) vision

44. Reduce most nearly means
    (A) grow
    (B) increase
    (C) repeat
    (D) shrink

45. Jog is to sprint as disagree is to
    (A) agree
    (B) cooperate
    (C) discuss
    (D) fight

46. Which word does *not* belong with the others?
    (A) ballet
    (B) dance
    (C) hip hop
    (D) salsa

47. Spectacle most nearly means
    (A) abandonment
    (B) disguise
    (C) extravaganza
    (D) punishment

48. Bequeath means the opposite of
    (A) benefit
    (B) leave
    (C) pass
    (D) steal

49. Which word does *not* belong with the others?
    (A) kitchen
    (B) house
    (C) bathroom
    (D) living room

50. Allege most nearly means
    (A) declare
    (B) deny
    (C) erode
    (D) tumble

51. Brenda doesn't eat meat. Paella contains meat. Brenda doesn't eat paella. If the first two statements are true, then the third is
    (A) True
    (B) False
    (C) Uncertain

52. Which word does *not* belong with the others?
    (A) dinner
    (B) hamburger
    (C) salad
    (D) steak

53. Achievement most nearly means
    (A) creation
    (B) defeat
    (C) movement
    (D) triumph

54. Instantaneous is to immediate as distraught is to
    (A) reassured
    (B) trouble
    (C) unconcerned
    (D) upset

55. Create means the opposite of
    (A) art
    (B) build
    (C) destroy
    (D) hate

56. Penguins are birds. Penguins cannot fly. Some birds cannot fly. If the first two statements are true, then the third is
    (A) True
    (B) False
    (C) Uncertain

57. Which word does *not* belong with the others?
    (A) build
    (B) draw
    (C) paint
    (D) sketch

58. Bewilder most nearly means
    (A) confound
    (B) curse
    (C) discover
    (D) explore

59. Which word does *not* belong with the others?
    (A) competition
    (B) running
    (C) skiing
    (D) swimming

60. Which word does *not* belong with the others?
    (A) engine
    (B) headlights
    (C) vehicle
    (D) windshield

Quantitative Skills

Questions 61-112, 30 Minutes

61. Examine the following and find the best answer:

    I. $2 \times -(4+7)$
    II. $(2 \times -4) + 7$
    III. $(2 \times -7) + 4$

    (A) I is greater than II, which is greater than III
    (B) I, II, and III are equal
    (C) I is smaller than II, which is smaller than III
    (D) II is greater than III, which is greater than I

62. Examine I, II, and III and find the *best* answer:

    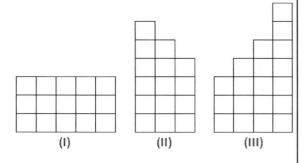

    (A) I = II > III
    (B) I = II = III
    (C) I < II < III
    (D) I = II < III

63. Which number should fill the blank in the following sequence: $-1000, 1000, \_\_\_, 1000, -1000$?
    (A) -999
    (B) -1000
    (C) 1000
    (D) -1002

64. Examine I, II, and III and find the *best* answer if $x = -1$.

    I. x^2
    II. $x(4-2)$
    III. $x - 1$

    (A) I is equal to III
    (B) II is equal to III
    (C) II is greater than I and III
    (D) I, II, and III are equal to each other

65. In the sequence $-0.3, 0.9, -2.7, 8.1...$, which should come next?
    (A) -24.3
    (B) -10.8
    (C) 10.8
    (D) 24.3

66. What number subtracted from 60 leaves you the median of 10, 6, 28, 15, and 17?
    (A) 16
    (B) 26
    (C) 32
    (D) 45

67. What number is 8 less than the average of 10, 20, 30, and 40?
    (A) 2
    (B) 17
    (C) 33
    (D) 92

68. Examine the angles *A*, *B*, and *C* and find the *best* answer.

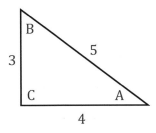

(A) ∠A + ∠C = ∠B
(B) ∠C < ∠B < ∠A
(C) ∠A < ∠C < ∠B
(D) ∠C > ∠B > ∠A

69. Examine the following and find the best answer:

   I. 2 + (7 × 3)
   II. (2 + 7) × 3
   III. 3 × (2 + 7)

(A) I is greater than II, which is greater than III
(B) I, II, and III are equal
(C) I is smaller than III and II, which are equal
(D) I is greater than III and II, which are equal

70. Examine the following and find the best answer.

   I. The area of a rectangle with a length of 8 and a width of 5
   II. The perimeter of a square with a length of 9
   III. The perimeter of an equilateral triangle with a side of 12

(A) I > II > III
(B) I > III > II
(C) I < II = III
(D) III = II < I

71. Examine the following and find the best answer.

   I. The area of the rectangle
   II. The area of the triangle
   III. The area of the square

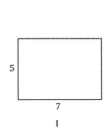 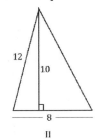 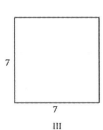

I   II   III

(A) I is less than II, and II is less than III
(B) II is greater than III, and III is greater than I
(C) I is greater than III, and III is greater than II
(D) I, II, and III are all equal

72. Which number should fill the blank in the following sequence: 11, ___, 1100, 11000?
(A) 110
(B) 121
(C) 1000
(D) 1010

73. Examine the following and find the best answer:

   I. −5 × (4 + 3)
   II. (−5 × 4) + 3
   III. (−5 × 3) + 4

(A) I is greater than II, which is greater than III
(B) I, II, and III are equal
(C) I is smaller than II, which is smaller than III
(D) I is greater than III, which is greater than II

74. Examine the bar graph and find the *best* answer.

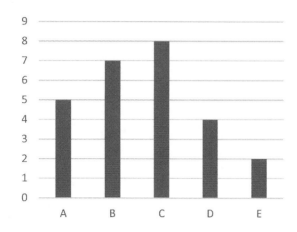

(A) B is greater than C
(B) The sum of D and E is less than B
(C) D is less than E
(D) The sum of A and B is equal to the sum of C and E

75. What number is 7 more than the product of 25% of 40 and $\frac{1}{2}$ of 14?

(A) 27
(B) 60
(C) 70
(D) 77

76. What number is $\frac{2}{3}$ of the median of 10, 30, and 100?

(A) 8
(B) 14
(C) 20
(D) 80

77. Examine I, II, and III and find the *best* answer if $x = 1$.

 I. x^5
 II. $5x$
 III. $5 + x$

(A) I, II, and III are all equal
(B) I and II are equal, and both are less than III
(C) II and III are equal, and both are less than I
(D) I is less than II, and II is less than III

78. Examine I, II, and III and find the *best* answer:

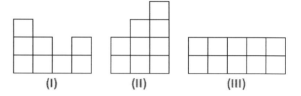

(A) I is greater than II which is equal to III
(B) I is equal to II and greater than III
(C) I is less than II which is less than III
(D) III is greater than II which is equal to I

79. Examine I, II, and III and find the *best* answer if $x = 3$.

 I. $2x$
 II. x^2
 III. 2^x

(A) I is less than II, and II is less than III
(B) I is less than III, and III is less than II
(C) I, II, and III are all equal
(D) II and III are equal, and II is greater than I

80. Examine the following and find the best answer.

   I. The perimeter of a regular pentagon with a length of 6
   II. The perimeter of a regular hexagon with a length of 5
   III. The perimeter of a regular octagon with a length of 4

   (A) I > II > III
   (B) I < II < III
   (C) III > I = II
   (D) I = II > III

81. Examine I, II, and III and find the best answer.

   I. 1 dime
   II. 1 nickel
   III. 1 penny

   (A) I < II < III
   (B) II + III < I
   (C) I + III < II
   (D) II + II > III

82. In the sequence 3, 0, −7, −10..., what comes next?
   (A) −17
   (B) −13
   (C) −7
   (D) −3

83. Examine I, II, and III and find the best answer if $x = 4$.

   I. $\frac{12}{x}$
   II. $3x$
   III. $5 - x + 3$

   (A) III is greater than I
   (B) II is greater than I, and I is greater than III
   (C) III is greater than I and II
   (D) I and III are equal

84. In the sequence 22, 19, 16, 12, 10..., one number is *wrong*. That number should be:
   (A) 9
   (B) 13
   (C) 17
   (D) 18

85. Examine I, II, and III and find the best answer.

   I. the slope of the line shown
   II. the slope of $y = 2x - 3$
   III. the slope of $-3x + y = 2$

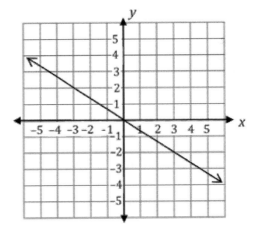

   (A) I > II > III
   (B) II > I > III
   (C) I < II = III
   (D) I < II < III

86. Examine I, II, and III, and find the *best* answer.

   I. 200% of 4
   II. $\frac{1}{3}$ of 24
   III. 50% of 18

   (A) I = II < III
   (B) I < II < III
   (C) I < II = III
   (D) III < I = II

87. The following circle graph shows the value of four variables. Find the *best* answer.

   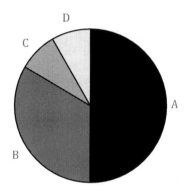

   ■ A ■ B ■ C □ D

   (A) $C + D = B$
   (B) $A + C = B$
   (C) $B + C + D = A$
   (D) $B + D = A$

88. Examine I, II, and III, and find the *best* answer.

   I. $\frac{3}{4}$ of 36
   II. 300% of 9
   III. 10% of 270

   (A) II < I < III
   (B) I = II < III
   (C) I = II = III
   (D) I = II > III

89. What is 10 less than the difference of 100 and 65?

   (A) 15
   (B) 20
   (C) 25
   (D) 45

90. What number divided by 8 is $\frac{2}{3}$ of 12?

   (A) 1
   (B) 8
   (C) 16
   (D) 64

91. Examine angles *A*, *B*, *C*, and *D* and find the *best* answer.

   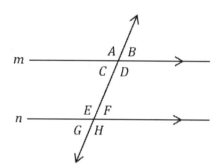

   (A) $\angle C = \angle B$
   (B) $\angle A = \angle B$
   (C) $\angle C = \angle D$
   (D) $\angle B = \angle D$

92. What number multiplied by 5 is equal to the median of 25, 40, 50, 60, and 15?

   (A) 5
   (B) 8
   (C) 38
   (D) 200

93. Examine I, II, and III and find the *best* answer.

   I. 10 inches
   II. 5 feet
   III. 2 yards

   (A) The sum of I and II is less than III
   (B) The sum of II and III is less than I
   (C) II and III are equal
   (D) I is greater than II

94. Examine I, II, and III and find the *best* answer:

   I.

   II.

   III.

   (A) I = III < II
   (B) II = III > I
   (C) II = III < I
   (D) I = II > III

95. Which number should fill the blank in the following sequence: 1, ___, 49, −343, 2401?
   (A) −6
   (B) −7
   (C) 7
   (D) 14

96. What number added to the difference of 14 and 9 is equal to the sum of 12, 20, and 19?
   (A) 27
   (B) 28
   (C) 45
   (D) 46

97. Examine I, II, and III and find the *best* answer.

   I. 5,000 feet
   II. 6,000 feet
   III. 1 mile

   (A) I is less than II, and II is less than III
   (B) III is greater than II
   (C) I is less than III, and III is less than II
   (D) I and III are equal

98. What number added to 6 is equal to the average of 8, 5, 10, and 13?
   (A) 3
   (B) 4
   (C) 14
   (D) 15

99. Examine I, II, and III and find the best answer.

   I. the slope of $4x + y = 12$
   II. the slope of the line shown
   III. the slope of $y = 4x - 8$

   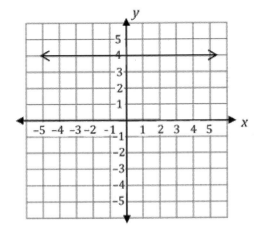

   (A) I < II = III
   (B) II < I = III
   (C) III > II > I
   (D) I = II = III

100. Examine I, II, and III, and find the *best* answer.

   I. 5.1414
   II. 5.141
   III. 5.14041

   (A) II < I < III
   (B) I < II < III
   (C) II > III > I
   (D) I > II > III

101. Examine I, II, and III, and find the *best* answer.

   I.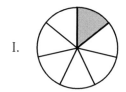

   II.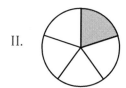

   III.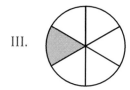

   (A) The three circles are equally shaded
   (B) I is more shaded than II, and II is more shade than III
   (C) II is the most shaded, and I is more shaded than III
   (D) I is less shaded than III, and III is less shaded than II

102. In the sequence 0, 11, 22, 33, 66..., what number should come next?
   (A) 77
   (B) 88
   (C) 99
   (D) 132

103. In the sequence $-7, -3, 2, 6...$, what number comes next?
   (A) -2
   (B) 10
   (C) 11
   (D) 12

104. Examine the angles in rectangle ABCD and find the *best* answer.

   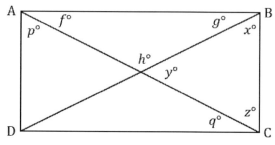

   (A) $g = x$
   (B) $h + y = f + g + h$
   (C) $y = q + z$
   (D) $f = h$

105. In the sequence $4, 3\frac{1}{2}, 3, 2\frac{1}{2}...$, what number should come next?
   (A) $1\frac{1}{2}$
   (B) 2
   (C) $2\frac{1}{2}$
   (D) $3\frac{1}{2}$

106. Examine I, II, and III and find the *best* answer.

   I. 40 minutes
   II. 1 hour
   III. 15 minutes

   (A) I = II
   (B) II > I + III
   (C) I + III > II
   (D) II - III < I

107. In the sequence $\frac{1}{2}, \frac{3}{4}, 1, 1\frac{1}{4}$..., what number should come next?
    (A) $1\frac{1}{2}$
    (B) $1\frac{3}{4}$
    (C) 2
    (D) $2\frac{1}{4}$

108. In the sequence 15, 19, 22, 27, 31..., one number is *wrong*. That number should be:
    (A) 23
    (B) 25
    (C) 26
    (D) 32

109. What number subtracted from 28 leaves you with the average of 26, 20, and 14?
    (A) 4
    (B) 8
    (C) 16
    (D) 48

110. Examine I, II, and III and find the best answer.
    I. the slope of $y = -2x - 10$
    II. the slope of $6x + 3y = 1$
    III. the slope of the line shown

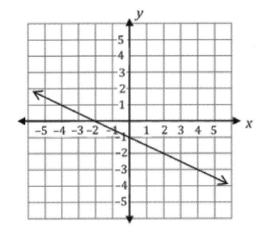

    (A) I > II
    (B) II > III
    (C) I < III
    (D) I = III

111. What number should fill in the blank in this series: −1, 3, 6, ___, −36?
    (A) −18
    (B) −12
    (C) 12
    (D) 18

112. Examine the line graph and find the *best* answer.

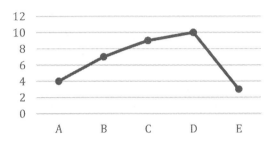

    (A) A and E are equal
    (B) B is greater than C
    (C) A plus B is greater than D
    (D) D plus E is less than A plus B

Reading

Questions 113-174, 25 Minutes

Tulips bloom only briefly; when they do, they are beloved the world over for their bright colors and soft petals. As familiar as the flower might be to modern Americans, tulips actually originated in Central Asia, first cultivated in Persia in the 10th century. The real boom in tulip popularity, however, began in Holland in the 16th century, when the <u>exotic</u> reputation of tulips drove wealthy traders and nobles alike to acquire the vibrant flower as a symbol of beauty and status. This intense interest in tulips came to be known as Tulip Mania.

At that time, along with growing interest in unusual foreign goods, Dutch society became fascinated with the natural world, with many members of the upper class studying nature and different cultures. Botanist Carolus Clusius introduced the public to tulips when he added the flower to his large botanical garden at the University of Leiden. Soon, tulips became famous throughout the country. Around this time, people also learned of how the Sultan of the Ottoman Empire prized the tulips in his garden. Soon, the national interest in tulips turned into a feverish quest by many to have their own tulip garden, just like the Sultan.

Unfortunately, though beautiful, tulips were not necessarily ideal plants for growing. They often suffered from diseases or flowered for only one week; on top of this, they had to be shipped from Turkey or Russia, making tulips very expensive and difficult to come by. Even though most everyone in Holland knew about tulips, they were still a luxury item; one that required time, patience, and wealth in order to grow for oneself. But for wealthy businesspeople who wanted to <u>flaunt</u> their financial success and social status, tulips were perfect.

Botanists soon discovered that planting the tulips' bulbs in the ground instead of the seeds could speed up the time between planting and flowering, making tulips slightly faster to produce. Though quicker to grow, the bulbs had to be created in labs and were expensive. They weren't even guaranteed to grow. But that did not stop the demand for these flowers, and prices for tulips continued to rise. Soon, people realized that a lot of money could be made buying and selling tulips; at this point, things got out of control. Many people spent enormous sums to purchase tulips to resell, only to find that, when the prices got too high, they were not able to make back the money they already spent. As a result, many individuals went bankrupt. Tulip Mania serves as a healthy reminder that greed for even the loveliest of things can be taken too far, and can have a negative effect on people's lives.

113. This passage is mostly about
(A) Dutch society in the 1500s.
(B) the intense popularity of tulips in Holland in the 16th century.
(C) the origins of the tulip.
(D) the effect that foreign goods can have on a country's economy.

114. All of the following contributed to the popularity of tulips EXCEPT their
(A) exotic origins.
(B) beauty.
(C) prized status to the Ottoman Sultan.
(D) susceptibility to disease.

115. Carolus Clusius and the Ottoman Sultan are both mentioned in paragraph two in order to
    (A) illustrate the Dutch public's interest in nature and exotic cultures.
    (B) present arguments for and against the popularity of tulips.
    (C) contrast the ways in which Dutch and Ottoman cultures differed.
    (D) provide examples of two wealthy men who became experts in trending topics.

116. It can be inferred from the passage that botanists were
    (A) a new type of scientist in the 1500s.
    (B) interested in finding ways for tulips to help cure diseases.
    (C) interested in making tulips easier to produce.
    (D) not respected by the Dutch public.

117. The word "exotic", as it is used in the passage, most nearly means
    (A) artificial.
    (B) stolen.
    (C) threatening.
    (D) unusual.

118. It can be inferred from the passage that, compared to the rest of society Dutch businessmen had all of the following EXCEPT
    (A) greater resources.
    (B) more leisure time.
    (C) a need to prove to others their economic prosperity.
    (D) advanced degrees in horticulture.

119. The word "flaunt", as it is used in the passage, most nearly means
    (A) describe.
    (B) display.
    (C) hide.
    (D) increase.

120. Based on the passage, it can be inferred that many tulip buyers
    (A) were able to find bulbs at a reasonable cost.
    (B) went to Persia themselves to buy the bulbs.
    (C) were more interested in selling tulips than planting their own gardens.
    (D) wanted to help the botanists learn more about this unusual plant.

121. According to the passage, which of the following is true?
    (A) Tulips are rarely found in the United States.
    (B) Tulips were primarily cultivated in ancient Greece.
    (C) Even people who had allergies to flowers spent great sums of money to purchase tulip bulbs.
    (D) The showcase at the university botanical garden helped thrust tulips into the spotlight

122. What would be the most appropriate title for the passage?
    (A) The Magical Spell of the Tulip
    (B) A Dutch Cultural History
    (C) The Sultan's Most Prized Possession
    (D) How to Grow a Stunning Tulip Garden

The idea of going up a tower that tilts to one side sounds a little terrifying. Shockingly, tourists from around the world have done just that for centuries. The Leaning Tower of Pisa is a very famous bell tower in Pisa, Italy, known for its characteristic four-degree tilt. After hundreds of years, the Leaning Tower still stands strong, not yet pulled down by gravity and time.

The Leaning Tower of Pisa has attracted visitors since construction began on the tower in 1173. With all the political and cultural changes occurring in Italy at the time, it took workers around two hundred years to finish building the tower! Though some might believe the tower was designed to lean, that is not the case. The tower's unique angle is a total accident, a result of an error in construction. The foundation, which sits at the very bottom of the tower, was laid too thin, making it too weak to adequately support the mammoth tower. By the time the construction of the second floor began, the tower had shifted and began to lean. Now, the tower is approximately 183 feet tall on the lowest side and 186 feet tall on the highest. The tower is so tall, it takes 294 steps to climb to the top! The Leaning Tower of Pisa is not just a fascinating tourist attraction, but also a functioning bell tower with seven bells—one for each note of the musical scale.

Over the years, many attempts have been made to straighten the Leaning Tower of Pisa and prevent it from leaning further down or collapsing. In the mid-1960s, construction began on the tower that lasted over twenty years. Then, in 1990, the bells were temporarily removed to relieve the weight at the top of the tower. Lots more work was done, including placing lead counterweights at the base of the tower, and after another several years of closure and construction, the tower reopened in 2001. Following this period of construction, engineers predicted that, despite its faulty foundation, the tower would remain stable for at least another three hundred years. Although the tower has been stabilized, it still has its characteristic famous lean, and likely will for many years to come.

123. What would be the most appropriate title for this passage?
    (A) Famous Bell Towers
    (B) The Tower of London
    (C) A Little to the Left: All about Pisa's Famous Tower
    (D) Travel Destinations in Italy

124. This passage is mostly about
    (A) the architect who designed the Leaning Tower of Pisa.
    (B) how to navigate the city of Pisa to find the tower.
    (C) the history and construction of the Leaning Tower of Pisa.
    (D) statistics on how many tourists visit the Leaning Tower of Pisa each year.

125. According to the facts in the passage the Leaning Tower of Pisa
    (A) has one large bell.
    (B) seven bells.
    (C) has four bells.
    (D) does not have any bells.

126. According to the passage, which of the following is true?
    (A) Construction on the tower was completed in 1173.
    (B) The tower will collapse by the end of the century.
    (C) It took about two hundred years to build the tower.
    (D) The Leaning Tower of Pisa was designed to lean.

127. The Leaning Tower of Pisa is named
    (A) for its location in Pisa, Italy.
    (B) after Stefan Pisa, who designed the tower.
    (C) after the Italian word, "pisa," which means tower.
    (D) Pisa, but is actually located in Florence, Italy.

128. The author would most likely agree with which of the following statements?
    (A) The Leaning Tower of Pisa is unsafe and should be torn down.
    (B) The Leaning Tower of Pisa is worth the maintenance the tower has taken over the years.
    (C) It's proven impossible to stabilize the Leaning Tower of Pisa.
    (D) It is common for old towers to lean.

129. You would probably find this passage in
    (A) a diary.
    (B) a hospital brochure.
    (C) a history book.
    (D) a sports magazine.

130. Which of the following can be inferred from the passage?
    (A) The Leaning Tower of Pisa attracts only European tourists.
    (B) The effort that went into maintaining the Leaning Tower of Pisa was wasted.
    (C) Tourists have lost interest in the Leaning Tower of Pisa in recent years.
    (D) Despite problems with the foundation, the Leaning Tower of Pisa itself is well-constructed.

131. As it is used in the passage, the word "mammoth" most nearly means
    (A) elephant.
    (B) extinct.
    (C) gigantic.
    (D) impressive.

132. As it is used in the passage, the word "relieve" most nearly means
    (A) comfort.
    (B) lessen.
    (C) relax.
    (D) unwind.

Claire woke up with a pit in her stomach. The excitement that she had felt in the last few weeks for her upcoming 12-mile hike of the Appalachian Trail had disappeared. Now she was left with a sense of <u>dread</u> and doubt. *What have I gotten myself into?* A whole week in the woods with people she didn't know, carrying a heavy backpack loaded full of basic meals and gear—*How did I ever think this would be fun?*

"Don't think about it. It's too late to back out now," she mumbled as she dressed.

Claire held back her tears when her mom dropped her off at the departure point with the other hikers. She groaned at the weight of her pack as she slipped it over her shoulders. As their guide talked about their route and shared basic survival tips, Claire eyed the other kids. Some seemed to already be friends; others seemed experienced; most seemed excited about the upcoming journey. All Claire could think of was the long week she had ahead of her.

Claire's fears were soon <u>reinforced</u>. Despite being in pretty good shape from competitive swimming, Claire quickly began to lose her breath, hiking through the winding uphill trail and carrying 20 pounds of gear. The first mile seemed like five, and by the end of the second, she felt like she'd climbed Mt. Everest. She was dying to rest, but didn't want to look like a wimp in front of the others. As she trudged up a steep, rocky slope, feeling the weight of her pack digging into her shoulders, Claire lost her footing and stumbled—she would've fallen down the hill if the girl behind her hadn't grabbed her arm.

"You okay?" the girl asked, as Claire regained her balance.

"Yeah. Thanks," Claire replied. She tried to sound casual.

"I'm Anne, by the way," the girl said. She extended her hand and smiled. "I was miserable when I started my first hike. Trust me: it gets better."

Claire gratefully shook Anne's hand and smiled back.

Claire and Anne talked the rest of the day as they hiked, and before long, they were fast friends. They learned they had lots in common, like their love of sushi and snowboarding. Anne shared some of her experiences from her first hiking trip, which included a terrifying but harmless encounter with a baby bear. Compared to that trip, Claire's first hike was a breeze. The conversation and laughter made the trail seem easier. When nightfall hit, Claire and Anne snuggled under a blanket to keep warm and fell asleep in front of the dying fire. *Maybe the hike will be as amazing as I hoped after-all.* Exhausted but at peace under the stars, Claire slept better than she had in a long time.

133. This story is mostly about
    (A) the joys of the outdoors.
    (B) a girl finding comfort on her first hike.
    (C) the tiring experience of trail hikes.
    (D) how to make new friends.

134. The "pit" in Claire's stomach is most likely caused by
    (A) her heavy backpack.
    (B) the filling dinner she had the night before.
    (C) the excitement of trying something new.
    (D) her fear regarding her upcoming hike.

135. As it is used in the passage, the word "dread" most nearly means
    (A) nervous excitement.
    (B) casual indifference.
    (C) anxious anticipation.
    (D) intense skepticism.

136. Based on the details of the passage, compared to Claire, the other hikers seem
    (A) confident and excited.
    (B) bored and restless.
    (C) inexperienced and confused.
    (D) sullen and defensive.

137. As it is used in the passage, the word "reinforced" most nearly means
    (A) alleviated.
    (B) confirmed.
    (C) delayed.
    (D) questioned.

138. According to the story, Claire nearly falls because
    (A) she is carrying a heavy load.
    (B) she is extremely tired from the trek.
    (C) she stumbles on the slopes.
    (D) all of the above.

139. According to the story, sushi and snowboarding are
    (A) what Claire and Anne will miss most about being away from civilization.
    (B) enjoyed by both Claire and Anne.
    (C) the only things that Claire and Anne have in common.
    (D) two skills easier to master than hiking.

140. From the story, it can be inferred that
    (A) hiking is easier than it sounds.
    (B) one does not need to have friends in order to have a good time.
    (C) only experienced hikers should attempt a 12-mile hike.
    (D) going through a difficult situation is easier when done with a friend.

141. Based on the story, Claire would most accurately be characterized as
    (A) self-conscious yet determined.
    (B) lazy yet open-minded.
    (C) spoiled yet intelligent.
    (D) aloof yet ambitious.

142. What would be the most appropriate title for the story?
    (A) The Worst Week
    (B) A New Friend for the Trail
    (C) A Bear's Trail
    (D) Best Friends Forever

Blankets, carpets, bedsheets, and clothes: fabrics play a crucial role in all of our lives. Some are soft, others rough. Some are natural, others synthetic. The most famous of all of these fabrics might be silk, a natural fabric known for its <u>luxurious</u> softness and shine. Though silk has a reputation as being simply a stylish and expensive fabric, it actually has a number of different strengths and a unique and interesting history to its production that makes it well worth the cost.

The Chinese were the first to recognize the potential of silk and to experiment with turning the material into fabric. In order for a fabric to be considered natural, it has to come from a plant or animal. The fibers that make silk come from the cocoons woven by silkworms when they begin their transformations from caterpillars into moths. Silk manufacturers then unwind the caterpillars' cocoons and spin them into a thin thread, making silk. This thread is then woven together with others in order to create silk fabric.

In addition to its elegance, there are many reasons why silk is an excellent choice of material for clothing. Though its softness suggests it might be fragile, silk is actually the strongest natural fabric in the world. Some silk fabrics can hold up to 100 times their own weight before breaking! Silk is great at absorbing heat in cold weather and moisture in warm weather, making it the perfect material to wear no matter the season. Lastly, silk fabric is woven very tight, which makes it difficult for insects such as mosquitos to pierce through. Not many materials can provide that kind of protection!

Though silk farming began in China thousands of years ago, silk fabrics are now manufactured in over sixty countries around the world. Still, silk remains expensive to produce and purchase, due in part to the intense labor required to harvest and weave the material. However, the benefits may outweigh the costs; other fabrics cannot beat the softness and strength of silk, and although it's expensive, silk fabric lasts a long time. Silk has a number of characteristics that make it not only one of the most <u>versatile</u> fabrics in the world, but also one of the most valuable.

143. What would be the most appropriate title for this passage?
    (A) The Life of a Silkworm
    (B) Natural vs. Synthetic Fabrics
    (C) A Fabric Worth the Cost
    (D) Creating Your Own Clothing

144. This passage is mostly about
    (A) how to sew with silk.
    (B) the pros and cons of wearing silk.
    (C) the life cycle of a silkworm.
    (D) a unique type of fabric.

145. According to the facts of the passage, silk
    (A) is no longer produced in China.
    (B) was discovered in China in 1950.
    (C) was first produced in China thousands of years ago.
    (D) is only produced by silkworms that live in China.

146. Based on the details of the passage, silk is
    (A) a highly absorbent fabric.
    (B) one of the least expensive fabrics to purchase.
    (C) too slippery to wear as clothing because of its soft texture.
    (D) too fragile a fabric to wear regularly.

147. According to the facts of the passage,
    (A) silk moths produce the majority of the world's silk.
    (B) silk is harvested from the cocoons of transforming silkworms.
    (C) all insects possess the ability to produce silk.
    (D) all caterpillars produce silk when they go through metamorphosis.

148. The author would most likely agree with which of the following statements?
    (A) Silk is too expensive to consider purchasing.
    (B) Silk is a good choice for bedsheets but not clothing.
    (C) Silk has a number of unique characteristics that make it one of the best natural fabrics.
    (D) Silk is easy to manufacture.

149. It can be inferred from the passage that
    (A) selling silk can be a difficult but ultimately profitable endeavor.
    (B) silk is too difficult and expensive to produce, so it's not worth selling.
    (C) making cocoons is exhausting for silkworms.
    (D) silkworms only produce silk in warm weather.

150. It can be inferred from the passage that silk fabrics are
    (A) easy to produce.
    (B) a cheap and accessible material for clothing.
    (C) stronger than cotton fabrics
    (D) most often used to make curtains and draperies.

151. As it is used in the passage, the word "luxurious" most nearly means
    (A) average.
    (B) elegant.
    (C) rough.
    (D) vivid.

152. As it is used in the passage, the word "versatile" most nearly means
    (A) even.
    (B) glossy.
    (C) multipurpose.
    (D) soft.

Vocabulary

153. The <u>optimum</u> result
    (A) aberrant
    (B) dreary
    (C) ideal
    (D) normal

154. He <u>frequently</u> forgets his keys
    (A) audibly
    (B) rarely
    (C) regularly
    (D) never

155. The <u>downtrodden</u> prisoner
    (A) appropriate
    (B) chosen
    (C) oppressed
    (D) questionable

156. A <u>regrettable</u> mistake
    (A) acceptable
    (B) appreciated
    (C) forgettable
    (D) unfortunate

157. A <u>fortuitous</u> encounter
    (A) advantageous
    (B) luminous
    (C) ruinous
    (D) zealous

158. An <u>unpleasant</u> odor
    (A) appreciated
    (B) concocted
    (C) horrible
    (D) inevitable

159. They <u>compared</u> their notes
    (A) ailed
    (B) bested
    (C) contrasted
    (D) deranged

160. To <u>compete</u> in a race
    (A) battle
    (B) deal
    (C) fine
    (D) train

161. To <u>verify</u> information
    (A) authenticate
    (B) berate
    (C) lose
    (D) partake

162. Embarked on an <u>arduous</u> journey
    (A) artful
    (B) challenging
    (C) esteemed
    (D) unlikely

163. To <u>complicate</u> a situation
    (A) authenticate
    (B) behoove
    (C) muddle
    (D) operate

164. <u>Supply</u> someone with food
    (A) eject
    (B) humiliate
    (C) prove
    (D) provide

165. The most <u>dreaded</u> option
    (A) acknowledged
    (B) feared
    (C) stolen
    (D) violated

166. A <u>conflicted</u> state of mind
    (A) ambivalent
    (B) duplicated
    (C) rescued
    (D) verdant

167. The hero's <u>bold</u> actions
    (A) daring
    (B) cautious
    (C) foolish
    (D) weak

168. A <u>compliant</u> servant
    (A) celebratory
    (B) flexible
    (C) obedient
    (D) typical

169. The train was <u>delayed</u>
    (A) acidic
    (B) hovered
    (C) late
    (D) mystic

170. The <u>dastardly</u> coward
    (A) audacious
    (B) dauntless
    (C) determined
    (D) spineless

171. The villain's <u>diabolical</u> plan
    (A) fiendish
    (B) heroic
    (C) misled
    (D) shy

172. The politician's <u>heinous</u> crimes
    (A) admirable
    (B) atrocious
    (C) behavioral
    (D) candid

173. The judge's <u>rational</u> decision
    (A) bizarre
    (B) logical
    (C) lost
    (D) playful

174. The <u>meek</u> followers
    (A) camouflaged
    (B) compliant
    (C) outrageous
    (D) tiny

Mathematics

Questions 175-238, 45 Minutes

175. Cindy is handing out treats to her 5 cats. If she hands out all the treats, and each cat gets the same number of treats, how many treats did she have to begin with?
    (A) 18
    (B) 19
    (C) 20
    (D) 21

176. A cube has a side length of 8 cm. What is its surface area?
    (A) 64 cm^2
    (B) 192 cm^2
    (C) 384 cm^2
    (D) 512 cm^2

177. Which of the following is equal to $\frac{9 \times 10^{-5}}{3 \times 10^2}$?
    (A) 3×10^{-3}
    (B) 3×10^{-7}
    (C) 3×10^3
    (D) 3×10^7

178. What is the perimeter of a square with an area of 4?
    (A) 2
    (B) 4
    (C) 6
    (D) 8

179. Assuming that x is a prime number, what is the LCM of $3x^2$ and $9x^5$?
    (A) $9x^2$
    (B) $9x^5$
    (C) $18x^5$
    (D) $27x^5$

180. What is the diameter of a circle with a circumference of 15π mm?
    (A) 5 mm
    (B) 7.5 mm
    (C) 10 mm
    (D) 15 mm

181. What is the GCF of 14, 42, and 28?
    (A) 4
    (B) 7
    (C) 14
    (D) 16

182. Which of the following is most appropriate for measuring the area of Yellowstone National Park?
    (A) kilograms
    (B) square feet
    (C) square inches
    (D) square kilometers

183. A rectangle has an area of 60 square centimeters. If the width of the rectangle is 4 cm, what is the perimeter of the rectangle?
    (A) 15 cm
    (B) 30 cm
    (C) 38 cm
    (D) 45 cm

184. Express $\frac{7}{8}$ as a decimal.
    (A) 0.0875
    (B) 0.857
    (C) $0.85\overline{7}$
    (D) 0.875

185. If the area of a circle is 144π sq ft, what is its circumference?
    (A) 12π ft
    (B) 14π ft
    (C) 24π ft
    (D) 72π ft

The Tutorverse
www.thetutorverse.com

186. What is the value of the expression $(9 \times 10^5) - (6 \times 10^4)$?
   (A) 3×10^1
   (B) 3×10^5
   (C) 8.4×10^4
   (D) 8.4×10^5

187. Express 1.25 as a fraction.
   (A) $1\frac{1}{4}$
   (B) $1\frac{2}{5}$
   (C) $1\frac{5}{20}$
   (D) $1\frac{25}{100}$

188. Which of the following units is most appropriate for measuring the amount of water in the shark tank of an aquarium?
   (A) gallons
   (B) grams
   (C) milliliters
   (D) quarts

189. Three squares connect to make a larger rectangle as shown below. If the area of each square is 36 mm², what is the perimeter of the rectangle?

   (A) 24 mm
   (B) 36 mm
   (C) 48 mm
   (D) 60 mm

190. What is the GCF of $12a^2b^3$ and $4a^3b^2$?
   (A) $3ab$
   (B) $4ab$
   (C) $4a^2b^2$
   (D) $4a^3b^3$

191. Solve: $-4x + 20 \leq 4x - 4$.
   (A) $x \geq -3$
   (B) $x \geq 3$
   (C) $x \geq 4$
   (D) All Real Numbers

192. In the regular pentagon shown below, what is the measurement of an internal angle?

   (A) 60°
   (B) 100°
   (C) 108°
   (D) 120°

193. Solve: : $6y - 11 > 18y$.
   (A) $y < \frac{-11}{12}$
   (B) $y > \frac{11}{12}$
   (C) $y > \frac{-11}{12}$
   (D) $y < -1$

194. What type of triangle is shown?

   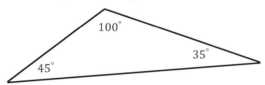

   (A) right
   (B) acute
   (C) obtuse
   (D) isosceles

195. If the equation of a line is $x = 8$, what is the slope of the line?
   (A) -8
   (B) 0
   (C) 8
   (D) The slope is undefined.

196. Which fraction is smallest?
   (A) $\frac{2}{3}$
   (B) $\frac{2}{4}$
   (C) $\frac{2}{5}$
   (D) $\frac{2}{6}$

197. Find the LCM of $4x$, $10xy^2$, and $5x^3yz^2$.
(A) $15x^2y^2z^2$
(B) $20x^2yz$
(C) $20x^3y^2z^2$
(D) $40x^3y^2z^3$

198. Which fraction is smallest?
(A) $\frac{1}{10}$
(B) $\frac{9}{100}$
(C) $\frac{98}{1,000}$
(D) $\frac{997}{10,000}$

199. What is the surface area of this object?

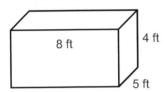

(A) 34 ft²
(B) 52 ft²
(C) 160 ft²
(D) 184 ft²

200. What is equivalent to a^3b^5?
(A) $(a^2b^2) \times (a^2b^4)$
(B) $(a^2b^3) \times (ab^2)$
(C) $(a^2b^5) \times (ab)$
(D) $(a^3b^3) \times (ab^2)$

201. What is equivalent to m^4n^6?
(A) $\frac{m^2n^4}{m^2n^2}$
(B) $\frac{m^5n^8}{mn^2}$
(C) $\frac{m^6n}{m^2n^5}$
(D) $\frac{m^6n^7}{mn}$

202. What is the slope of a line parallel to the line $y = -\frac{3}{4}x - 2$?
(A) -2
(B) $-\frac{4}{3}$
(C) $-\frac{3}{4}$
(D) $\frac{3}{4}$

Problem Solving

203. What is $7.451 - 2.183$ rounded to the nearest tenth?
(A) 5.2
(B) 5.268
(C) 5.27
(D) 5.3

204. An animal shelter has a total of 40 dogs and cats. The ratio of dogs to cats is 3:2. How many cats are there?
(A) 5
(B) 16
(C) 20
(D) 24

205. Roberto is working on his math homework. He can complete 18 math problems per hour. How long will it take him to complete 30 problems?
(A) $\frac{3}{5}$ hours
(B) $1\frac{3}{5}$ hours
(C) $1\frac{2}{3}$ hours
(D) 12 hours

206. What is $5 - 4.27$ rounded to the nearest tenth?
(A) 0.7
(B) 0.73
(C) 1.3
(D) 1.7

207. What is the value of $\sqrt{18} + \sqrt{8}$?
    (A) 3
    (B) $3\sqrt{2}$
    (C) $\sqrt{26}$
    (D) $5\sqrt{2}$

208. A stop sign, which has eight sides, is an example of what kind of polygon?
    (A) hexagon
    (B) kite
    (C) octagon
    (D) parallelogram

209. Solve: $132 + (-28) - (-12) =$
    (A) 92
    (B) 106
    (C) 116
    (D) 148

210. 0.15 kilometers equals
    (A) 15 meters
    (B) 150 meters
    (C) 1500 meters
    (D) 15000 meters

211. Solve: $\frac{11}{12} - \frac{3}{4} =$
    (A) $\frac{1}{6}$
    (B) $\frac{2}{12}$
    (C) $\frac{8}{48}$
    (D) $\frac{8}{8}$

212. Jordan, Chris, and Dominic are competing in a javelin throwing competition, and they each get three throws. The data is included in the chart below. What is the approximate range of all their javelin throws?

    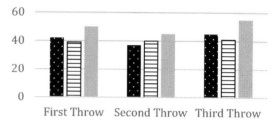

    (A) 10m
    (B) 13m
    (C) 18m
    (D) 55m

213. Which information is best displayed on a line chart?
    (A) driveway lengths
    (B) gas mileage over time
    (C) number of tests taken
    (D) difficulty of books read for school

214. Daisy purchased a new car for $3,000. After two years, her car was worth $1,200. By what percent did the value of Daisy's car decrease after two years?
    (A) 40%
    (B) 45%
    (C) 55%
    (D) 60%

215. Three students sell boxes of candies at the school fair. Each box of candy costs $3.25. The first student sold 3 boxes, the second sold 8 boxes, and the third sold 9 boxes. How much money did the three students earn in candy sales?
    (A) $9.75
    (B) $26.00
    (C) $55.25
    (D) $65.00

216. Percy must get to the airport, which is 30 miles away, in 45 minutes. How fast does he have to drive to make it on time?
    (A) 40 miles per hour
    (B) 45 miles per hour
    (C) 60 miles per hour
    (D) 65 miles per hour

217. Which of the following is NOT equivalent to $25\frac{1}{5}$%?
    (A) 0.252
    (B) $\frac{25.2}{100}$
    (C) $\frac{126}{500}$
    (D) 25.2

218. If the prime factorization of 24 is $2^x \times 3^y$, then what does $x + y$ equal?
    (A) 2
    (B) 3
    (C) 4
    (D) 5

219. Solve: $15 + (-3) + (-18) =$
    (A) -6
    (B) -5
    (C) 0
    (D) 36

220. How many meters is 4,320 centimeters?
    (A) .432 meters
    (B) 4.32 meters
    (C) 43.2 meters
    (D) 432 meters

221. Dana and Polly are biking together at a speed of 12 miles per hour. Polly's house is 3 miles further down the road than Dana's. How much longer will she bike for?
    (A) 10 minutes
    (B) 12 minutes
    (C) 15 minutes
    (D) 20 minutes

222. The numbers in the following Venn diagram indicate how many students can play a particular instrument or instruments. How many students can play both the flute and piano?

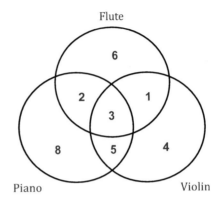

   (A) 2
   (B) 3
   (C) 5
   (D) 16

223. Solve for x: $4 - x = 5x - 8$
    (A) -1
    (B) 1
    (C) 2
    (D) 3

224. Which of the following is NOT equal to 550%?
    (A) $\frac{11}{2}$
    (B) 5.5
    (C) $\frac{165}{30}$
    (D) 550

225. Solve: $7 - 0.006 =$
    (A) 6.006
    (B) 6.94
    (C) 6.994
    (D) 7.994

226. The following graph shows the number of goals scored by the Wildcats. In how many games did the team score fewer than 5 goals?

NUMBER OF GOALS SCORED BY THE WILDCATS

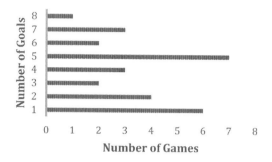

(A) 7 games
(B) 9 games
(C) 15 games
(D) 22 games

227. Which of the following is equivalent to $\sqrt{x^6}$?
(A) x^2
(B) x^3
(C) x^4
(D) x^5

228. A store sells three different types of pants: 20% are khakis, 60% are jeans, and the remaining 40 pairs of pants are slacks. How many jeans does the store have?
(A) 100
(B) 110
(C) 120
(D) 135

229. If the average of 8, 9, and x is equal to the average of 7 and x, what is the value of x?
(A) 9
(B) 10
(C) 11
(D) 13

230. A survey is taken of the 6th, 7th, and 8th grade students at a local middle school of whether they spend more time on the internet or watching television. The data is recorded in the table below. If a student is randomly selected from those who spend more time on the internet, what is the probability that the student is a 7th grader?

	Internet	Television	Total
6th grade	12	16	28
7th grade	15	15	30
8th grade	20	8	28
Total	37	39	86

(A) $\frac{15}{76}$
(B) $\frac{15}{75}$
(C) $\frac{15}{37}$
(D) $\frac{1}{2}$

231. In a classroom, the ratio of girls to boys is 5 to 3. If there are 15 girls in the class, how many boys are there?
(A) 6
(B) 9
(C) 12
(D) 25

232. What is the best description for this shape?

(A) isosceles right triangle
(B) parallelogram
(C) rhombus
(D) scalene right triangle

233. A group of 120 adults are surveyed about how they get their news. 40 said that they watch television news, 60 said that they read the internet, and 50 said that they do not follow the news at all. How many adults use only the internet to get their news?
    (A) 10
    (B) 20
    (C) 30
    (D) 70

234. Christine went shopping on Thursday afternoon at her local mall. She purchased a blouse for $45, a hat for $12, and a pair of shoes for $37. If she started the day with $108, how much money does she have left after making the purchases?
    (A) 104
    (B) 86
    (C) 26
    (D) 14

235. At the beginning of a game, a bag is filled with 5 red marbles, 4 green marbles, 3 purple marbles, and 9 clear marbles. Jasmine goes first and randomly selects a red marble, which she keeps in her hand. If Horatio goes next and selects a marble at random, what is the probability that he gets a green marble?
    (A) $\frac{4}{21}$
    (B) $\frac{1}{5}$
    (C) $\frac{5}{21}$
    (D) $\frac{1}{4}$

236. Solve for x: $-4x = 12 \times 0.25 \times 3$
    (A) -3
    (B) -2.25
    (C) 2.25
    (D) 3

237. If $2^x = 128$, then $x =$?
    (A) 6
    (B) 7
    (C) 12
    (D) 64

238. The ratio of pennies to nickels to dimes in Clarence's money jar is 10:4:3. If he has 51 coins in his money jar, how many pennies does he have?
    (A) 10
    (B) 12
    (C) 17
    (D) 30

Language Skills

Questions 239-298, 25 Minutes

For questions 239–278, choose the sentence that contains an error in punctuation, capitalization, or usage. If there is no error, select choice (D).

239. (A) All of her books has sad endings.
     (B) The only hero who can save us is not here.
     (C) Her favorite mug is shattered.
     (D) No mistake.

240. (A) They decorated the tree together every Christmas Eve.
     (B) He had a dentist appointment on Wednesday, March 7.
     (C) Her favorite dog breed is the german shepherd.
     (D) No mistake.

241. (A) The Concert would take place at the Hollywood Bowl.
     (B) Every actor dreams of acting on Broadway.
     (C) Marty was waiting for the bus on Bond Street.
     (D) No mistake.

242. (A) Ruby is very bright.
     (B) They dance impressive.
     (C) Chandler was a talented musician.
     (D) No mistake.

243. (A) She likes her pudding more than her mother's.
     (B) I love baking both cookies and brownies, but during the holidays, I prefer to bake it more.
     (C) She couldn't stand her brother's singing.
     (D) No mistake.

244. (A) A variety of show's played at the local theater.
     (B) The actor's script was ridiculous.
     (C) Candy, brownies, and cookies were offered.
     (D) No mistake.

245. (A) Dominic will continue to invest in the stock market in the future.
     (B) The cereal boxes are all open in the pantry.
     (C) When he realized he was going to be late, Terry is jumping out of bed.
     (D) No mistake.

246. (A) He has the longest hair in the family.
     (B) Kelsey is more blonder than Samiya.
     (C) Her book was the most successful of the year.
     (D) No mistake.

247. (A) If you are a billionaire, then I was Mickey Mouse!
     (B) Alterations to her dress are expected to take hours to complete.
     (C) The day after tomorrow will be her cousin's birthday.
     (D) No mistake.

248. (A) The Universe contains billions of stars.
     (B) The first question on the test was difficult.
     (C) Only the university could give degrees.
     (D) No mistake.

249. (A) There were barely any cookies left.
     (B) She won't never leave her house.
     (C) She specialized in refusing things.
     (D) No mistake.

250. (A) She left the party and driving home.
     (B) He skied, snow boarded, and dirt biked.
     (C) The sky was both cloudy and sunny.
     (D) No mistake.

251. (A) She was more ready to try new things.
     (B) Taylor is taller than her older sister.
     (C) She was the most boldest artist of her generation.
     (D) No mistake.

252. (A) Deserts are difficult environments to thrive in.
     (B) The british are known for their love of tea.
     (C) Only the president can declare a war.
     (D) No mistake.

253. (A) It's going to be a difficult few days.
     (B) She's always been there for her friend.
     (C) Caroline's friends were always late.
     (D) No mistake.

254. (A) If you receive a perfect score on the exam, it led to many opportunities.
     (B) The wedding is going to take place in the park next summer.
     (C) She will only attend the concert if her brother drives her there.
     (D) No mistake.

255. (A) They placed ten books on hold.
     (B) It was another hot summer.
     (C) The winter freezing.
     (D) No mistake.

256. (A) This summer, we're going to relax, have fun, and did new things.
     (B) They hoped to succeed and to make lots of money.
     (C) Their business was failing and suffering.
     (D) No mistake.

257. (A) They didn't have time for that.
     (B) It was late; she was going home.
     (C) Isn't it time to leave? asked Cheryl.
     (D) No mistake.

258. (A) They went to the store, walked around, and bought some make up supplies.
     (B) She wanted to join the team and help her team members succeed.
     (C) They painted the mural and then they washed it away.
     (D) No mistake.

259. (A) The island of Cuba is an independent country.
     (B) Only King George was able to enter the premises.
     (C) She hoped to plant an Orange Tree in the back yard.
     (D) No mistake.

260. (A) The children were helpless.
     (B) His boss was furious.
     (C) They fought back weakly.
     (D) No mistake.

261. (A) This past year has been completely exhausting.
     (B) The weather is expected to changed after noon.
     (C) She will ride the train home and then make dinner tonight.
     (D) No mistake.

262. (A) Elizabeth loves her mother very much.
     (B) The cow spends their days eating grass.
     (C) Bob went to visit his brother last weekend.
     (D) No mistake.

263. (A) The daisies flourished.
     (B) She was late.
     (C) Every day the same.
     (D) No mistake.

264. (A) She envied her brother's intelligence.
(B) Like it or not, it has to be done.
(C) If Maria wins then she gets the money.
(D) No mistake.

265. (A) John barely never runs late.
(B) He doesn't have any money to pay his bills.
(C) Mary didn't check the weather before leaving her apartment.
(D) No mistake.

266. (A) It wasnt time for us to go yet.
(B) It's too early for the sun to be up.
(C) She was never wrong.
(D) No mistake.

267. (A) Mathematics, a challenging subject, are fundamental to learning physics.
(B) A cheetah races across the plains in pursuit of its prey.
(C) The mayor has the perfect solution to this problem.
(D) No mistake.

268. (A) The presidents aim, which was to bring the parties together, would be difficult to achieve.
(B) Mirabel's brothers arm was broken when he fell from the tree.
(C) Ron couldn't believe that his sister spoiled the ending of the movie.
(D) No mistake.

269. (A) They refused to stop the train.
(B) After running, she rested.
(C) Forgot to say hello.
(D) No mistake.

270. (A) Sarah and Dominique would go back to school in the fall.
(B) They learned about World War II in history class.
(C) Rikio studied japanese in college.
(D) No mistake.

271. (A) She couldn't see through the fog.
(B) Emily hasn't seen him since that day.
(C) Forgetting to set her alarm clock; the star athlete was late for her big game.
(D) No mistake.

272. (A) All planets orbit around the Sun.
(B) She always went to Canada during the Summer.
(C) They traveled to Egypt to see the pyramids.
(D) No mistake.

273. (A) Jade's birthday was their favorite day of the year.
(B) Our dogs came running up to us.
(C) His tie was so long he had to tuck it into his jacket.
(D) No mistake.

274. (A) Beth returned Jake's wallet to him.
(B) Their schedules allowed them to get more work done.
(C) They determined the car was in fact theirs.
(D) No mistake.

275. (A) She said, "I'm sorry."
(B) All the people, even the children, have to leave.
(C) "Thats great!" shouted Michael.
(D) No mistake.

276. (A) Budapest, Hungary is an affordable destination in Europe.
(B) They admired the vibrant blue color of the Mediterranean Sea.
(C) There are several different provinces in Canada.
(D) No mistake.

277. (A) The United states has only fifty states.
(B) Colorado has great opportunities for skiing.
(C) The smallest state is Rhode Island.
(D) No mistake.

278. (A) Only peonies were planted in Maggie's garden.
(B) His dog who had a loud bark was annoying the neighbors.
(C) She's only trying to keep her children safe.
(D) No mistake.

Spelling

For questions 279–288, choose the sentence that contains an error in spelling. If there is no error, select choice (D).

279. (A) Kristie had an overall cheerful demeanor.
(B) He didn't want to interrupt their discussion.
(C) Jamal hoped to one day study medecine.
(D) No mistake.

280. (A) The seasons changed right outside her window.
(B) The alterations to her dress were perfect.
(C) Although she won, she still felt downtrodden.
(D) No mistake.

281. (A) The shipwreck was legendary on that island.
(B) As a scientist, he was interested in the concept of parralel universes.
(C) The infection spread quickly and was impossible to stop.
(D) No mistake.

282. (A) The occurence was considered rare by experts.
(B) This time won't be anything like the last one.
(C) She hated being compared to her sister.
(D) No mistake.

283. (A) The public had access to that information to.
(B) She was persistent in her pursuit of her goals.
(C) The teacher expressed disapproval of her pupils.
(D) No mistake.

284. (A) He forgot to put his mask on before boarding the train.
(B) They were a very religious family.
(C) They publically admitted their mistake.
(D) No mistake.

285. (A) He was a successful business partner.
(B) The suprise birthday party was planned for Saturday.
(C) She couldn't wait for the celebration.
(D) No mistake.

286. (A) She walked along the river every morning.
(B) He ran harder than anyone else on the team.
(C) Her tounge swelled up in an allergic reaction to the soup.
(D) No mistake.

287. (A) His eyes were wide open.
(B) She bet her sister she couldn't balance on the beam.
(C) He fooled his mother into believing his homework was done.
(D) No mistake.

288. (A) Her apetite was ruined by the atrocious sight.
(B) They hurried to catch their train at the station.
(C) She expressed discomfort at the proposal.
(D) No mistake.

Composition

289. Which of these sentences would best fit at the end of the paragraph?

    (1) Making a peanut butter and jelly sandwich is easy to do. (2) First, gather your ingredients and utensils: bread, peanut butter, jelly, a plate, and a butter knife. (3) Using the butter knife, spread peanut butter on one slice of bread and jelly on the other.

    (A) Be sure to wash your knife thoroughly.
    (B) Put the slices together and you have a sandwich that is ready to eat.
    (C) You can choose whether to use crunchy or smooth peanut butter.
    (D) Some people do not like peanut butter and jelly sandwiches.

290. Choose the word or words that is a clear connective to complete the sentence.

    The stairs in the old house were falling apart; _____ they are unsafe to walk on.

    (A) however,
    (B) in addition,
    (C) therefore,
    (D) none of these

291. Choose the word that is a clear connective to complete the sentence.

    Samson was a very smart cat; _____ he loved sleep on his owner's lap.

    (A) additionally,
    (B) unfortunately,
    (C) carefully,
    (D) none of these

292. Which of these best fits under the topic "Eating Healthy"?

    (A) Eating at restaurants can be expensive.
    (B) Fruits and vegetables are part of a healthy diet.
    (C) Exercise is important for health.
    (D) none of these

293. Which sentence does *not* belong in the paragraph?

    (1) Basketball is a popular team sport. (2) Anyone can learn how to play. (3) It is great exercise and lots of fun. (4) Outdoor sports are more fun than indoor sports.

    (A) Sentence 1
    (B) Sentence 2
    (C) Sentence 3
    (D) Sentence 4

294. Which of the following themes could be effectively explored in a one-paragraph passage?

    (A) Banking 101
    (B) Animals of the World
    (C) Skydiving Safety
    (D) none of these

295. Which of the following themes could be effectively explored in a one-paragraph passage?

    (A) Building Model Airplanes
    (B) How to Write a Thank You Card
    (C) Learning to Speak Japanese
    (D) none of these

296. Choose the word that best completes the sentence.

    Bruce cheered _____ when his teammate scored the winning goal.

    (A) surprisingly
    (B) nervously
    (C) excitedly
    (D) frightfully

297. Where should the sentence, "Consider adopting a rescue animal; you will save a life and have a new best friend!" be placed in the paragraph below?

    (1) Adopting an animal from a shelter is a great thing to do. (2) Many shelter animals have been rescued from situations where they did not receive proper care. (3) These loving animals are looking for new homes and better lives.

    (A) Between sentences 1 and 2
    (B) Between sentences 2 and 3
    (C) After sentence 3
    (D) The sentence does not belong in the paragraph.

298. Which of the following sentences offers the *least* support for the topic "The History of the Automobile"?

    (A) The development of automobiles dates back over one hundred years.
    (B) The Model T, a prominent early automobile, first debuted in 1908.
    (C) Driving a car requires a driver's license.
    (D) Early automobiles did not have radios.

Scoring Practice Test 2

Using your answer sheet and referring to the answer key at the back of the book, calculate the percentage of questions you answered correctly in each section by taking the number of questions you answered correctly in that section and dividing it by the number of questions in that section. Multiply this number by 100 to determine your percentage score. The higher the percentage, the stronger your performance in that section. The lower the percentage, the more time you should spend practicing that section.

Note that the actual test will not evaluate your score based on percentage correct or incorrect. Instead, it will evaluate your performance relative to all other students in your grade who took the test.

Record your results here:

Section	Questions Correct	Total Questions	Percent Questions Correct
Verbal Skills	_____	60	_____%
Quantitative Skills	_____	52	_____%
Reading Comprehension	_____	62	_____%
Mathematics Achievement	_____	64	_____%
Language	_____	60	_____%

Remember that, depending on the curriculum at your school, there may be material on this test that you have not yet been taught. If this is the case, and you would like to improve your score beyond what is expected of your grade, consider outside help from an adult (such as a tutor or teacher) who can help you learn more about the topics that are new to you.

Answer Key

The keys are organized by section, and each question has an answer associated with it. Remember: there are detailed and searchable answer explanations available online at www.thetutorverse.com/books. Be sure to obtain permission before going online.

Answer Keys

This section provides the answer solutions to the practice questions in each section of the workbook including the diagnostic test, exercises, and practice tests. **Remember: there are detailed answer explanations available online at www.thetutorverse.com/books. Be sure to obtain permission before going online.**

Diagnostic Test

Quantitative Skills

1. C	8. C	15. B	22. D	29. A	36. D	43. A	50. C
2. C	9. D	16. A	23. C	30. B	37. C	44. B	51. D
3. A	10. B	17. B	24. C	31. A	38. B	45. D	52. C
4. C	11. D	18. D	25. B	32. B	39. D	46. C	
5. D	12. B	19. A	26. A	33. C	40. C	47. B	
6. D	13. C	20. B	27. D	34. B	41. A	48. B	
7. C	14. A	21. C	28. B	35. B	42. B	49. A	

Mathematics

53. B	61. C	69. B	77. D	85. D	93. C	101. B	109. B
54. D	62. D	70. D	78. B	86. B	94. A	102. B	110. A
55. D	63. B	71. A	79. C	87. B	95. C	103. C	111. A
56. D	64. C	72. B	80. D	88. B	96. C	104. D	112. A
57. C	65. C	73. C	81. D	89. C	97. B	105. D	113. D
58. B	66. C	74. A	82. D	90. C	98. B	106. D	114. D
59. A	67. C	75. D	83. A	91. C	99. C	107. B	115. C
60. A	68. A	76. B	84. D	92. B	100. D	108. B	116. C

Exercises

Quantitative Skills

Number Series (Sequence)

Arithmetic	14. C	28. C	41. C	55. D	68. C	82. D	96. A
1. D	15. A	29. D	42. D	56. C	69. D	83. C	97. C
2. C	16. B	30. B	43. B	57. C	70. D	84. C	98. D
3. A	17. D	*Geometric*	44. B	58. C	71. B	85. A	99. A
4. D	18. C	31. B	45. A	59. C	72. D	86. D	100. D
5. B	19. D	32. C	46. D	60. B	73. C	87. B	101. A
6. B	20. B	33. A	47. A	*Other*	74. D	88. C	102. C
7. C	21. C	34. B	48. A	61. C	75. B	89. C	103. C
8. D	22. B	35. A	49. D	62. B	76. C	90. A	104. B
9. A	23. A	36. B	50. D	63. A	77. D	91. C	
10. B	24. B	37. B	51. D	64. B	78. B	92. D	
11. C	25. C	38. B	52. C	65. D	79. B	93. B	
12. A	26. C	39. B	53. C	66. B	80. A	94. D	
13. D	27. A	40. A	54. D	67. A	81. D	95. C	

Answer Keys

Geometric Comparison

Angles
1. D
2. A
3. C
4. C
5. C
6. A
7. A
8. C
9. D
10. D
11. B
12. C
13. B
14. C
15. C
16. A

Polygons
17. A
18. C
19. B
20. D
21. B
22. A
23. D
24. A
25. D
26. B
27. C
28. B
29. A
30. A
31. D
32. C

Non-Geometric Comparison

Algebraic
1. A
2. C
3. C
4. D
5. B
6. A
7. D
8. A
9. C
10. C
11. B

Counting
12. C
13. D
14. D
15. C
16. A
17. C
18. B
19. D
20. D
21. D

Fractions, Decimals, Percent
22. D
23. D
24. B
25. B
26. C
27. D
28. C
29. B
30. A
31. D
32. D
33. A

Graphs
34. A
35. A
36. B
37. D
38. D
39. A
40. C
41. C
42. A
43. C
44. C
45. A
46. D
47. A
48. B

Measurements
49. C
50. A
51. C
52. B
53. A
54. B
55. D
56. A
57. A
58. C
59. C
60. A
61. B
62. D
63. C

Order of Operations
64. A
65. C
66. C
67. A
68. D
69. B
70. D
71. D
72. D
73. A
74. C
75. B
76. B
77. C
78. C
79. A

Slope
80. D
81. A
82. B
83. B
84. B
85. B
86. C
87. C
88. B
89. D
90. A
91. D
92. D
93. C
94. D

Number Manipulation (Reasoning)

Fractions, Decimals
1. B
2. C
3. C
4. C
5. B
6. B
7. C
8. B
9. D
10. D
11. B
12. A
13. C
14. B
15. A
16. D
17. C
18. D
19. B
20. B

Whole Numbers
21. D
22. A
23. D
24. B
25. C
26. B
27. B
28. C
29. A
30. B
31. B
32. D
33. B
34. C
35. C
36. D
37. D
38. A
39. D
40. C

Mathematics Concepts

Algebraic

Inequalities
1. A
2. C
3. C
4. B

Slope
5. A
6. D
7. A
8. D
9. D
10. B
11. C
12. C
13. D
14. B

Geometry

Angles
1. C
2. C
3. B
4. A
5. D

Area/Perimeter
6. D
7. A
8. C
9. C
10. B
11. D
12. B
13. C
14. B
15. A
16. D
17. A
18. D

Circles
19. D
20. B
21. B
22. C
23. C
24. D
25. C
26. B
27. C
28. D
29. D
30. D
31. B
32. C
33. C

Polygons
34. D
35. D
36. A
37. B
38. D
39. B
40. A
41. A

Surface Area/Volume
42. C
43. D
44. D
45. D
46. C
47. A
48. B
49. C
50. A
51. D

Measurements

Appropriate Units
1. C
2. C
3. B

Answer Keys

Numbers & Operations

Comparing Fractions	Converting Fractions, Decimals, Percents	9. A	15. C	20. C	Scientific Notation	30. C	37. C
		10. D	Exponents	21. C		31. D	38. B
1. A		Divisibility	16. C	Multiples	25. C	32. C	
2. A	6. D	11. A	17. D	22. C	26. B	33. A	
3. D	7. B	12. A	18. B	23. B	27. B	34. B	
4. C	8. C	13. B	Factors	24. D	28. D	35. D	
5. B		14. C	19. C		29. B	36. D	

Mathematics Problem Solving

Algebraic Concepts

Algebra Word Problems	7. C	15. C	22. D	27. B	35. D	Variable Exponents	47. B
	8. D	Proportions	23. C	28. A	36. C		48. A
1. B	9. C	16. D	24. C	29. B	37. C	41. B	49. A
2. D	10. D	17. A	25. C	30. D	38. B	42. A	50. D
3. C	11. C	18. A	Solving Algebraic Equations	31. A	39. D	43. B	
4. C	12. B	19. D		32. B	40. A	44. C	
5. D	13. D	20. B		33. D		45. A	
6. B	14. C	21. C	26. C	34. A		46. A	

Data & Probability

Averages	8. C	Graphs	23. B	Probability	38. D	Venn Diagrams	52. D
	9. D	16. C	24. C	31. B	39. B		53. C
1. C	10. C	17. B	25. B	32. A	40. A	46. C	54. D
2. D	11. B	18. B	26. C	33. A	41. C	47. D	55. B
3. D	12. A	19. C	27. B	34. B	42. A	48. A	
4. A	13. D	20. A	28. B	35. A	43. A	49. C	
5. C	14. A	21. D	29. B	36. A	44. D	50. C	
6. C	15. B	22. D	30. A	37. D	45. A	51. B	
7. B							

Measurements

Speed	4. B	8. D	Units	14. A	18. D	22. C
	5. C	9. D	11. A	15. B	19. D	23. A
1. C	6. C	10. D	12. B	16. B	20. C	24. A
2. A	7. A		13. A	17. B	21. A	25. B
3. C						

Numbers & Operations

Arithmetic	14. C	25. A	37. D	50. A	62. D	75. A	87. D
	15. D	26. B	38. B	Roots	63. B	76. D	88. B
1. C	Operations with Fractions and Decimals	27. C	39. A	51. B	64. C	77. D	89. D
2. D		28. C	40. D	52. B	65. C	78. A	90. D
3. C		29. A	Percents	53. A	66. B	79. C	91. C
4. B		30. D	41. C	54. C	67. D	80. C	92. A
5. C	16. B	Percent Word Problems	42. C	55. A	68. C	Word Problems	93. C
6. C	17. A		43. A	56. B	69. A		94. C
7. C	18. D		44. A	57. D	70. A	81. B	95. D
8. D	19. A	31. D	45. B	58. B	Vocabulary	82. D	
9. B	20. B	32. C	46. A	59. A	71. C	83. B	
10. D	21. A	33. B	47. C	60. A	72. B	84. A	
11. C	22. A	34. C	48. D	Rounding	73. A	85. A	
12. C	23. A	35. A					
13. B	24. D	36. D	49. C	61. C	74. C	86. B	

The Tutorverse
www.thetutorverse.com

Practice Test 1

Verbal Skills

1. B	9. C	17. C	25. C	33. D	41. C	49. A	57. C
2. B	10. D	18. B	26. A	34. D	42. A	50. B	58. C
3. A	11. C	19. A	27. C	35. D	43. B	51. A	59. D
4. B	12. D	20. C	28. A	36. A	44. B	52. B	60. C
5. B	13. A	21. A	29. A	37. A	45. B	53. B	
6. B	14. C	22. B	30. C	38. B	46. A	54. C	
7. A	15. D	23. A	31. A	39. A	47. A	55. D	
8. B	16. B	24. C	32. D	40. D	48. C	56. D	

Quantitative Skills

61. D	68. D	75. B	82. D	89. D	96. B	103. B	110. A
62. B	69. C	76. B	83. D	90. A	97. A	104. C	111. C
63. A	70. A	77. C	84. B	91. D	98. C	105. A	112. B
64. C	71. D	78. A	85. A	92. A	99. B	106. B	
65. D	72. A	79. C	86. B	93. B	100. C	107. A	
66. D	73. B	80. C	87. D	94. B	101. A	108. C	
67. D	74. A	81. B	88. D	95. A	102. D	109. B	

Reading

113. A	121. B	129. B	137. A	145. B	153. D	161. C	169. C
114. A	122. B	130. A	138. C	146. A	154. A	162. C	170. D
115. C	123. D	131. D	139. B	147. C	155. C	163. A	171. D
116. A	124. C	132. C	140. A	148. A	156. A	164. C	172. A
117. B	125. A	133. D	141. C	149. D	157. A	165. C	173. D
118. D	126. D	134. D	142. C	150. A	158. D	166. D	174. B
119. C	127. C	135. C	143. D	151. C	159. C	167. A	
120. C	128. B	136. D	144. C	152. B	160. C	168. B	

Mathematics

175. B	183. A	191. B	199. A	207. B	215. A	223. C	231. B
176. B	184. D	192. B	200. B	208. B	216. A	224. A	232. A
177. A	185. B	193. B	201. B	209. B	217. B	225. C	233. C
178. B	186. C	194. C	202. A	210. D	218. B	226. B	234. B
179. B	187. C	195. C	203. C	211. C	219. A	227. D	235. B
180. D	188. A	196. D	204. C	212. D	220. A	228. A	236. C
181. C	189. A	197. C	205. D	213. C	221. D	229. C	237. C
182. D	190. B	198. A	206. B	214. C	222. D	230. D	238. A

Language Skills

239. A	247. B	255. B	263. B	271. C	279. C	287. B	295. B
240. B	248. C	256. A	264. C	272. A	280. B	288. B	296. B
241. B	249. A	257. C	265. B	273. C	281. D	289. A	297. A
242. B	250. B	258. B	266. D	274. B	282. B	290. B	298. B
243. D	251. B	259. A	267. C	275. D	283. C	291. B	
244. C	252. B	260. C	268. A	276. B	284. A	292. C	
245. C	253. B	261. C	269. B	277. D	285. B	293. D	
246. A	254. A	262. A	270. A	278. D	286. C	294. B	

Practice Test 2

Verbal Skills

1. B	9. B	17. B	25. B	33. D	41. D	49. B	57. A
2. C	10. B	18. C	26. A	34. C	42. B	50. A	58. A
3. B	11. C	19. D	27. D	35. B	43. C	51. A	59. A
4. C	12. C	20. A	28. C	36. C	44. D	52. A	60. C
5. C	13. B	21. A	29. C	37. C	45. D	53. D	
6. D	14. B	22. D	30. B	38. D	46. B	54. D	
7. C	15. D	23. C	31. A	39. B	47. C	55. C	
8. A	16. B	24. C	32. C	40. A	48. D	56. A	

Quantitative Skills

61. D	68. D	75. D	82. A	89. C	96. D	103. C	110. C
62. D	69. C	76. C	83. A	90. D	97. C	104. B	111. A
63. B	70. D	77. D	84. B	91. A	98. A	105. B	112. C
64. B	71. A	78. C	85. D	92. B	99. C	106. B	
65. A	72. A	79. B	86. A	93. A	100. D	107. A	
66. D	73. C	80. C	87. C	94. B	101. D	108. A	
67. B	74. B	81. B	88. C	95. B	102. A	109. B	

Reading

113. B	121. D	129. C	137. B	145. C	153. C	161. A	169. C
114. D	122. A	130. D	138. D	146. A	154. C	162. B	170. D
115. A	123. C	131. B	139. B	147. B	155. C	163. C	171. A
116. C	124. C	132. C	140. D	148. C	156. D	164. D	172. B
117. D	125. B	133. B	141. A	149. A	157. A	165. B	173. B
118. D	126. C	134. D	142. B	150. C	158. C	166. A	174. B
119. B	127. A	135. C	143. C	151. B	159. C	167. A	
120. C	128. B	136. A	144. D	152. C	160. A	168. C	

Mathematics

175. C	183. C	191. B	199. D	207. D	215. D	223. C	231. B
176. C	184. D	192. C	200. B	208. C	216. A	224. D	232. D
177. B	185. C	193. A	201. B	209. C	217. D	225. C	233. C
178. D	186. D	194. C	202. C	210. B	218. C	226. C	234. D
179. B	187. A	195. D	203. D	211. A	219. A	227. B	235. B
180. D	188. A	196. D	204. B	212. C	220. C	228. C	236. B
181. C	189. C	197. C	205. C	213. B	221. C	229. D	237. B
182. D	190. C	198. B	206. A	214. D	222. C	230. C	238. D

Language Skills

239. A	248. A	257. C	266. A	275. C	284. C	293. D
240. C	249. B	258. D	267. A	276. D	285. B	294. D
241. A	250. A	259. C	268. B	277. A	286. C	295. B
242. B	251. C	260. D	269. C	278. B	287. D	296. C
243. B	252. B	261. B	270. C	279. C	288. A	297. C
244. A	253. D	262. B	271. C	280. D	289. B	298. C
245. C	254. A	263. C	272. B	281. B	290. C	
246. B	255. C	264. C	273. A	282. A	291. A	
247. A	256. A	265. A	274. D	283. A	292. B	

The Tutorverse
www.thetutorverse.com

Made in the USA
Columbia, SC
25 April 2024

34889265R00107